RETHINKING TESTIMONIAL CINEMA IN POSTDICTATORSHIP ARGENTINA

NEW DIRECTIONS IN NATIONAL CINEMAS

Robert Rushing, *editor*

RETHINKING TESTIMONIAL CINEMA IN POSTDICTATORSHIP ARGENTINA
Beyond Memory Fatigue

Verónica Garibotto

Indiana University Press

This book is a publication of

Indiana University Press
Office of Scholarly Publishing
Herman B Wells Library 350
1320 East 10th Street
Bloomington, Indiana 47405 USA

iupress.indiana.edu

© 2019 by Verónica Garibotto

All rights reserved

No part of this book may be reproduced or utilized in any form or by any means, electronic or mechanical, including photocopying and recording, or by any information storage and retrieval system, without permission in writing from the publisher. The paper used in this publication meets the minimum requirements of the American National Standard for Information Sciences—Permanence of Paper for Printed Library Materials, ANSI Z39.48-1992.

Manufactured in the United States of America

Cataloging information is available from the Library of Congress.

ISBN 978-0-253-03850-0 (cloth)
ISBN 978-0-253-03851-7 (paperback)
ISBN 978-0-253-03852-4 (ebook)

1 2 3 4 5   23 22 21 20 19

Contents

	Preface and Acknowledgments	*vii*
	Introduction: Redefining Testimonial Cinema	*1*
1	Knowledge and Feeling: Testimonial Documentary and Fiction in the 1980s	*38*
2	Indexicality and Counterhegemony: Testimonial Documentary in the 1990s	*73*
3	Distortion and History in Post-2000 Second-Generation Performative Documentaries	*105*
4	Emotion and History in Post-2000 Second-Generation Iconic Fictions	*140*
	Afterword: From Counterhegemony to Hegemony	*172*
	Works Cited	*177*
	Index	*195*

Preface and Acknowledgments

As is often the case with research projects, this one was born, over a decade ago, of an impossibility. In 2005, while contemplating topics for my doctoral dissertation, I attended several panels and read various texts on the representation of history in contemporary Argentine culture. I soon noticed a dominant trend, both in Latin American and US scholarship. The vast majority of the contributions—particularly those concerning the links among culture, history, and politics—focused on filmic or literary narratives of the 1976–1983 dictatorship. These narratives, usually told in the first person by a camp survivor or a child of disappeared parents, were mostly analyzed from the standpoint of trauma theory—that is, most interpretations addressed how trauma, memory, and mourning emerged in or resulted from these stories. For my own autobiographical reasons (when I was six weeks old, my father was deeply wounded in a bomb attack claimed by Montoneros), I had always been interested in Argentine politics and especially in understanding the 1970s and its effects. So, at first, I believed I had found my niche. "Postmemory," "melancholy," and "grief"—for me, these terms held the mesmerizing power of a revealed truth. Yet, after some time had passed, I felt unable to join the conversation. I had the impression that there was nothing new that could be said about trauma, memory, and mourning. I thought that there was no way one could read these narratives without repeating what other people had observed. I became convinced that it was unnecessary to continue addressing this corpus, given the volume of contributions that already existed.

Confronted with these impossibilities, I decided to be pragmatic: I would set the topic aside, avoid all presentations on trauma at future conferences, and write a dissertation on something "new": the nineteenth century. The release of Beatriz Sarlo's book *Tiempo pasado* at the end of that same year reinforced my decision. Sarlo, arguably the most emblematic intellectual in Argentina, published a strong critique of first-person narratives, declaring what I thought would be the death of memory culture. Moreover, a number of academics concurred with Sarlo, and several memory narratives, like Albertina Carri's film *Los rubios*, explicitly represented their own exhaustion, staging what Andreas Huyssen has described as "memory fatigue" (3). That was the end of my dilemma: I forgot about the topic, returned to the nineteenth century, and wrote a dissertation that eventually developed into my first book.

But memory culture did not die, despite Sarlo's statements and Carri's parody. Quite the contrary; the Kirchner administration (2003–2015) continued to try former military officers, to allocate public funds for the creation of TV programs denouncing past dictatorial violence, and to give voice to human rights organizations like Madres de Plaza de Mayo. Furthermore, films and novels on the dictatorship became especially prolific, as children born to missing parents grew up and became adults willing to tell their own stories. Since 2005, at least eighteen of these second-generation survivors have created their own narratives based on their childhood experiences. Although I had resolved to forget the topic, several questions—to borrow the language of trauma theory—began to haunt me. Was getting rid of memory culture the only answer to the problems that Sarlo and Huyssen had identified? Was it indeed impossible to say something meaningful about these texts that accounted for a vast portion of Argentine culture and continued to mobilize people's feelings? Could I somehow redefine the theoretical approach to find new lines of inquiry and insight?

This book is an attempt to overcome my initial sense of impossibility. Its primary goals are to critically examine traditional approaches to testimonial cinema (trauma theory and subaltern studies), to propose an alternate interpretive framework at the intersection of semiotics and theories of affect, and to reread Argentine films produced between 1983 and 2016 from this latter standpoint. I expect that this renewed analysis will contribute to understanding the specific place of first-person narratives in contemporary Argentine culture and to overcoming the existing fatigue surrounding the topic (*el temita* [the topic], as academic, writer, and second-generation survivor Mariana Eva Perez, also known as *la princesa montonera* [the Montonero princess], has brilliantly called the fossilized discourse on the dictatorship). Although I focus on Argentina, my readings could also apply to other contexts in which narratives about recent political conflicts have shifted from alternative versions of history to hegemonic, iconic accounts: Spanish, Chilean, Uruguayan, and Brazilian postdictatorship narratives; accounts of apartheid South Africa; and Holocaust testimonies, to name but a few. In this sense, I see postdictatorship Argentina as a case study for rethinking testimonial cinema in a larger context, one that goes beyond trauma and subaltern theories. I also believe that an approach combining semiotics and affect theories could be helpful in pursuing an ideological analysis of the links between film and historical representation more broadly.

In spite of what it might have felt daily, as I sat in front of the computer trying to organize ideas, writing this book has truly been a collective endeavor. A number of colleagues and friends shared their own thoughts, time, and resources to make my work possible, and I am forever grateful for their generosity. First and foremost, I am grateful to Joanna Page, Jorge Pérez, and Laura Podalsky, who wrote several letters of recommendation, including the ones that allowed me to receive a Hall Center Humanities Research Fellowship in the spring of 2017. This fellowship provided the release time from teaching and service that was instrumental to giving the final touches to the manuscript—and I am also grateful to the Hall Center staff and other fellows for enabling such a welcoming, productive environment. John Beverley, Andrea Cobas Carral, and Antonio Gómez selflessly dedicated their time to reading different sections, sharing important sources, and/or helping me develop my ideas. John Beverley's thought-provoking work on *testimonio* is actually what sparked my interest in conceiving of this corpus in testimonial terms—even if, as I note in the introduction, some of his arguments need to be rethought for the Argentine case. I will never be able to thank him enough for all the things that he has taught me, including that a lucid scholar can also be a genuine listener and a modest, generous person. Paola Bohórquez inspired me with productive conversations on the links between culture and psychoanalysis. Jorge Pérez supported me in multiple ways that go beyond letters of recommendation and that include (but are not limited to) grant applications and words of encouragement. Gonzalo Aguilar, Albertina Carri, Geoffrey Maguire, Paola Margulis, Pablo Piedras, Ximena Triquell, and Noa Vaisman kindly sent me their own materials. Andrés Di Tella dedicated Facebook time to clearing my doubts on his work. Javier Barroso, Stuart Day, Betsaida Reyes, and Margot Versteeg located important bibliographic references and new sources. Juan Pablo Cinelli and Astrid Riehn provided valuable contact information. Ari Linden, the KU Writing Center, and especially Robin Myers helped me polish grammar and style. Lina Muñoz Márquez and Juan Pablo Román Alvarado helped me with formatting. Keah Cunningham and Jonathan Perkins, from KU's EGARC, spared me several headaches with their magical editing of the book's screen grabs. The students in my doctoral seminar on testimonial narratives in the spring of 2015 infused energy to my writing with their enthusiastic opinions.

This project was also possible thanks to several grants from the University of Kansas: General Research Funds (2014, 2015, and 2017), Research Excellence Funds (2018), a sabbatical leave in the fall of 2016, and travel awards from the College of Arts and Sciences, the Center for Latin American and Caribbean Studies, and the Department of Spanish and Portuguese. These travel grants allowed me to gather research materials in Argentina and to present my work at the Society for Cinema and Media Studies, the American Comparative Literature Association, the Latin American Studies Association, CineLit, the Annual International Conference on Communication and Mass Media, and the Pacific Ancient and Modern Languages Association. I benefitted from the participants' comments at each of these conferences as well as from the friendly audiences at the Hall Center for the Humanities, the Department of Spanish and Portuguese, the Department of Film and Media Studies, and the Center for Latin American and Caribbean Studies at the University of Kansas.

A modified, shorter version of the introduction was published as "Pitfalls of Trauma: Revisiting Postdictatorship Cinema from a Semiotic Perspective" in *Latin American Research Review* 52.4 (fall 2017): 654–667. Modified sections of the fourth chapter were published as "Private Narratives and Infant Views: Iconizing 1970s Militancy in Contemporary Argentine Cinema" in *Hispanic Research Journal* 16.3 (June 2015): 257–272 and as "Iconic Fictions: Narrating Recent Argentine History in Post-2000 Second-Generation Films" in *Studies in Hispanic Cinemas* 8.2 (March 2012): 175–188. Many thanks to the editors and reviewers for their helpful comments. Special thanks to Janice Frisch and Maya Bringe at Indiana University Press for their professionalism and to the two anonymous readers for their time and dedication. Their careful suggestions definitely resulted in an improved final version. Their caring tone and their commitment to helping me refine my arguments renewed my confidence in our academic community.

This book owes part of its driving impulse to my parents, Liliana and Enrique Garibotto, who, despite a very difficult background, raised their four children without ever transpiring an ounce of either self-pity or resentment. On the contrary, they always made us feel privileged for having a "different" father, and they always encouraged us to pursue our own ideological journeys. As a result, they got an academic, a translator, an ophthalmologist, and a boxer with very different, sometimes conflicting, political views. This freedom was certainly crucial to my feeling entitled to choose a topic that is sensitive to our family. Finally, I am particularly grateful to Rafael Acosta Morales, my partner and colleague, whose sharp suggestions made this book, especially the introduction, far more ambitious than what I had originally conceived and who arrived to my life unexpectedly to fill every day with light and joy. Rafa, Cabrón, and our soon-to-be born Rafita are the reasons I wake up every morning feeling like the luckiest person on earth.

RETHINKING TESTIMONIAL CINEMA IN POSTDICTATORSHIP ARGENTINA

Introduction
Redefining Testimonial Cinema

AFTER INTERVIEWING DOZENS of witnesses, listening to many confusing accounts, and trying to make sense of their contradictions, the main character in Carlos Gamerro's novel *El secreto y las voces* reaches an unsettling conclusion: "*Esperaba una conspiración de silencio, no una de locuacidad*" [I was expecting a conspiracy of silence, not a conspiracy of voices] (73).[1] I find that this deduction expresses an ongoing perception of Argentine postdictatorship testimonial narratives—that is, narratives, enunciated by protagonists or witnesses, of the military regime that ruled the country between 1976 and 1983.[2] Published in 2002, Gamerro's novel is the fictional detective story of a man who returns to his hometown to investigate the details surrounding a neighbor's disappearance back in 1977. Having expected to encounter only silence, he instead meets a group of people who simply cannot stop talking. They talk about the missing man, police officers, other neighbors, and especially their own private lives. They provide specific descriptions and endless speculations. They corroborate their recollections with dates, names, and figures. By the end of the trip, however, the detective has realized that the testimonies contradict one another. The proliferation of voices is more deceptive than the conspiracy of silence he had anticipated. In fact, it is only when he decides to read these voices against the grain—to read the silences within the voices—that an actual story comes to light. Paradoxically, as he harbors his suspicions about these firsthand accounts and places the legitimacy of direct experience into parentheses, he comes into closer contact with recent history.

The year 2003 witnessed another groundbreaking parody of testimonial narrative: Albertina Carri's film *Los rubios*. Challenging conventional documentary strategies, Carri talks about her missing militant parents while exposing the difficulties of representation. She uses Playmobil toys to reenact imaginary versions of the kidnapping, recalls her own past through the voice of an actress who appears on screen at the same time as Carri herself does, discusses the narrative structure in front of the camera, and exhibits the film crew and backstage area. Moreover, her documentary is based on interviews that destabilize the premises at the very heart of testimonial cinema. Questions and answers are overtly scripted. Memories shared by her parents' friends are treated with no greater or lesser relevance than the gossip spread by street children born at least twenty years after their disappearance. And the interviewees participate in fictional scenes in which the actress portraying Carri asks them for family details. More than a testimonial film, *Los rubios* is a performance of a testimonial film: a hypermediated narrative whose reality effect is explicitly undermined before the audience's eyes.

I see Carri's documentary and Gamerro's novel as two paradigmatic examples of a reticence toward postdictatorship testimonial narrative that began around the early 2000s and still exists today (at least as I write this introduction in 2017). Other cases in point are *M* (2007), a documentary in which Nicolás Prividera simultaneously unveils the fate of his disappeared mother and questions the authority of his own findings; *Historia del llanto: un testimonio* (2007), a novel by Alan Pauls, in which the banality of the story being told echoes the oxymoron in the title—an entire history of something as private as crying contained in a single testimony; and Mariano Pensotti's play *Cuando vuelva a casa voy a ser otro* (2016), in which audio of a 1970s-era activist is turned into background music for a conservative political campaign. A similar reticence is evident in academic discourse. In *Tiempo pasado* (2005), Beatriz Sarlo, an intellectual who in fact helped testimonial narrative achieve canonicity, denounces the negative impact of subjective experience on the representation of the past. Historians Hugo Vezzetti (2009) and Emilio Crenzel (2010) critically assess the figure of the victim in testimonies from the early democracy, and Cecilia Vallina edits an anthology of interdisciplinary articles entitled *Crítica del testimonio* (2009), in which a number of scholars heatedly discuss the value of such narratives.[3]

This reticence, while perceptible since the early 2000s, is quite surprising. If we take a look into postdictatorship history, we can see that such distrust is unprecedented. For roughly two decades (1983–2000), testimonial narrative was viewed primarily, especially by progressive thinkers, as a privileged type of narrative in Argentina.[4] In 1983, Raúl Alfonsín, the first democratically elected president after the military regime, commissioned a group of intellectuals to investigate past human rights violations. *Nunca más*, the compilation of testimonies resulting from this commission, prepared the way for the genre to take center stage. Originally conceived as legal evidence in trials unfolding throughout 1985, these narrations soon went beyond the judicial sphere, inspiring literary and filmic products such as Alicia Partnoy's *The Little School* (1986), a collection of stories on the author's experience in a clandestine detention center, and Lourdes Portillo and Susana Blaustein's *Las Madres: The Mothers of Plaza de Mayo* (1985), a documentary exploring the struggle of the women in this organization. In the early democracy, when it was imperative to rethink the role of left-leaning intellectuals, the genre became a key pillar in the definition of a new ethics. Was it still possible for progressive thinkers to participate in the public sphere? Were their voices still capable of producing social change? Could narrative still hold political potential? Was it still able to represent history? The testimonial genre provided a viable means of solving these questions: firsthand experiences directly engaged the public sphere, disclosing hidden aspects of the recent past and creating social consensus against its atrocities. If the figure of the revolutionary intellectual had collapsed along with 1960s and '70s revolutionary projects, the figure of the post-dictatorship intellectual came to life along with the testimonial genre.[5]

In the 1990s, the appeal of testimonial narrative intensified following decrees, issued by President Carlos Menem, that released members of the military who had been imprisoned as a result of the 1985 trials. As the Menem administration attempted to erase recent history, memory texts became increasingly prolific. Victims' relatives produced new narratives contesting official amnesia, including Juan Gelman and Mara La Madrid's *Ni el flaco perdón de dios*, a 1997 book compiling testimonies from the children of missing people. Former militants insisted on the genre's importance in fighting against the official erasure—as in Martín Caparrós and Eduardo Anguita's *La voluntad* (1997), three volumes interviewing 1970s-era activists. An effective tool for raising dissident voices, testimonial narrative was widely produced, analyzed, and praised for its political effects.

The contemporary reticence is surprising not only when compared to its celebratory reception in previous decades but also when contrasted with the central status of testimonial narrative between 2003 and 2015. During the Kirchner administration, the imperative to remember developed into public policy, marking a shift from Menemist discourse in the 1990s. The reopening of trials against members of the regime, the conversion of military facilities into museums, and the insistence on disclosing the junta's illegal actions once again brought the recent past to the fore. Human rights organizations like Abuelas de Plaza de Mayo, Madres de Plaza de Mayo, and H.I.J.O.S. gained visibility as government supporters, placing survivors' and relatives' voices at the very center of social rhetoric. Public funds facilitated the creation of films and TV programs that addressed past military violence, like *Televisión x la identidad* (2007), a state-sponsored series on babies born in captivity. Children of disappeared people grew into adults capable of crafting their own stories, which sparked a new wave of testimonial production; for instance, second-generation documentaries like Natalia Bruschtein's *Encontrando a Víctor* (2005) and plays such as Lola Arias's *Mi vida después* (2010). Paradoxically, however, as the government made the dictatorship into the core substance of official discourse, a number of artists, intellectuals, and even second-generation survivors like Carri and Prividera showed their misgivings about testimonial narrative. It was precisely as the genre reached the center of the public sphere that reluctance arose.[6]

Could this reticence be interpreted, then, as the result of an excess? It may well be, after three decades of increasing production, that the testimonial genre has reached a saturation point. One might conjecture that there is nothing else to say. Perhaps, as Carri's documentary suggests, stories about the dictatorship have become so repetitive that they more often obscure history than reveal undisclosed aspects of it. Maybe, as Gamerro's novel implies, the proliferation of voices is more confusing than a conspiracy of silence. In this sense, Argentine reticence is attuned to global changes. The general disappointment with memory texts seems to announce their universal death. Dominick LaCapra asserts that, after decades of euphoria, we are witnessing a backlash against the concepts of memory and trauma in the humanities and social sciences (*History* 110). Kali Tal observes that literatures of trauma have passed through three consecutive stages: sacralization, assimilation, and appropriation (59). First regarded as quasi-religious artifacts, they were then analyzed as historical documents and finally treated as self-help texts whereby the reader him- or herself lives through the traumatic experience, neutralizing potential political effects. Kimberly Nance follows Tal's periodization in stating that Latin American testimonial narratives have ceded to less politically charged memoirs and that critical reception has run the gamut from celebration to pessimism, from praise to mourning (137–178). Tzvetan Todorov warns about an overabundance of representations that can paradoxically result in oblivion (12–13). Andreas Huyssen, in a preface to *Present Pasts* (notably dated 2003), makes an assertion that has been quoted innumerable times since then: "Today, we seem to suffer from a hypertrophy of memory.... After more than a decade of intense public and academic discussions of the uses and abuses of memory, many feel that the topic has been exhausted. Memory fatigue has set in" (3). Yet, as Huyssen goes on to say, the call to move on and dismiss discourses of memory merely reproduces the industry's fast-paced mechanisms of declaring obsolescence. Moreover, moving on impedes any explanation for the current obsession with memory itself as a symptom of the present. In other words, it is more fruitful to analyze this obsession than to let it go. Rather than discarding memory texts for their repetitive excess, it is necessary to acknowledge them (and their exhaustion) as discourses of the present.

Rethinking Testimonial Cinema takes this acknowledgment as its starting point. My primary intuition is that understanding memory fatigue as a symptom of the present is especially relevant in the Argentine case—where, as I have just mentioned, this fatigue sets in precisely when memory reaches the center of social discourse. Why is it, as the imperative to remember the dictatorship is widely regarded as moral imperative, that people who have been advocating for such recognition (like left-leaning intellectuals and second-generation survivors) abruptly come to distrust memory texts? Why is it that people who have been active in contesting Menemist amnesia (Sarlo, Gamerro, Vezzetti) are suddenly suspicious of the testimonial genre? Analyzing the stakes behind this unexpected distrust is more useful than merely moving on. Rather than reading this attitude toward testimonial narrative as a reticence about the past, it would be more productive to read it as a reticence about the present.

Reading Testimonial Narratives in Contemporary Argentina

The controversy surrounding Sarlo's 2005 book is a helpful context for elucidating this present-driven discourse. An examination of the debate helps us understand how testimonial narrative is being read and hints toward an explanation for the existing distrust. In *Tiempo pasado,* Sarlo argues that the subjective turn prevalent in contemporary Argentine culture has made memory discourse the only acceptable means of representing the past. Yet, far from illuminating history, this type of discourse (with testimonial narrative at its core) fits within a preestablished framework that precludes historical examination. According to Sarlo, though memory texts refer to the past, they do not actually address it. Their narratives resort to crystallized images but never fully explore history— a lack of efficacy caused by the fact that memory discourse relies on subjective experience, thus eliciting empathy, preventing critical distance, falling short of a broader collective scope, and avoiding empirical verification. This is why, she argues, we should only turn to testimonial texts for legal purposes. If we truly want to explore the past, we need to examine nonautobiographical literature and good academic history (16), as these two fields go beyond the problems entailed by personal experience alone and therefore permit (a more adequate) historical knowledge.

Although it is not the core of Sarlo's argument, which targets, above all, the repetitive aspects of contemporary discourse, the binary of "memory texts" versus "nonautobiographical literature/good academic history" sparked multiple reactions defending the testimonial genre. Relying on an interpretive tradition that focuses on the genre's popular edge, some scholars have seen Sarlo's dichotomy as a normative gesture that aims to preserve an intellectual status quo. José Rabasa, for instance, questions Sarlo's "iron-fisted critical stance" and "hegemonic deconstructivism" (179) and reminds her that testimonies can produce a popular history that "counters the hegemony of state historiography" (174). Alicia Partnoy claims that Sarlo's view is grounded in a patronizing conception that grants intellectuals the authority to dismiss testimonial authors' voices and then translate their experiences. "Sarlo's findings," Partnoy states, "nurture a view of the testimonial author as . . . on the one hand, the native informant, on the other, the native spoken for" ("Cuando vienen" 1666). John Beverley takes the critique a step further and places this normative gesture within a regional context. For him, *Tiempo pasado* is a model example of a neoconservative turn within the Latin American left. He reads this turn as a defensive reaction against the growing hegemony of popular voices that are increasingly displacing intellectual expertise.

In this line, Sarlo's disavowal of testimonial narrative masks a concern with how this type of narrative erodes boundaries and standards of disciplinary authority. Her reluctance hides an antipopular and antimulticultural ethos that aims to preserve intellectuals' power: "First there is a rejection of the authority of subaltern voice and experience, and an extreme dissatisfaction with or skepticism about multiculturalism.... Second, there is a defense of the writer-critic or traditional intellectual... in the process of being displaced by new political forces and actors... who more often than not do not come from the intelligentsia" (Beverley, "Neoconservative Turn" 76).

Rabasa, Partnoy, and Beverley base their defenses on what has become a dominant approach in reading Latin American testimonial narrative, especially after Beverley himself wrote a number of seminal essays in response to Rigoberta Menchú's account of the Guatemalan civil wars: subaltern theory. In the early 1990s, laying the foundations for this interpretive tradition, Beverley defined *testimonio* as a graphemic narrative told in the first person by a narrator who is also the real protagonist or witness of the events she or he recounts and who belongs to a subaltern or popular social class or group. *Testimonio* serves these previously voiceless and anonymous popular-democratic subjects by constituting a means of speaking for themselves rather than being spoken for.

Despite being a dynamic form with a complex generic history, Beverley suggested that *testimonio* emerged as a genre in the 1960s, in parallel to the struggles for national liberation. Grounded in the conviction that the personal is political, *testimonios* are told in the first person yet are concerned with a problematic collective situation that the narrator undergoes alongside others. In *testimonio*—as opposed to autobiography, which relies on the image of a coherent, self-conscious subject who appropriates literature as a means of self-expression—the "I" has the status of what linguists call a "shifter" or a linguistic function that anyone can indiscriminately assume. It is an affirmation of the authority of a single speaking subject, but it cannot affirm a self-identity that is separate from a group or class situation marked by oppression. Since, in many cases, this narrator is someone who is illiterate, the production of a *testimonio* often involves mediation by an intellectual, journalist, or writer, permitting the entry into literature of persons who would normally be excluded from direct literary expression. *Testimonio*, Beverley claimed (anticipating his later critique of Sarlo's position), thus challenges both the notion of the intellectual as society's leading voice and the integrity of literature as a discipline (*Against Literature* 69–99).[7]

While subaltern theory has served as a defense of the testimonial genre, trauma theory has provided further justifications for contesting Sarlo's text. Alejandro Kaufman argues that *Tiempo pasado*'s normative gesture does not wholly consider that testimonial narrative entails an experience of mourning, which is necessarily subjective and private. Validating these texts for their factual claims, as Sarlo does, would be as deceptive as legitimizing a psychological process by appealing to objectivity. Trauma and horror, he concludes, raise concerns that should be neither normative nor epistemological but solely ethical ("Aduanas" n.p.). Diego Tatián also stresses that testimonies should be distinguished from other narratives in that they result from an individual traumatic experience. He asserts, however, that experience itself is what grounds these discourses in fact as opposed to reason, making them relevant for history as a discipline. According to Tatián, someone who endured a traumatic experience attests to the existence of that experience and thus helps create an alternative history, one that illuminates the facts denied by official history (50–63).

Kaufman's and Tatián's are not isolated voices. Since the 1990s, trauma theory has also been a leading framework for interpreting testimonial texts globally.[8] Shoshana Felman and Dori Laub's *Testimony* and Cathy Caruth's *Unclaimed Experience* map out the connections among trauma, memory, testimony, and history, setting the stage for what has become a common reading. Drawing from Sigmund Freud and Bessel van der Kolk, they define "trauma" as "an overwhelming experience of sudden or catastrophic events in which the response to these events occurs in the often delayed and uncontrolled appearance of intrusive phenomena" (Caruth, *Unclaimed* 11). Trauma is caused by a lack of preparation in response to a sudden stimulus, preventing that stimulus from being processed at the time. This traumatizing experience, perceived but not fully grasped, returns in the form of a symptom. A wound that goes undetected until it haunts the individual, trauma emerges as an unwitting reenactment of an episode that one cannot leave behind. Yet trauma, these scholars stated, is more than pathology. It is also the voice of a past truth that cries out and remains otherwise unavailable. Contradicting suspicions regarding access to history, trauma allows for a recuperation of the past. It is within this possibility that the importance of testimonial narrative becomes apparent. Testimony is composed of traumatic memories that have not settled into understanding and hence conveys truths that are unspoken—and yet inscribed in the text. A precocious mode of accessing reality, testimony becomes "at once historical and clinical . . . a medium of historical transmission and the unsuspected medium of a healing" (Felman and Laub 9). Testimonial texts thus go beyond their legal aspects. They serve a liberating, healing purpose; they carry historical knowledge; and they elicit ethical responses.

Findings in trauma theory have had particular resonance in the field of post-dictatorship studies, where psychoanalysis was already a privileged discourse, especially in the Southern Cone. In the 1990s—marked by Walter Benjamin's writings, impacted by recent shifts in cultural criticism, and attuned to the discipline's historical influence across the region—foundational scholars like Nelly Richard, Alberto Moreiras, and Idelber Avelar appealed to psychoanalysis in unveiling the complex relationship between narrative and history. Trauma, symptom, memory, and mourning proved to be useful concepts for understanding how cultural production reacted to what Richard famously called the neoliberal "techniques of forgetting" (33), the strategies of silence and oblivion encouraged by the neoliberal regimes of the 1990s. It is probably due to the popularity achieved by psychoanalysis as well as to the privileging of Benjamin's Freudian dimension over his historical-materialist dimension (a telling preference in terms of how the critical conversation shifted from party politics to identity politics after the collapse of 1960s and '70s revolutionary projects) that trauma theory remains prominent in postdictatorship studies into the present day.[9] Books such as Nora Strejilevich's *El arte de no olvidar* (2006) and Edurne Portela's *Displaced Memories* (2009) base their analyses on the premise that clinical discourse is suitable for reading the representation of history in catastrophic narratives.[10] Several of the articles included in a 2013 volume edited by Erna Pfeiffer also follow this path. Moreover, trauma theory has become a leading paradigm for reading postdictatorship cinema. Scholars appeal to the discipline for understanding cinematic strategies. Film critics and journalists pepper their reviews with clinical vocabulary. Graduate students ground their dissertations in the hypotheses put forward by Felman and Laub.[11]

Even if we set aside the main points under discussion, the dispute over *Tiempo pasado* has a crucial value as a discourse of the present. Not only does it register the existing reticence against testimonial narrative, but it also documents the primary interpretive frameworks through which this type of narrative is being read. In this book, I argue that such frameworks, though highly constructive in the 1990s and when reading early testimonial production, have become less fruitful in contemporary Argentina and when reading later manifestations of the genre. Trauma and subaltern theories yield ahistorical analyses that cannot fully account for the postdictatorship scenario, especially after the 2000s. Hence, rather than discussing the internal features of testimonial texts (first-person narration, subjective history, appeals to empathy, fragmentary representations of the past), we need to rethink our theoretical approach. Redefining the interpretive focus can help us explain the contemporary reticence and redesign an intellectual ethics more in keeping with Argentina's political juncture today.

I find this latter point to be the main drawback of *Tiempo pasado*'s critique. Although the essay alludes to several challenges facing testimonial narrative in Argentina, it eventually attributes most of them to a textual feature: the use of the first person. This conclusion undermines Sarlo's arguments. On the one hand, she questions the authority of subjective experience without considering how subaltern and trauma studies have addressed this issue. In particular, both Beverley's canonical texts and Arturo Arias's compilation *The Rigoberta Menchú Controversy* respond, one by one, to her main concerns: the link between the individual and the collective dimensions, the role of empathy, and the tension between testimonial truth and empirical verification. On the other hand, the binary posed by "memory texts" versus "non-autobiographical literature/good academic history," aside from sparking various critical reactions, forecloses the existence of the testimonial genre as such. In short, if we follow the logic of Sarlo's essay, the only recourse for testimonial texts is for them to *not* be testimonial texts. Yet, even if the genre ceased to exist, the problems that Sarlo observes would remain, as they are not tied to subjective experience. Nonautobiographical literature, for example, can also be formulaic, fit a preestablished framework, and elicit empathy. The use of the third person does not guarantee a collective dimension, nor does it preclude a text from focusing on everyday details.

Increasingly, then, in the way that Sarlo's examples and counterexamples challenge the essay's leading binary, it grows clear that subjective representation is not in fact the central problem. At the beginning, consistent with her argument, Sarlo praises both *The Little School* (Partnoy's literary mixture of the first and the third person) and Pilar Calveiro's and Emilio De Ípola's books, written by two survivors who have decided to explain the dictatorship from an academic perspective. However, in subsequent pages, Sarlo commends testimonies that emerged from H.I.J.O.S.—texts explicitly grounded in subjectivity—and criticizes those included in *La voluntad*, a compilation of militants' testimonies with the goal of recuperating a collective perspective on the 1970s. In other words, a close look into *Tiempo pasado* reveals that memory fatigue is not indeed related to the subjective representation of history. The repetition of preexisting patterns goes beyond internal textual features. The problem lies instead, I argue, in how testimonial narrative is being read. Regardless of their content or leading voice, all texts (from subjective stories in H.I.J.O.S. to *The Little School*'s third-person sections) fit within the same preestablished (ahistorical) analysis. It is on the level of interpretation, not in the text itself, that the access to history has become a problem. What the controversy sparked by *Tiempo pasado* ultimately reveals is less the exhaustion of the genre than the need for a new approach to that genre.

Testimonial Narratives beyond Subaltern and Trauma Theories

But what is the trouble with the existing frameworks? In what sense do subaltern and trauma theories yield ahistorical analyses? Why are they unable to fully account for the postdictatorship scenario, especially after the 2000s? In the case of subaltern theory, these questions can be answered initially by looking back at its primary tenets and trying to assign them a referent. Who is the popular-democratic subject whose voice the testimonial text conveys? Who is the subaltern witness speaking for a marginalized class or group? In postdictatorship Argentina, testimonial subjects are usually intellectuals, or, as is true for relatives of disappeared people, mostly members of a white, urban middle class whose agenda does not necessarily coincide with that of an oppressed social group. Indeed, most testimonial subjects join Sarlo in belonging to the nation's leading intelligentsia. When Beverley states that Sarlo's disavowal of the genre is guided by an anti-multicultural and antipopular feeling, he overlooks the Argentine specificity, transferring canonical theories on *testimonio* to a context where they do not quite apply.[12] We could say, in fact, that when reading these texts from a subaltern studies standpoint, we may actually be preserving subalternity. Grouping all testimonial subjects under the *subaltern*, *multicultural*, or *popular* label fails to acknowledge particular victims who remain underrepresented in postdictatorship narrative: for example, working-class, gay, and indigenous people.[13] Moreover, although testimonial subjects were oppressed, anonymous, and voiceless in the past (during the dictatorship and arguably in the 1990s as well), they have been on center stage for over a decade, even becoming key pillars for the Kirchner administration—when, in Ludmila Da Silva Catela's words, there is an "*estatización de la memoria*" (state-controlled memory) ("Prólogo"11). To put it simply, testimonial narrative is no longer a subaltern narration of history; it has become, as I analyze in the last two chapters, a hegemonic version: that is, a particularity that has taken up "incommensurable universal signification" (Laclau 70).[14] In contemporary Argentina, subaltern theory faces a problem similar to the one already noted by Javier Sanjinés and Gustavo Verdesio in another context: it relies on a static view of subaltern identity, one that does not recognize historical change (Verdesio 16).[15]

That being said, it could be argued that, even if not an expression of a subaltern group, testimonial narrative is nonetheless a popular (i.e., massive, "low-culture") type of narrative. This is what Partnoy and Beverley imply when criticizing Sarlo's binary: "The political and ethical authority conceded to *testimonio* threatens, in Sarlo's view, to destabilize the authority of both imaginative literature and the academic social sciences" (Beverley, "Neoconservative Turn" 73). Yet, these statements are built on a slight displacement that occurs when summarizing Sarlo's dichotomy: it does not bring testimonial discourse into outright opposition with literary and academic discourse. Rather, Sarlo traces differences between "memory texts," "non-autobiographical literature," and "good academic history." The displacement, though subtle, is telling: Sarlo's adjectives (*nonautobiographical*, *good*) are certainly grounded in a normative gesture, but normativity is unrelated to disciplinary or artistic boundaries. There are also, Sarlo implies, "bad" literary and academic texts facing the same challenges as memory texts. Her choice of examples and counterexamples is again indicative of this view: As I mentioned earlier, Sarlo celebrates H.I.J.O.S.'s narratives and instead criticizes those produced by scholars and intellectuals for compilation in *La voluntad*. Although she explicitly states her discomfort toward the fetishization of memory texts and the commodification of the recent past (17), the argument that she feels threatened by the increasing hegemony of popular-subaltern texts or groups is somewhat overstated. Subaltern theory seems to have exported a set of given concepts into a particular context where they do not really fit—a disparity evidenced in Partnoy's use of the word *native* ("Cuando vienen" 1666) when alluding to the testimonial author. Although this framework is potentially productive (and I will revisit some of its concepts to examine 1980s and '90s testimonial production and to analyze the testimonial genre's hegemonization), it risks overlooking the specificity of postdictatorship narrative—and, above all, it does not quite explain the phenomenon of post-2000 reticence, which is a necessary starting point for redefining an intellectual ethics after the so-called return of the left in the region.

Although subaltern theory resurfaced during the controversy, it is trauma theory, as mentioned earlier, that has dominated postdictatorship readings, due in large part to the regional prominence of psychoanalysis. Nonetheless, it would be misleading to argue that the entire psychoanalytic framework fails when approaching postdictatorship cultural production. Given that such narratives have resulted from catastrophic events, this framework can illuminate, among other things, how people cope with catastrophes and how discourse embodies unconscious aspects. Analyses of documentaries featuring second-generation survivors, for example, have shed light on how children experience traumatic events and on how memory acquires layers. There are also two well-known traditions that do not entirely fall within this critique: one—on which I rely throughout the book—that blends psychoanalysis, semiotics, and sometimes Marxism, and another that sees cinema as a useful medium for exploring concepts such as identification, fetishism, scopophilia, the gaze, fantasy, and pleasure.[16] Several problems arise, however, when appealing to psychoanalytic clinical discourse to interpret history—a move that, via trauma theory, has become quite common when reading testimonial narratives.[17]

A first hint of this incompatibility between history and clinical discourse is found in the choice of theoretical concepts that are not easily translated from one to the other. One of these is trauma. An occurrence that is unwittingly reenacted, trauma as a concept must be reconsidered when analyzing a narrative that tends to be carefully organized—and thus, to put it in psychoanalytic terms, self-reflectively foregrounds its own symptoms. Testimonial subjects are not patients who seek help after a haunting recurrence but people who have decided to speak publicly about a specific event affecting society, even in the case of real victims in a documentary. Moreover, testimonial discourse is not uncontrolled, symptomatic rhetoric to be used in reconstructing hidden traumatic circumstances but rather a discourse that openly addresses those circumstances. Even if we agreed with the psychoanalytic premise that any type of discourse contains unconscious aspects, we could not establish a symmetrical parallel between a narrative representing a past catastrophe and the clinical narrative delivered by a traumatized subject. At this point, the distinction between experience and event becomes relevant. As LaCapra explains, while the traumatizing event (say, torture or kidnapping) is time-specific and datable, the traumatic experience (the delayed effects of the catastrophic event) is not; it has an elusive aspect because it has not expired (*History* 45). Trauma theory seems to juxtapose event and experience, a juxtaposition that ascribes the qualities of the traumatic experience to the representation of the traumatizing event. In other words, trauma theory uses concepts associated with the subjective sphere to assess the collective realm, often obliterating a larger (political, historical) dimension—and relegating the testimonial subject to the role of a traumatized victim who passively suffers an unexpected occurrence.[18]

A good example of this obliteration can be found in a dispute over revolutionary violence that put left-leaning intellectuals at odds with each other. In 2004, the journal *La Intemperie* published an interview with Héctor Jouvé, a former member of a guerrilla group that aimed to create a Guevarist *foco* (guerrilla focus) in northern Argentina in the 1960s. At some point in the interview, Jouvé suggested that the armed group itself had committed a crime by killing two of its members who had broken down psychologically. The philosopher Oscar Del Barco, a former activist himself, responded to the interview with a letter assuming responsibility and exhorting his fellows to follow the same path. Armed struggle, he proposed, needed to be reassessed, even if this entailed acknowledgment of its possible mistakes. Del Barco's response sparked innumerable reactions in academic journals and cultural magazines. What I find most interesting is that, with a couple of exceptions, such as Eduardo Grüner's analysis of the generalization implied by the notion of the revolutionary left, most replies addressed the (overtly political) topic with clinical psychoanalytic discourse. Juan Bautista Ritvo, for example, studied Del Barco's critique of violence in terms of Freudian "sublimation" (130). Alejandro Kaufman stated that it would be redundant to discuss the letter's assertions because they had emerged as an act of anamnesis rather than an argued presentation. Instead of an invitation to political reflection, according to Kaufman, Del Barco's confession was an untimely reenactment of a trauma that he had forgotten: the experience of war violence (145–147). Jorge Jinkis, the editor of the journal, made an explicit case for a clinical psychoanalytic reading, arguing that Del Barco had proposed an impossible exercise based on an unstable first person: his guilt had materialized through a politics of feelings that had transferred the *I* to a *we*, asking readers to suppress their own murderous desires (120–122). Leonor Arfuch read the entire debate as a symptom of the traumatic disorientation of the intellectual left (107).

I find this controversy particularly telling as an example of how such a framework can preclude further examination.[19] Although we could agree that testimonial discourse conveys unconscious aspects, that memory can be analyzed in Freudian terms, and that it is possible to read traumatic experience as a collective experience (especially when focusing on similarity effects triggered by a political event), the above-mentioned responses clearly demonstrate the drawbacks of clinical discourse for assessing the political realm.[20]

We could indeed say that such limitations become doubly problematic in the postdictatorship context. Scholars working on authoritarian regimes agree that the military based their supremacy on the dismantling of the intellectual field, the abolition of collective forms of expression, and the privatization of the public sphere.[21] Censorship, forced exile, imprisonment, and death went hand in hand with an official discourse that emphasized private notions like *home* and *family*. *Domesticity* became the leading military ideologeme, creating a rift between the private and public fields and between the individual and collective realms. Thus, in failing to establish a compelling link between the private and public domains, the framework of clinical psychoanalytic discourse seems to endure dictatorial logic. The almost exclusive focus on concepts such as trauma, mourning, and experience further separates both dimensions. In this sense, we must agree with Sarlo on the challenges posed by the subjective turn. Yet, these limitations confirm that the problem has less to do with subjective representation than with subjective interpretation.[22]

Moreover, the conflation of the private and collective spheres paradoxically undermines the possibility of testimonial narratives engendering historical transmission. The attitude toward history as a hidden truth that has been unconsciously inscribed in texts waiting to be deciphered converts them into thriller-like narratives. Once the truth has been discovered, once the secret has been revealed, the search is over. Via trauma theory, history becomes a fixed, latent, stable referent that simply needs to be brought into the realm of cognition. Trauma theory ends up being, as Thomas Elsaesser observes, an account of "recovered referentiality" (201) or, to put it in Leys's terms, a "pathos of the literal" (266); an account that concludes with the assertion that there exists a hidden, static, literal referent to be unveiled by the cultural scholar. This literal stasis is implied in Felman's theorization. For instance, she claims: "Psychoanalytic theory is nothing other than a finally available statement of a truth that, at the outset, was unknown but was gradually accessed through the practice and the process of the testimony" (16). But what happens if that truth was actually known from the start? What happens if that truth is being openly addressed and has been repeated and reemphasized for several decades? Then psychoanalytic theory (we could say, slightly tweaking Felman's words) gradually revolves around the testimony's own process and practice toward finally accessing a statement that had actually been available all along.

Conceiving of narratives as pieces in a clinical dialogue gives rise to another undesired backlash: they become redundant. Based on unchanging conceptions of mourning, trauma, and memory, trauma theory provides an interpretive formula that treats all of them identically, extracting a common meaning. Independently of their content, all narratives end up yielding the same analysis; regardless of their specific textual configuration, they result in a single possible interpretation. In this sense, trauma theory comes closer to what Christian Metz has called a "nosographic approach": an approach that treats cultural products (in particular films) as symptoms and thus "accords no intrinsic importance to [their] manifest content, which becomes simply a kind of (discontinuous) reservoir of more or less isolated clues whose immediate purpose is to reveal the latent.... Everything remains the same except the sharp distinction between the normal and the pathological... and with it the indifference to the filmic text as such" (*The Imaginary* 25–26). As I explain in chapter 3 in further detail, the omission of textual differences also entails an oversight of diachronic transformations in the representation of history, disregarding how testimonial narrative has changed over the years. In this way, discussing the military regimes in the early democracy, as hidden aspects of recent history first came to light, seems no different than addressing them after decades of continuous findings. Early allegories become as revealing as second-generation films being produced today. Trauma theory ultimately reads *La historia oficial*, Luis Puenzo's 1985 film unveiling the atrocities of the Argentine dictatorship for the first time, the same way as it reads *Los rubios*, Carri's documentary exposing the iconic nature of those same facts after twenty years of repetitive representation. Thus, although trauma scholars want testimonial narratives to serve as means of historical transmission, analyses embedded in longstanding conceptions of individual experience actually end up impeding access to history.[23]

In noting this problem, I am not trying to accuse trauma theory of forgetting certain facts. As Paul Ricœr has compellingly shown, forgetting is a necessary condition for remembrance (542). What I intend to highlight here is that this type of reading does not fully incorporate a historical perspective. History becomes a fixed, frozen background, framing a repetitive analysis of the process of trauma and mourning. Although this approach might have helped to study early manifestations of the testimonial genre—and although I rely on some of its concepts when addressing 1980s and '90s cultural production—it does not truly account for changes over time. In this sense, I agree with Huyssen when he warns that psychoanalysis has formed a thick discursive network that obstructs the political and historical layers of memory discourse (8–9). Or, to put it in the discipline's own terms, it has sealed memory discourse into compulsive repetition. If a primary feature of the traumatic symptom is that it is an out-of-context experience, we could say then that these out-of-context analyses have become traumatic and symptomatic readings.²⁴ The Argentine dictatorship remains what LaCapra calls a "founding trauma" (*History* 56; *Writing* 81): a traumatic event that shatters identity yet paradoxically becomes its basis. In other words, while a founding trauma provides a means to understanding history, it also becomes an obsession that undermines the possibility of engaging the present. Hence, LaCapra admits, existing critiques constitute "an important challenge that needs to be addressed: to develop a careful approach that does not become psychologizing, consumingly theoretical, oblivious to larger social and political problems, narrowly subservient to identity politics, or the object of a fixation whereby history is identified with trauma and one sees trauma everywhere" (*History* 112).²⁵

Restoring Historicity: Testimonial Cinema at the Intersection of Semiotics and Affect

But how can we develop such an approach? Is there any way for interpretations of testimonial narrative to avoid excessive psychologizing, hypertheoretical analysis, or fixations on trauma and mourning? How likely are we to address testimonial texts without submitting to a narrow conception of identity politics? Is it possible to delve into these subjective stories without overlooking larger political problems? In this book I argue that, in order to develop this kind of approach, we need to recover a concept that has been missing from subaltern and trauma theories: historicity. By "historicity" I do not only mean the textual representation of history but also the particular qualities that texts adopt as a result of their inscription in history. This inscription manifests itself on two different, interrelated planes. Synchronically, texts are marked by their present of enunciation; that is, they are impacted by the tensions and impulses of a certain historical moment. Texts simultaneously convey existing social discourses and contribute to creating these discourses. They belong to (and contribute to the creation of) particular ideological and discursive formations. In other words, texts have historicity because they emerge within a concrete, particular present—and because they are being read in that concrete, particular present. Yet, as LaCapra famously stated, "History is always in transit" (*History* 1). Texts are not only inscribed in the present but also diachronically impacted by temporality; they are marked by earlier historical moments (whose residual components, as Raymond Williams would say, largely constitute their present [53]), and they are open to the future. Texts might anticipate and shape historical moments yet to come. They might also be read at a forthcoming historical moment, thereby achieving new meanings. As Vezzetti observes, criticizing the repetitive interpretations of the Argentine dictatorship: "*Hay una profunda historicidad de la memoria, que se conjuga siempre desde un presente: eso se expresa en las formas de la producción pero también de la apropiación del testimonio*" [Memory has profound historicity, which is always conjugated in the present: it is expressed in testimony's forms of production, but also in its appropriation] ("El testimonio" 25). An analysis that attends to testimonial narrative's historicity on both the synchronic and diachronic planes, then, must simultaneously contemplate three interrelated levels of interpretation: the textual representation of history, the dialectical (mutually constructed) relationship between this textual representation and the narrative's present of enunciation, and its temporal (diachronic) localization in history.[26]

An example from a well-known film might help clarify this intersection. Interpreting *La historia oficial* while attending to its historicity means first analyzing how history is being represented within the narrative: how Gaby's illegal adoption discloses hidden aspects of the military years, how the connections between US corporations and Gaby's adoptive father alludes to the economic interests behind the coup d'état, how the initial indifference of Gaby's adoptive mother points to a general social attitude, etc. Second, paying attention to historicity entails dialectically linking this internal representation to the film's present of enunciation. How does the internal portrayal shape social discourses in the early democracy, when the question of who should be brought to court is being debated? And, conversely, how do social discourses in the early democracy enable the emergence of this particular depiction? For example, how does an existing notion of family—largely enabled by an earlier military discourse praising domesticity—provide a common ground for fictional representation at this sensitive moment? Finally, acknowledging historicity means recognizing that Puenzo's film both engages past narratives and continues to be read over time. How does *La historia oficial* build on or challenge pre-1980s Argentine cinema? What does the film say in the 1990s, in the wake of the Menemist decrees releasing the imprisoned members of the military junta? How does it speak to us in 2017, when the tragic fate of the disappeared and their children is already known and has occupied center stage at least since *kirchnerismo*?

Paying special attention to these three interrelated levels of interpretation, *Rethinking Testimonial Cinema* engages in synchronic and diachronic readings of testimonial films produced in the 1980s, in the 1990s, and since the 2000s—three distinctive moments marked by different social and official discourses on the dictatorship. This periodization is meant, however, less as a rigid classification than as a pointer to broad, progressive tendencies. Not all the films produced in each of these moments represent the dictatorship the same way. The filmmaker's particular history, class, gender, and ideology—to name but a few important parameters—certainly yield diverse representations. The choice of genre and the advent of particular political events also impact, as I suggest throughout the book, the connection with history in different ways. Moreover, marking a specific year as the beginning for each period is somewhat arbitrary: representation patterns certainly do not expire December 31 and begin January 1.

I came across this arbitrariness especially when investigating films shot around the year 2000. Some seemed to be more in line with the critical edge of the genre typical of the 1990s, and others began to show a kind of exhaustion more typical of the 2000s—which is why I included films shot in the same year in chapters 2 and 3, even though each chapter deals with two different periods. Yet, despite running the risk of falling into arbitrary generalization, I believe that this periodization allows us to better understand testimonial cinema's historicity—for example, we can better understand, as I claim in chapter 4, the ideological implications of post-2000 fiction films that return to an earlier 1980s format.[27] I expect that these synchronic and diachronic analyses will overcome the existing fatigue affecting the topic and contribute to an understanding of testimonial narrative's specific place in Argentine culture.

Although the book sometimes refers to other media, its primary focus is cinema. The reason is twofold. On the one hand, in a world dominated by audiovisual imagery, as Robert Rosenstone claims (29), cinema is the main source of historical knowledge—a claim that certainly applies to the Argentine case, where cinema has been the leading artistic field in representing the dictatorship precisely since the release of the Academy Award–winning *La historia oficial* in 1985. Cinema has served as a document preserving fragments of the afilmic realm, a register of social attitudes, and an agent capable of shaping feelings and beliefs; this is why the close-knit relationship between film and history has been singled out since early theorizations on the medium.[28] On the other hand, film's indexical, symbolic, and iconic dimensions allow for a more nuanced reading of the testimonial genre's inscription in history. Thus, in order to avoid a loss of historicity, I propose—in line with a contemporary trend in film scholarship—that we revitalize a semiotic approach.

As Philip Rosen has carefully explained, although semiotics emerged in film scholarship mainly via Peter Wollen's rereading of André Bazin in 1969, it was almost immediately superseded by other discourses that emphasized the role of subjectivity, such as poststructuralism and feminist theory. Sharing an antirealist conception of representation, these approaches replaced discussions of referentiality with issues like subject-positioning, desire, and sexual difference (1–8).[29] Since the early 2000s, however, a group of film scholars has been arguing that a revitalization of key concepts in Peircean semiotics, in particular "indexicality," is useful for rethinking the links between film and history. As I will further address in the first two chapters, indexicality doubly endows the filmic image with historical qualities. First, it points to the image's existence at a particular historical moment and thus brings traces of that moment into the filmic world. Because the image is composed of a referent that belongs to the present of enunciation, we can find this present within the film. For instance, in Carlos Echeverría's *Juan, como si nada hubiera sucedido* (1987), we see journalist Esteban Buch walking through the streets, knocking on doors, and entering military facilities in search of clues about a man's disappearance in southern Argentina. Thus, although the documentary aims to reveal what happened during the dictatorship, it is full of indexical images of the 1980s (i.e., the film's present of enunciation). Put simply, thanks to indexicality, we can actually see fragments of the 1980s, of the documentary's "present," within the film—something that would not be possible in a literary piece. As Mary Ann Doane observes, "The indexical sign is the imprint of a once-present and unique moment, the signature of temporality. As pure indication, pure assurance of existence, it is allied with contingency" (16).

Second, indexicality endows film with history because it points to the past. Given that the profilmic object was placed in front of the camera prior to the image being viewed, filmic images become "indexical traces": "for their spatial field and the objects depicted were in the camera's presence at some point prior to the actual reading of the sign" (Rosen 20). In other words, the scenes from the 1980s, in which Buch interviews former military officers, belong to the documentary's present of enunciation, but by the time we see them, this present is already past—a fact that would be true even if we viewed these scenes a mere five minutes after they were shot. Thus, because films, unlike TV broadcasts, cannot transmit the present simultaneously, they resort to all kinds of representational strategies in order to differentiate the present from the past. Its nonimmediacy makes the cinematic field more explicitly and visually historical than others: a "representation of history . . . marked by history and prompted to find formal solutions for its own paradoxical non-simultaneity" (Andermann, *New Argentine* 155). In *Juan*, where distinguishing between the dictatorial past and the democratic present is of the utmost importance, these solutions include the incorporation both of television images to mark scenes as belonging to the present and of photographic images to emphasize the past.[30]

Building on this semiotic trend, I argue that the symbolic and iconic dimensions, even though they have not received the same attention as indexicality in recent film scholarship, are also crucial for restoring historicity. If we agree that social discourse is historically situated, then we can read generic conventions and verbal language historically. Because genres change over time, we can read films diachronically based on generic repetitions and variations, a practice I engage especially in chapter 3 when addressing the parodic nature of second-generation performative documentaries. The decades-long repetition of certain features associated with the testimonial genre (e.g., a first-person account of history, interviewees able to delve into private details as well as to offer political commentary, and photos attesting to the existence of the missing person) allows us to read performative documentaries like María Inés Roqué's *Papá Iván* (2000) as parodic distortions that indicate the exhaustion of the genre. Moreover, since verbal language is historically specific, we can connect words and expressions to particular historical moments, as I analyze mostly in chapter 4. In second-generation fiction told from a child's perspective, such as *Infancia clandestina* (2012), there is an anachronistic contrast between children's contemporary phrases and an adult, 1970s-era vocabulary.

Finally, as I also show in the last chapter, iconicity helps us understand the diachronic inscription of filmic images in history. As Peirce explained, iconicity results from the mixture of repetition and stability (78). Because a sign is repeatedly connected to a stable referent, an icon is formed. For a sign to be considered iconic, a particular image must be continually linked to an invariable referent. An everyday example helps illustrate this: it is because a particular shape regularly refers to a women's restroom that people are able to visually associate the shape with the restroom. Since this image always evokes a space that remains constant, people are able to choose the appropriate space when seeing the image. A case in point are post-2000 fiction films like Daniel Bustamante's *Andrés no quiere dormir la siesta* (2009), where several iconic signs (a garage-style door leading to a detention camp, a woman giving birth in chains, a black hood in the middle of the night, and a green Ford Falcon) evoke a (stable) referent that for three decades we have called "military dictatorship." Thus, in resulting from repetition over time, iconicity helps elucidate the diachronic itinerary of filmic images. It contributes to an understanding of how these images, like history itself, are always in transit.[31]

However, semiotics alone cannot illustrate the historicity of the filmic image—especially when it comes to testimonial cinema, where both representations of the dictatorship and feelings associated with these representations have persisted over time. I therefore believe that, in order to restore historicity, a semiotic approach must be complemented with an affect-based approach. Indeed, the interrelatedness between feelings and history lies at the center of what Patricia Ticineto Clough calls "the affective turn": the theoretical importance of affect for a number of academics in the humanities and social sciences since at least the early 2000s (1).[32] Affect scholars rely on an assumption that has important implications for reading cultural artifacts: they claim that feelings are culturally, socially, and historically variable as opposed to universal, private, and static. Michelle Rosaldo, for example, has studied how in Ilongot society, unlike in more vertical societies like the Japanese, "shame" arises occasionally and is mostly linked to sporadic situations of inequality (93). In another case, Carol Stearns has examined how the ability to moderate anger in early modern Britain was seen as a marker of upper-class belonging, whereas the manifestation of anger was perceived as insanity in those at the bottom of the socioeconomic hierarchy. This perception, she argues, was both class related and historically specific. It was not until the late seventeenth century that the notion of anger truly took shape, along with a new conception of a merciful God. Before this period, "anger" was closer to the feeling that today we call *sadness* (170–190).

The cultural, social, and historical variability of feelings has prompted scholars such as Brian Massumi to make a vital distinction for the argument that I develop in this book: the distinction between *affect* and *emotion*. Massumi defines emotion as "the socio-linguistic fixing of the quality of an experience which is from that point onward defined as personal" (28). A result of social convention, emotion has meaning and can thus be verbalized. In other words, we can say that we are angry because our present-day society acknowledges a particular feeling that we all understand as anger. Although we experience this emotion as personal and private, we can understand it and name it because there is social consensus around its existence. Affect, on the contrary, is intensity before signification or coding. As such, it is "unqualified" and is not "ownable" or "recognizable" (28). Whereas emotion is a feeling that has been socially inscribed, affect is a feeling that could be considered as a presocial intensity, because its meaning has not been socially codified. While emotions are "qualified intensity" (28) because they have been conceptualized, conventionalized, and named, affects have not been semantically defined. As Kathleen Stewart puts it, affects are "obtuse and erratic, in contrast to the 'obvious meaning' of semantic message and symbolic signification" (3). This distinction between affect and emotion helps us perceive that feelings, like conventions and meanings, vary culturally and socially—that is, an affective intensity might be named as a specific emotion in one particular culture or social group and not in another. It also shows us that feelings are always in transit. Going back to Stearns's example, British people experienced an intensity (an affect) that only in the late seventeenth century became an emotion with a specific name: anger.

There is disagreement, even among affect scholars, with respect to the connections between emotion and affect. Alison Jaggar and Rosaldo, for example, use these terms interchangeably (50–68, 84–99). Ticineto Clough explicitly disagrees with Massumi and argues that affect is not a presocial intensity but rather "a nonlinear complexity out of which the narration of conscious states such as emotion is subtracted" (3). Lawrence Grossberg understands affect as a structured plane of effects by which power is mobilized and performed, while emotion exists at the intersection of affect and narrative ideology (28). Similarly to Grossberg, Sara Ahmed understands emotions as "affective economies, where feelings do not reside in subjects or objects, but are produced as effects of circulation" (*Cultural* 8). For her, then, emotions are a form of cultural politics that creates boundaries, allowing the individual and the social to be delineated as if they were objects. Without distinguishing between emotion and affect, geographers Joyce Davidson, Liz Bondi, and Mick Smith propose a "non-objectifying view of emotions as relational flows, fluxes or currents, in-between people and places rather than 'things' or 'objects' to be studied or measured" (3). In spite of their varying definitions, these scholars agree on a basic point that aligns with my argument:

the historicity of feelings. Thus, although other possibilities for naming these concepts are certainly available, I follow the distinction between emotions as explicitly codified feelings and affects as nonconceptualized feelings, because I find it especially productive for reading historicity in postdictatorship cinema.[33]

Taking this distinction into account, scholars like Metz, Massumi, and Jill Bennett claim that the event of image reception is always, as Massumi puts it, "bi-level" (24). On the one hand, it is marked by what Massumi calls "quality," what Metz calls "visual series," and what Bennett calls "communicative dimension": a response to the content and meaning of the image. On the other, it also contains what Massumi understands as "intensity," Metz as "proprioceptive series," and Bennett as "transaction": a response to the materiality of the image that is nonverbal, corporeal, and manifested in the skin (Bennett 7; Massumi 24–25; Metz, *Film* 10–11). If the former falls within the realm of emotion (that is, of qualified intensity), the latter can be understood as affect. Put simply, films not only reflect, transmit, or unsettle already existing and recognizable feelings (i.e., emotions), but can also shape new feelings (i.e., affects). Rather than only translating experiences with which the audience emotionally identifies, films depict unnamed sensations that are felt and that serve as catalysts for critical inquiry (Bennett 25). Films can create new affective configurations and not only document previously codified feelings. In this sense, cinema becomes both a historical register and a historical agent. Film is representational and also "generative" (Bennett 153)—and, in this sense, nonrepresentational.

Cecilia Sosa has indeed explored this generative capacity of affect for the Argentine case. In her insightful book *Queering Acts of Mourning*, Sosa draws from queer and performance theories to develop an alternative framework for understanding the affective transmission of trauma beyond family settings. If, at least until 2003, human rights organizations' discourses had adopted an idea of mourning based on the wounded family—as seen, for example, in the discourses surrounding Madres and Abuelas de Plaza de Mayo—this idea has been displaced onto a collective sense of co-ownership of trauma beyond blood ties. In this light, postdictatorship films such as *Los rubios* and *M* can be seen as queer narratives that challenge hegemonic notions of biology-based trauma, contest victimizing accounts, and open new lines of affective transmission (1–12). The Argentine grief, Sosa argues, does not allow for a linear historicism. As these films show, there is "an archive of feelings" (*Queering* 7) composed of intensities and sensations that have not settled and that enable nonnormative acts of mourning.[34]

Although ultimately aiming at a different goal (i.e., to understand alternative forms of processing collective trauma), Sosa's findings rest on the premise that I have been emphasizing in these paragraphs: theories of affect are central to historical readings of postdictatorship cinema. These theories help us perceive, as

Sosa claims, queer archives of feeling and also, as evidenced in the diachronic itinerary of my book, how testimonial films generally went from shaping new affects to solidifying already codified emotions. Radical activism in the 1970s is a cogent example. While testimonial films in the early democracy shaped a highly sentimental image of militancy that was new to the era and that helped foster new democratic feelings, post-2000 fiction films like *Infancia clandestina* repeat and intensify an existing emotional discourse on left-leaning militancy, arguably precluding the emergence of alternative types of sensation. By the same token, while in the 1980s the referent "military dictatorship" was built on new affective images, over the decades it has become part of what Jaggar calls "emotional hegemony" (60): the predominant norms, values, and feelings whereby societies ensure their own perpetuation. Moreover, the interrelatedness between feelings and cognition that lies at the heart of affect theories—that is, the idea that they constitute an overarching dimension rather than existing as two separate realms—helps us read testimonial cinema as a multifaceted phenomenon appealing equally to the body and to the mind. Both what is represented and the feelings associated with these representations are crucial to understanding what is at stake in testimonial films, which is why an approach combining semiotics and affect theories is more suitable for engaging in a historical interpretation of the genre. It allows us to read both its representational and nonrepresentational dimensions historically.

While the combination of affect and semiotics retains the most important findings of each framework, it also fills their gaps. On the one hand, affect theory helps analyze the nonvisual aspects that escape a semiotic approach, which is necessarily based on visual representation. On the other, semiotics provides a firmer ground against speculation—a risk often encountered by affect theories and by theories of spectatorship more broadly. In this sense, I agree with David Rodowick when he states that "claims made about processes of identification in actual spectators, powerful and important as they may be, are speculative. . . . One must accept fundamentally that these positions exist only as potentialities that are ultimately undecidable with respect to any given spectator" (viii). The combination of semiotics and affect enables us to shift the focus from potential spectatorship to the representation of feelings on screen and over time. To continue with the example of militancy in post-2000 fiction, these two combined frameworks show us how, in *Infancia clandestina*, the use of close-up and slow-motion shots intensifies feelings linked to an iconic image of the 1970s. A diachronic look into postdictatorship cinema suggests that these feelings, rather than being affects, have gradually turned into qualified intensities that are part of Argentina's emotional hegemony during *kirchnerismo*.[35]

Moreover, the mixture of semiotics and affect theories sheds light on a connection I address repeatedly throughout the book: the connection among genre, ideology, and history. Although (as I explain in the paragraphs below and as I further develop in the first chapter) I argue that "documentary" and "fiction" should not play any role in defining testimonial cinema, I also believe that the uses of these two genres entail different ideological implications. For example, while second-generation documentaries tend to challenge hegemonic representations of the dictatorship and unsettle emotions, second-generation fiction tends to enhance codified feelings and enable hegemony. *Papá Iván* and *Los rubios* are two good examples of the former. Roqué and Carri manipulate indexicality (for instance, they include photos and letters and then erase their referential markers) to question dominant narratives about the 1970s—a manipulation especially enabled by documentary.[36] By contrast, as seen in the second-generation fiction films mentioned earlier, the use of fiction allows for narratives legitimizing dominant and official representations. This dichotomy is far from unequivocal. Not only—as several scholars have observed (Nichols 50–60; Plantinga 20–35; Chanan, *The Politics* 4–16)—is it difficult to establish clear-cut boundaries between documentary and fiction, but also, as Aguilar has outlined, Argentine cinema has been dominated by hybridity since the 1990s (*Otros mundos* 64). The vast majority of documentaries include fictional strategies, like in Carri's incorporation of her own presence as a survivor by means of Playmobil toys and an actress who plays her. Many fictional works integrate documentary sections, as in Gastón Biraben's *Cautiva* (2005), where a completely fictional plot follows archival footage of the 1978 FIFA Soccer World Cup. In this sense, establishing a clear boundary between documentary and fiction is an impossible task. Analyzing different uses of the two genres, however, illuminates the important ideological consequences that this difference entails, particularly for the enhancement or diminishment of feeling, iconicity, and indexicality.

Drawing mostly from semiotics, theories of affect, and scholarship on the ideological uses of documentary and fiction, *Rethinking Testimonial Cinema* explores the multiple ways in which historicity has permeated testimonial films. Although each chapter refers to a number of films that share similar patterns, I have chosen to focus on an essential two or three in order to effectively engage in close analysis. In the first chapter, I primarily reexamine two films that have received conflicting appraisals: Echeverría's documentary *Juan, como si nada hubiera sucedido* and Héctor Olivera's fiction film *La noche de los lápices* (1986). While Olivera's melodramatic fiction, based on the testimony of a camp survivor, has been dismissed as a naïve, self-purging, and emotional narrative, *Juan* has been praised as an exception within the early democracy: a highly reflexive documentary that bears little resemblance to the unsophisticated, sentimental generic fictions of its time. Predominantly relying on Chanan and Doane's views of indexicality, I reread *Juan*'s "exceptional" reflexivity, conflicting temporalities, and reconfigured television strategies, on the one hand, as materializations of the open-ended possibilities that characterized a still-uncertain democracy, and on the other, as aspects in line with other 1980s documentaries such as *Todo es ausencia* (Rodolfo Kuhn, 1984), *Malvinas: historia de traiciones* (Jorge Denti, 1983), *No al punto final* (Jorge Denti, 1986), *A los compañeros la libertad* (Marcelo Céspedes and Carmen Guarini, 1987), and *Las Madres* (Lourdes Portillo and Susana Blaustein, 1985). Rather than establishing a contrast between *Juan* and melodramatic fiction, I then reexamine *La noche de los lápices* from an affect-based standpoint to highlight the role of fictional testimonies as historical agents, while remaining attuned to what was happening in the 1980s. Ultimately, this chapter aims to dismantle the rigid binaries driving the opposite reactions toward the two films (knowledge/feeling, documentary/fiction) and to propose a redefinition of testimonial cinema: one that allows for a more comprehensive understanding of how testimonial films in the early democracy fostered civic participation, shaped new affects, and offered an alternative version of history.

Chapter 2, "Indexicality and Counterhegemony: Testimonial Documentary in the 1990s," pays special attention to theories on the links between documentary and history, focusing on films that, even as they refer to the 1970s, stage the 1990s. Such films include Andrés Di Tella's *Montoneros: una historia* (1994) and David Blaustein's *Cazadores de utopías* (1996), which interview first-generation political activists, and Blaustein's *Botín de guerra* (1999), which gives voice to the second-generation experiences. At a moment when official discourses grounded in neoliberalism aim to push forward and forget the recent past, these documentaries—as well as others shot at roughly the same time, like Di Tella's *Prohibido* (1997), Andrés Habegger's *(h)istorias cotidianas* (1998–2000), and Carmen Guarini and Marcelo Céspedes's *H.I.J.O.S., el alma en dos* (2000)—portray testimonial subjects, organize historical sequences, and materialize temporality in stark opposition to such discourses. Relying on several formal solutions to distinguish present and past—including the use of archival footage, historically marked indexical signs, and spatial displacement—these films both create new affects around 1970s-era militancy and disclose a frozen, alien present: a present radically different from the one praised by the neoliberal narrative of progress and modernity that permeates the afilmic realm. The testimonial documentaries of the 1990s thus take an antiofficial and counterhegemonic stance: they oppose official discourses, counter hegemonic narratives, and bid for hegemony.

In the third chapter, I reconsider the widely discussed *Papá Iván* and *Los rubios* to suggest that the use of documentary in post-2000 second-generation performative cinema indicates the increasing hegemonization of testimonial film and exposes the exhaustion of trauma and subaltern theories. By way of generic distortion, these films indirectly show that testimonial cinema went from being an alternative type of narrative to occupying a hegemonic place in contemporary Argentina. In other words, these films not only perform (self-inscribe) the filmmaker, but also perform (repeat, expose, and parody) hegemony. Although I find these documentaries paradigmatic of a broader trend that includes Laura Bondarevsky's *Che vo cachai* (2003), Natalia Bruschtein's *Encontrando a Víctor* (2005) and *Tiempo suspendido* (2016), Gabriela Golder's *En memoria de los pájaros* (2000), Prividera's *M*, and Carri's *Cuatreros* (2016), the chapter deliberately focuses on the overanalyzed *Papá Iván* and *Los rubios* in order to examine the gaps surrounding the concepts of memory, postmemory, trauma, and mourning—the very concepts that drive these films' most popular interpretations. Toward the end of the chapter, I address *Televisión x la identidad*, a documentary-fiction hybrid, in claiming that the increase in hegemony runs parallel to a progressive fictionalization of the testimonial genre.

Building on this argument, in the closing chapter I address post-2000 fiction films by second-generation filmmakers that return to a child's or a teenager's perspective and to an earlier (1980s) format, such as Biraben's *Cautiva*, Pablo Agüero's *Salamandra* (2008), Bustamante's *Andrés no quiere dormir la siesta*, Paula Markovitch's *El premio* (2011), and Ávila's *Infancia clandestina*. In these films, which I call "iconic fictions," the cinematic images' iconic dimension takes over their indexical dimension. Making use of scholarship on the links among iconicity, feeling, and ideology, I argue that this predominance strengthens consensus against the military regime yet precludes further examination. Likewise, such increase in iconicity solidifies emotions yet blocks the configuration of alternative sensibilities. My analyses thus conflict to some extent with the assertion that a child's or a teenager's perspective can provide the basis for a successful historical representation—an assertion underlying recent scholarship on childhood, adolescence, and cinema. While many of these films certainly challenge traditional notions of family, domesticity, and childhood, they also contribute to the formulation of the 1970s as a global iconic sign attuned to the logic of immediate response that is typical of late capitalism. Moreover, these films are cogent examples of the hegemonic role that testimonial cinema, especially fiction, plays during *kirchnerismo*.

Rethinking Testimonial Cinema, then, traces a concrete historical and political itinerary. The book charts the ideological trajectory of testimonial films from counterhegemony to hegemony. It is of course possible to analyze other narratives, genres, and artistic fields historically. As Ana Forcinito proposes throughout her book, *testimonial* is a flexible adjective that can describe films, novels, and pieces of juridical evidence, to name but the most common examples in postdictatorship Argentina (11–39). In many respects, literature and theater, for example, have followed a similar path to that of cinema. Moreover, nontestimonial films depicting the recent past share numerous features with testimonial films on the same topic—and even exhibit a similar fatigue. Jordana Blejmar, Leonor Arfuch, and Ana Ros have indeed considered several of the films that I analyze as part of a broader corpus that includes literature, theater, and photography, and that they have respectively called "autofiction" (4), "narratives of the self" (14), and "self-aware memory" (5). For Blejmar, autofictions—that is, narratives that combine autobiography and fiction or fictionalizations of the self and an imaginative investment of the past—account for a new cultural formation of memory in Argentina that begins in 2003 (2–9). These narratives, among which she includes *Los rubios* and *Diario de una princesa montonera*, deploy a playful memory to provocatively represent the dictatorship and toy with trauma. According to Blejmar, this playful aesthetic allows them to access areas of the dictatorial past previously unexplored by more conventional testimonies, to avoid conclusive syntheses, to present alternative forms of witnessing, and to display the connection between documentary evidence and imaginative investment common to all types of memory (5–6).

Arfuch also notices a transformation in first-person narratives around the year 2000. These new narratives of the self, she suggests, go across generic boundaries to stage a different type of subjectivity characterized by simultaneity, multiplicity, and historicity (21). Unlike earlier testimony-based accounts, the more recent narratives emphasize what Arfuch calls *"valor biográfico"* (biographical value) and *"valor memorial"* (mnemonic value) (23). They highlight their intersubjective stance and the interdependence of past and present. This emphasis enables us to recover traumatic experiences that are not explicitly represented (82). Similarly, Ros argues that since 2003, the second generation has created cultural products that conceive of memory as an open-ended and dialogic process (5). As opposed to the more totalizing memories of the first generation, this new type of memory is aware of the impossibility of faithful reconstruction. This recognition helps in the active transmission of trauma and allows for successful mourning and for challenging perspectives on institutionalized narratives (39–46). Even when my book focuses on a rather different corpus (in terms of both temporal framework and artistic medium) and adopts a different theoretical standpoint (in particular with respect to trauma), many of its conclusions, especially those in chapter 3, apply to Blejmar's, Arfuch's, and Ros's cultural products as well. Although, for the reasons outlined above, I find cinema to be particularly relevant for historical analysis, my intention is less to engage in a generic or field-specific reading than to illuminate the (often-neglected) connections between history and representations of the dictatorship.

Despite the fact that this book's primary goal is not to pursue a generic or field-specific reading, I do not want to begin analyzing films without first proposing a redefinition of testimonial cinema more in line with its historicity. While it is a popular concept in postdictatorship scholarship, "testimonial cinema" has been less precisely defined than intuitively used. In his classic *Cine y políticas*, for example, Gustavo Aprea frequently employs the adjective *testimonial* in alluding, rather pejoratively, to 1980s fictional films that denounce the dictatorship via a transparent story of poor artistic value (32–37, 95–97)—a somewhat different approach than the one he adopts in *Filmar la memoria*, where he sees testimony as an inherent component of audiovisual documentary (40–49, 121–152). With *La historia oficial* as his core example, Aprea suggests that these testimonial melodramas appeal to naïve and linear narratives that put aesthetics at the service of morality. Blejmar initially opposes "testimony" to "fiction" (5, 6, 16, 24) but later claims that autofictions are "testimonial" (198), and Arfuch distinguishes narratives of the self from testimony-based accounts (23, 77). Ricardo Manetti proposes that testimonial films can be either documentary or fiction because films give testimony to their historical context regardless of genre (257).

Ana Amado, on the contrary, affiliates testimonial cinema with documentary—an affiliation shared by other Argentine academics, such as Pablo Piedras (*El cine* 27) and Antonio Gómez ("First-Person" 50). For Amado, testimonial films are first-person documentaries in which, as subaltern scholars would say, the individual stands in for a larger group—or, in Gómez's view, the "I" is grounded in a collective "we" ("Displacing" 66). The referential value of this first person is what sustains the genre: *"si se la despoja de toda información biográfica, la función documental de su discurso tambalea . . . y el testimonio pierde su objeto y su centro"* [if stripped of all biographical information, the documentary function of its discourse teeters . . . and the testimony loses its object and its center] (Amado 129).

Jens Andermann also seems to emphasize the primacy of documentary when he claims that one of the major strands in contemporary Argentine cinema comprises "testimonial documentaries from the perspective of the survivors' generation" (*New Argentine* 108). Although I agree that many of these features are constitutive of the testimonial genre (a referential first person, an individual who stands in for a larger group, and a denunciation of the past), I argue—in line with Manetti's view—that the distinction between documentary and fiction should not play a role in the definition of testimonial cinema. Not only, as I noted earlier, is this distinction far from clear-cut, but it is also ultimately based on a dichotomy (feeling/reason) that, as theories of affect have shown, is not as rigid as usually perceived. In spite of the ideological undertones entailed by specific uses of documentary and fiction, to which I pay close attention throughout the book, it is unnecessary, and in fact potentially misleading, to appeal to these uses in order to define testimonial cinema as a genre.[37]

Steering clear of the binary "documentary/fiction," then, in this book I use the phrase "postdictatorship testimonial films" to refer to filmic narratives—whether documentary or fictional—enunciated by protagonists or witnesses of the military regime that ruled Argentina between 1976 and 1983. When I say *enunciated*, I am following Émile Benveniste's distinction between two subject positions involved in any discursive event: the speaking subject and the subject of speech. The first is the agent responsible for enunciation, the individual who utters an instance of discourse, which we colloquially call the speaker. The second is the discursive element with which the discoursing individual identifies, the representation the speaker makes for her- or himself, generally conveyed by the first-person pronoun *I* (200–225). A number of scholars, especially Colin MacCabe and Kaja Silverman, have adapted Benveniste's theory for the cinematic field, differentiating between "level of enunciation" and "level of fiction": "The level of enunciation is in effect that of production—of camera movement, editing, composition, sound-recording, sound-mix, script, etc. The level of fiction designates the narrative with which the spectator of the finished film is encouraged to 'find' him or herself" (Silverman 47). In this model, the speaking subject is the agent responsible for the level of enunciation. The subject of speech is the figure or figures most central to the level of fiction—that is, the main characters or cluster of characters in the finished filmic narrative that are equivalent to the first-person pronoun in a sentence. To these two subject positions, Silverman adds a third that she calls the "spoken subject": "the subject who is constituted through identification with the subject of the speech" (47). In other words, the spoken subject is the one produced through discourse, the *you* activated by the finished narrative, the viewer who is being addressed and hailed.

Metz has compellingly argued that this conception of enunciation, originated in the field of linguistics, is excessively tied to the idea of persons. In the case of cinema, he claims, markers of enunciation should not be personal but rather coextensive with film—and traceable in each shot, which should be regarded as a distinct utterance (*Impersonal* 3–24). He therefore proposes that, instead of "speaking subject" or "subject of speech," we call what happens in cinema "source of enunciation" (*Impersonal* 4). This concept goes beyond deictic personal pronouns and takes into account the type of anaphoric reference more typical of the cinematic field—that is, a type of reference that points to some previous information contained in the utterance and not in the circumstances of enunciation. "When enunciation marks itself in the cinematic utterance," Metz argues, "it is not, or at least not principally, by means of deictic indicators but by means of *reflexive* constructions" (*Impersonal* 10, emphasis in the original). Film bears its own source within itself, in the composition of every shot. Three discursive levels could be identified: the primary level of enunciation, the secondary level that corresponds to the primary enunciator in charge of a story, and a third level that corresponds to temporary enunciators and that is always diegetic (*Impersonal* 171). I find Metz's arguments persuasive. I believe, however, that the more subject-based theory of enunciation is still relevant for the case of testimonial films, in which it is precisely a deictic first person that sustains the genre—even when several times, as we will see for example in chapter 3, deixis is complicated, challenged, or parodied. Throughout my book, I thus retain Benveniste's distinction yet pay close attention to Metz's observations regarding the shot as distinct utterance and the role of temporary, anaphoric enunciators.

When I state that testimonial films are narratives of the military regime *enunciated* by protagonists or witnesses, then, I mean that either the subject of speech or the speaking subject was the (real) protagonist of the (real) events represented in the narrative. In some cases, these two subjects coincide, like in *Papá Iván*, a film that features second-generation survivor Roqué as both writer-director and protagonist. In other cases, they do not, like in *Botín de guerra*, where filmmaker David Blaustein offers us first-person accounts by relatives of disappeared people without being one himself. I believe that this focus on enunciation lets us retain the most important concepts advanced by subaltern and trauma theories (e.g., the role of the first person, its status as a shifter, and the genre's dynamic form) while eluding the most problematic: the ahistoricity of the notions of trauma and subalternity. Argentine scholar Ximena Triquell has also provided an oft-quoted classification that is grounded both generally in enunciation and specifically in the role of the spoken subject. Triquell distinguishes between three consecutive stages. In the first stage (1984–1986), the spoken subject becomes a witness to the events being told. At stake in these films, which she calls "*cine-testimonio*" (testimonial cinema), is the truth of the represented events. The second stage, "*cine-denuncia*" (1987–1989) (denunciatory cinema), is marked by a transformation in the role of the spoken subject. He or she is addressed less as a witness than as an agent who is encouraged to stand up against injustice. By contrast, the films of the third stage (1990–1994) are called "*cine-testamento*" (testifying cinema) because they are mostly memory narratives, documenting a past in danger of oblivion. Triquell's categorization takes an important step in a direction that is meaningful for this book: it helps us observe the historical transformation of postdictatorship films and to shy away from the documentary/fiction dichotomy. I contend, however, that the figures of the speaking subject and the subject of speech, as opposed to the spoken subject, allow for an alternative periodization that is more relevant for a historical reading of postdictatorship cinema—a periodization that illustrates how these films went from being alternative types of narratives to creating global iconic signs.

Finally, a word about the privileging of a nation-centered perspective is in order. As I acknowledged at the beginning of this introduction, memory fatigue is by no means exclusive to the Argentine context. There certainly is—as Huyssen, Todorov, and Tal suggest—a global disappointment with the genre that may be related to the shift from counterhegemony to hegemony. Moreover, I am aware that, as Kathleen Newman has famously claimed, cinematic styles are no longer understood as the result of closed nation-centric determinants, but rather of a dynamic cross-border dialogue. Instead of viewing films as passive reflections of a single national culture, they should be regarded as "contact zones" marked by transnational flows of cinematic exchange (9). This definition should be even starker in the case of genre films, which, as Luisela Alvaray observes, have always constituted "the Esperanto of film language" (80). However, I believe that the specific case of postdictatorship testimonial cinema calls for local readings as the most useful way to illuminate a global context. If, as I further develop in the closing chapter, the Argentine dictatorship has become a global icon, local analysis of the ideological trajectory of testimonial films representing the dictatorship can help "deiconize," historicize, and politicize the referent. In other words, I maintain in this particular case that a nation-centered interpretation can contribute toward a much-needed "decentering" perspective of world cinema (Newman 4).

Notes

1. All translations from Spanish into English in this chapter are Robin Myers's. All translations from Spanish into English in the following chapters are mine, unless otherwise noted.

2. I return to the definition of testimonial narratives later in the introduction. There has been considerable debate on the "post" in "postdictatorship." It has been criticized for connoting closure; it has been used as a synonym for *anti*; and it has also been used in a temporal context (see Richard; Vezzetti, *Pasado y presente*). Throughout this book, I refer to the term in a strictly temporal sense, as a reference to the period following the fall of the dictatorship (1983–today). Although replacing "military dictatorship" with "civil-military dictatorship" would probably be a more accurate way to acknowledge the participation of nonmilitary citizens in state terrorism, I use the former for language economy. Furthermore, for the reasons outlined in chapter 1, I prefer not to use "genocide" or "dirty war." See both Avelar and O'Donnell for an explanation of the emergence of Southern Cone dictatorships from an economic standpoint. See both Brunner and Shumway for sociological and historical perspectives on authoritarianism. See Vezzetti, *Pasado y presente*, for a comprehensive view that includes economic, sociological, and historical perspectives and which conceives of the dictatorships as global, regional, and local phenomena.

3. See Vezzetti, *Pasado y presente* and *Sobre la violencia revolucionaria*; Crenzel, *Los desaparecidos*.

4. Testimonial narratives have mostly been praised—with the exception of 1980s fictional narratives. I address this exception in chapter 1.

5. See Gilman for an overview of the notion of the revolutionary intellectual in Latin America during the 1960s and '70s.

6. In this book, I use *second generation*, as does Marianne Hirsch, to refer to second-generation survivors of collective or cultural trauma (*Family Frames* 23)—not only to those who share family ties with first-generation victims but also to those who connect with the latter through what Hirsch calls "retrospective witnessing by adoption" ("Surviving Images" 10). According to Hirsch, as opposed to the first generation, who had direct exposure to traumatic events, the second generation only "remembers" the narratives of these events. It thus relies heavily on cultural representations and visual images such as photographs. Hirsch's

concept is problematic in at least two ways. First, any type of memory is always necessarily mediated by and reliant on representation. Second, in the postdictatorship context, the generational distinction is not as straightforward, as children abducted and orphaned by the military, rather than having been exposed to the first-generation survivors' memories, were directly exposed to traumatic events themselves. I still find, however, Hirsch's concept relevant for this book. The emphasis on the visual, repetitive, and highly mediated aspects of second-generation discourses helps explain several of the features that characterize the films analyzed in the last chapters. Additionally, this more encompassing definition that goes beyond blood ties enables, as I also examine in those chapters, a more comprehensive view of post-2000 cultural production that includes filmmakers who did not lose their parents during the dictatorship (like Daniel Bustamante, Gastón Biraben, or Gabriela Golder) yet grew up in the midst of a traumatic environment that they recreate, and sometimes parody, in their filmic narratives. In this sense, I follow Jordana Blejmar and Natalia Fortuny's claim that, despite its inaccuracies, "second generation" still "pay[s] testament to a new generational formation of cultural memory in Latin America" (3) and Cecilia Sosa's suggestion that the notion enlightens two crucial dimensions that have become of central importance in recent Argentina: "the extent to which conventional family ties can be displaced, reversed and even 'countersigned'; and the way in which the particular features of the new generation's production can generate alternative engagements among expanded audiences, which have not been directly affected by loss" ("Humour" 75). I address in more detail the debates on the applicability of Hirsch's notions for the Argentine case in the third chapter.

7. For additional interpretations of *testimonio* from a subaltern studies standpoint, see Achugar and Beverley; Arias, Arturo; Beverley, *Testimonio: On the Politics of Truth* and *Subalternity and Representation*; Gugelberg; Guha; Jara and Vidal; Nance; Rodríguez; Sommer; Williams, Gareth. For a brief history of testimonial narrative in Latin America, see Nance 167–178. For further information on the history of Latin American subaltern studies and its connections to South Asian subaltern studies, postcolonial theory, and post-Marxism, see Latin American Subaltern Studies Group; Verdesio.

8. In this book, I will follow Susannah Radstone's definition of trauma theory: a theory that conceptualizes "trauma" by combining deconstruction, poststructuralism, psychoanalysis, and clinical work. As Radstone explains, this trend has been the "new theoretical orthodoxy" ("Trauma Theory" 10) in memory studies since the 1990s and is best represented by the works of Felman, Laub, and Caruth. For further details on this trend and its dominance within trauma and memory studies, see Radstone, "Trauma Theory" and "Trauma and Screen Studies"; Kaplan, Ann (especially, 21–41); Elsaesser; Traverso and Broderick. For a genealogy of the notion of trauma that pays careful attention to contradictions and instability, see Leys. For additional examples of readings based on this theoretical paradigm, see Antze and Lambek; Caruth, *Trauma: Explorations in Memory*; Douglass and Vogel; Herman; Kaplan, Ann; Santner; van der Kolk, McFarlane, and Weisaeth.

9. For canonical works in postdictatorship studies influenced by psychoanalysis, see Avelar; Gundermann; Richard; Richard and Moreiras. See Bosteels; Plotkin; Vezzetti, *Aventuras de Freud en el país de los argentinos* for further details on the importance of psychoanalysis in the region. See Casullo for additional references on the impact of Benjamin's work. See Avelar 39–85 for an explanation of how the critical paradigm changed after the dictatorships.

10. Interestingly enough, Portela claims that her readings are more influenced by Caruth's critics than by Caruth herself. Yet, most of her assertions and analyses are grounded in

Caruth's basic premises. This can be noted, for instance, when she describes *Displaced Memories* as "an analysis of the symbolic uses of language that communicate the traces and/or symptoms of trauma" (40) or when she states that the memories of the three authors addressed in her book search for "collective, fragmented, intertwined, and successive truths that could help to reconstruct the past" (23).

11. See Jelin, *Los trabajos de la memoria* for an overview of the influence of memory and trauma studies in postdictatorship scholarship. See Nisenson for an example of journalism and the articles in Paulinelli, ed., for an example of film criticism. A 2016 search on Proquest's Dissertations and Theses database indicates that since 2000 there have been fifty-five doctoral theses on Argentine film and trauma. The majority of these works quote Caruth, Felman, and Laub. Most were written after 2009.

12. In this sense, I agree both with Achugar when he suggests that Latin America sometimes works as a screen on which to project US academic concerns ("Leones" 212) and with a common critique of subaltern studies that Beverley summarizes as follows: "'Studies' [sic] represent a North American problematic about identity politics and multiculturalism ... that have been displaced onto Latin America, at the expense of misrepresenting its diverse histories and social-cultural formations" (Verdesio 64). Although I mostly concur with Beverley's points in this article regarding the "neoarielismo" of Latin American intellectuals, and although I also believe that academic debates in Argentina could benefit immensely from subaltern theory (an approach that, as Sarlo's book evidences, is often too quickly dismissed), some of its tenets must be revisited in order to account for the specific case of Argentine postdictatorship narratives.

13. See Crenzel, *Los desaparecidos*, 11–24 for an explanation of how the focus on middle-class victims has subsumed other social groups. See Jelin, "Víctimas" for an analysis of how the correlation between victimhood and family ties has precluded the emergence of other voices and other possible affiliations.

14. I conceived of this book when *kirchnerismo* was in full flower and Mauricio Macri had not yet taken office. I believe, however, that my assertions remain applicable despite the obvious changes in public discourse. Although we could probably say that testimonial narratives are no longer found at the center of *official* discourse, they are still the *hegemonic* way of representing the dictatorship. I address my use of *official*, *hegemonic*, and *counterhegemonic* (as well as the reasons for not using *posthegemonic*) in more detail in the second chapter. I return to testimonial narratives during *macrismo* in the conclusion.

15. See the articles in Castro-Gómez and Mendieta, eds., and in Verdesio for a summary of the most common critiques of subaltern theory.

16. See Silverman; Laclau and Mouffe for further details on the connections among psychoanalysis, semiotics, and Marxism. See Copjec; Metz, *The Imaginary Signifier*; Mulvey; Žižek for the primary references in the Lacanian tradition.

17. In this book I only focus on the problems posed by psychoanalytic clinical discourse in assessing historical dimensions. Although not directly related to my project, there are many other critiques of psychoanalysis as a discipline, and they span a broad range of perspectives. See, for example, Deleuze and Guattari; Gellner; Grünbaum; Irigaray; Jameson, *The Political Unconscious*; Popper; Zajko and Leonard. Interestingly, the difficulty of connecting the private and the collective realms is a recurrent critique that goes beyond the clinical context. In the first pages of *The Political Unconscious*, Fredric Jameson hints at an explanation as he traces the emergence of the discipline in the late nineteenth century.

According to Jameson, psychoanalysis developed due to the capitalistic separation of the private and the public spheres, which paved the way for the appearance of "desire" and "sexuality" as individual drives. Since its inception, he suggests, psychoanalysis has run the risk of remaining locked within the private realm, unless the individual is decentered in the direction of the collective (61–69). Ernest Gellner raises a similar critique. The chief psychoanalytic goal of individual adjustment leads to political quietism (xv). The discipline's ritualistic, esoteric, and elitist nature makes it a highly individual practice, leading to what he calls "the embourgeoisment of the psyche" (139–149). Moreover, many affect scholars, frequently consulted for this book, criticize psychoanalysis for generalizing subject formation and omitting differences of class, race, ethnicity, and nationality (see Harding and Pribram 8–15 for an overview of this critique).

18. As Leys explains, there are two opposing views of "trauma." While mimetic theories state that the subject hypnotically and unconsciously repeats the traumatic experience, antimimetic theories see trauma as a purely external event befalling a passive yet fully constituted subject (5–10; 298–301). These views, Leys argues throughout her book, often emerge together in quite contradictory ways. I thus agree with both Leys and Radstone when they claim that Felman, Laub, and Caruth's theory is one of those instances. Though their theory emphasizes the lack of recall that is typical of the mimetic view, it primarily relies on the idea of an external event coming upon the subject. As Radstone contends, this conception poses at least two problems. First, the notion of a passive yet fully constituted subject contradicts the theory's explicit affiliation with deconstruction. Second, it makes way for a number of Manichean binaries (inside and outside, trauma and normality, victims and perpetrators). See Radstone, "Trauma Theory" for a compelling analysis of how the emphasis on the antimimetic view is grounded in a partial reading of Freud's "unconscious," which leads to a problematic conflation of "event" and "experience" and of "history" and "memory." See Leys 275–292 for further details on Caruth's partial reading of Freudian psychoanalysis. See A. Kaplan, 32–41, for a broader conception of trauma that combines both conscious and unconscious aspects.

19. Another example is the common use of clinical concepts to appraise military officers' behavior. Explaining the existence of torturers by appealing to concepts such as "psychopathy," for example, is not only misleading (what are the odds of so many psychopaths emerging at the same time?), but it also prevents a necessary examination of broader causes. A similar objection can be raised against Eric Santner's classic *Stranded Objects* when he analyzes German post-Nazi stasis as a reaction to the loss of the Father or to Ann Kaplan's analysis of the gap left by the 9/11 destruction of the Twin Towers as castration (11–13).

20. Jouvé's interview, Del Barco's letter, and the responses have been collected in Belzagui, ed. See Andermann, Derbyshire, and Kraniauskas for a summary of the controversy. See Dove for an interesting analysis of how the dispute invites a reconsideration of the link between politics and ethics.

21. See Avelar; Balderston, comp.; Brunner; Dalmaroni; Richard, ed.; Sosnowski, comp.; Vezzetti, *Pasado y presente*.

22. Well-known scholarship on memory and trauma studies has been devoted to bridging the gap between the individual and collective realms. Several scholars have distinguished among "individual memory" (i.e., memory as experienced by an individual), "collective memory" (i.e., the shared pool of knowledge and information constitutive of collective consciousness), "social memory" (i.e., the shared memories whereby a specific group builds

its social identity, with special emphasis on how this memory affects the present), "cultural memory" (i.e., memory embodied in cultural artifacts), and "sites of memory" (i.e., memory as materialized in space). Others have focused on the (unstable and mutually constructed) connections between one or more of these concepts of memory and "history," broadly understood as the public representation of the collective past. Parallel distinctions to the ones between forms of memory have been made between "individual," "collective," "social," and "cultural" trauma. See Alexander, Eyerman, Giesen, Smelser, and Sztompka; Candau; Connerton; Freud; Halbwachs; Herman; Jelin, *Los trabajos de la memoria*; Koselleck; Nora; Ricœr; van der Kolk for classical examples of these two lines of scholarship. Although many of the above-mentioned concepts are implicit in my analyses, I do not delve into these categories, for two principal reasons. First, postdictatorship readings have generally relied on the most clinical tendency of trauma theory, as defined earlier. Second, as I explain in the sections below, I believe that the concept of historicity better captures the goal of my book, which is to read testimonial cinema synchronically and diachronically.

23. Other problems in trauma theory have been noted as well. Radstone cites three aspects that should be reconsidered: first, the role of the reader/analyst and the undiscussed notion of empathy that positions her or him above others; second, the fascination with trauma; and third, the contradiction encountered when analyzing texts representing catastrophes while relying on the idea of trauma as irrepresentability ("Trauma Theory" 22–26). Traverso and Broderick claim that this master paradigm neglects local specificities and assumes that people in the third world experience trauma as theorized in the first (3). Maureen Turim suggests that trauma scholars focus on the event without considering that trauma can be read formally, for example, in flashbacks and editing (234). In a similar vein, Jill Bennett argues that trauma theory privileges referential meaning, overlooking art's unique capacity to contribute to the politics of testimony in nonrepresentational ways (3–4). Although these are important critiques, in this book I am more interested in exploring trauma theory's loss of historicity, which I think is the most salient drawback in the postdictatorship context.

24. I owe this insight, as well as many helpful clarifications on psychoanalysis, to Paola Bohórquez.

25. We could say, in fact, that this challenge is especially applicable to Caruth, Felman, and Laub. They essentially consider every text after World War II, even those that do not involve an individual or historical catastrophe, to be a traumatic text. Although the claim that sustains their view (that narrative in general is in crisis) is quite compelling, the state of seeing trauma everywhere runs the risk of rendering texts, history, and trauma irrelevant—a risk that we encounter when reading postdictatorship narratives.

26. For an overview of scholarship that conceptualizes "historicity" at the intersection of these three levels, see Jameson, *The Political Unconscious*; *The Geopolitical Aesthetic*; LaCapra, *History in Transit*; and Williams, Raymond. This three-level notion differs from that of Copjec, who, referring to Foucault, claims: "We are calling historicist the reduction of society to its indwelling network of relations of power and knowledge" (6). When I say that we need to recover historicity, I do not want to suggest that nobody else has read these films attending to their historical context but that the two dominant approaches to testimonial cinema have tended to neglect this notion. As evident in my analyses, Aguilar, *Otros mundos*; Andermann, *New Argentine Cinema*; Amado; Burucúa; Feld and Stites Mor, eds.; Margulis, *De la formación a la institución*; and Page are good examples of scholarship that pays careful attention to several of these films' context. My book can be seen as an attempt to systematize some of these readings and to make their theoretical backbone more explicit.

27. Although they are not specifically concerned with establishing stages within the post-dictatorship era, my periodization mostly coincides with those proposed by Tamara Falicov, Gonzalo Aguilar, Joanna Page, and Ana Forcinito. Falicov alludes to three distinct stages marked by significant changes in state-led cultural policies: the mid-1980s, marked by the revelatory impulse of democratization; the '90s, marked both by new cinematic legislation and by neoliberal politics; and the post-2001 cinema of the crisis. Neither Aguilar (*Otros mundos*) nor Page focuses on the distinctions between the '90s and the 2000s, but both assert that '90s cinema is clearly different from that of the early democracy. Among these differences, they highlight the predominance of the documentary (Aguilar, *Otros mundos* 64) and the strong visibility of the postmemorial generation and their critique of revolutionary violence (Page 152–179). Despite not referring to cinema, the first chapter of Forcinito's *Los umbrales del testimonio* examines testimonial narratives based on three stages characterized by different juridical scenarios (41–72).

28. For general references on the connections between film and history, see Burke; Chapman; Ferro; Rosen; Rosenstone. In his useful book on film and history, James Chapman breaks down this relationship into six categories. According to this classification, film historians may be interested in cinema as a record of the past, in the history of film styles, in the history of the film industry, in the history of film as a business, in the history of film audiences, or in films as social documents—in how films somehow represent the societies in which they are produced and consumed (4). Although my analyses contemplate more than one of these categories (for example, stylistic changes are important in understanding second-generation parodies of the testimonial genre, and the goals of the film industry are important in understanding the role of the fictional testimony in the 1980s), I aim to contribute mainly to the first and the last. I am mostly interested in seeing how testimonial films have created and represented the referent that we call *military dictatorship* and in how they have built and documented their own present of enunciation.

29. Relying mainly on Peirce, film semioticians view cinema as a sign system encompassing indexical, iconic, and symbolic signs. Cinematic images are primarily indexical signs because a real referent is required for their configuration: profilmic objects must be located in front of the camera while being shot, in order for an image to be formed. At the same time, filmic images are iconic signs because they visually resemble the referent. In *La historia oficial*, for instance, the close-up of Gaby's face looks like that very face. Finally, filmic images also include symbolic signs; that is, signs that do not establish an existential or a visual connection to the referent, but rather a conventional one, like verbal language, plot, and genre codes. See Metz, *Film Language*; Wollen; Silverman; Prince for classical examples in this tradition. Certainly, semiotics cannot be completely isolated from questions of subjectivity and is not necessarily at odds with psychoanalysis. As Silverman explains, semiotics involves the study of signification, which—as Lacan's theory has shown—cannot be disengaged from the human subject (3–43). Or, as Metz puts it, "Any psychoanalytic reflection on the cinema might be defined in Lacanian terms as an attempt to disengage the cinema-object from the imaginary and win it for the symbolic . . .; that is to say, in the field of films as in other fields, the psychoanalytic itinerary is *from the outset a semiological one*" (*The Imaginary* 3, emphasis in the original). In this book, I am not attempting to separate these realms (an impossible task). Instead, I suggest that an approach emphasizing semiotics over a clinical psychoanalytic interpretation is more suitable for reading testimonial films historically.

30. See Rosen; Chanan, *The Politics of Documentary*; Doane, "The Indexical and the Concept of Medium Specificity" and *The Emergence of Cinematic Time* for examples of

the revitalization of semiotics. The 2016 first-ever English translation of Metz's *Impersonal Enunciation, or the Place of Film* can also be seen as a cogent index of this renewed interest. Andermann, *New Argentine Cinema*; and Aguilar, *Otros mundos* are good examples of how the notion of indexicality has helped connect film and history in post-2000 Argentina.

31. Peircean semiotics is more complex than what I have just outlined, and one of my goals is to address that complexity. First, in Peirce's view, we have direct experience but indirect knowledge of reality: we know that there is a world of things, but we have no intellectual access to that world unless we represent it. He thus distinguishes between two types of referents ("objects"): the "immediate object," the object as represented in the sign, and the "dynamic object," the object as it really is. Since I am interested in elucidating how the dictatorship becomes a sign (i.e., how it is being represented), in this book, the word *referent* corresponds to Peirce's immediate object, to the referent within the semiosis. Second, the symbolic, the indexical, and the iconic dimensions always overlap in a single sign. I analyze the ideological consequences of this triadic relationship in the fourth chapter. See Silverman, especially pages 20–25 and Wollen 97–107, for an explanation of overlapping functions in Peircean semiotics.

32. For an overview of theories of affect, see Ahmed, *The Cultural Politics of Emotion*; Cartwright; Gregg and Seigworth; Hardt; Harding and Pribram; Thrift; Ticineto Clough and Halley, eds.; Tomkins. For an exploration of affect theory in Latin America, see Macón and Solana; and Moraña and Sánchez Prado. For an examination of how Anglo-North American affect theory applies to the Latin American case, see Algarra and Noble. For a study of affect in contemporary Latin American cinema, see Podalsky. Although, as just mentioned, affect has become central especially since the 2000s, the notion is by no means new to film scholarship. Indeed, Metz's *Film Language* provides a clear example of an early theorization that takes into account both the semiotic and affective components of the filmic image (see especially 3–15).

33. There are, of course, other important implications of the affective turn and other possibilities for reading affect in cultural artifacts. See Butler; Connell; Jaggar; Macón and Solana; Sedgwick for examples of how a reconsideration of emotion has impacted gender and sexuality theories. See Davidson, Bondi, and Smith on how this reconsideration has impacted the field of geography, and see Brennan for the fields of psychology, psychoanalysis, biology, and neuroscience. See Ahmed, *The Cultural Politics of Emotion* and *The Promise of Happiness*; Appadurai; Berlant; Clarke, Hoggett, and Thomson; Williams, Simon; for examples of scholarly work focusing on the links between affect, political power, and inequality. See Lupton; Lutz; Rosaldo for an overview of how the idea of feelings as culturally constructed has paved the way for a less ethnocentric understanding of different societies and for a more diverse account of subject formation.

34. Sosa's readings are in line with other readings that also interpret part of my book's corpus from the perspective of gender and/or queer theory. In *Disappearing Acts*, Diana Taylor explores in depth the connections among gender, performance, and nation in Argentina's dictatorship and first decade of the postdictatorship, especially how gendered discourses empowered organizations such as Madres de Plaza de Mayo. In *Memoria y autobiografía*, Leonor Arfuch claims that women's postdictatorship testimonies help recover women's agency (103). A similar interpretation can be found in Ana Forcinito's *Los umbrales del testimonio*, where she argues that such testimonies make it possible to perceive gender violence as human rights violence (101–132). Constanza Burucúa analyzes in *Confronting the "Dirty*

War" how certain films allow for a successful, gendered-based representation of memory (110–154). Along the same lines, Pablo Piedras suggests that some contemporary documentaries by women filmmakers use the generic codes of the road movie to displace conventional approaches to memory ("Contemporary" 219–221). Although not my primary focus, I believe that these perspectives are good indications of the multiple possibilities that emerge when we rethink the postdictatorship corpus from the standpoint of affect, and I will thus return to some of their insights in the following chapters.

35. This is precisely why *Rethinking Testimonial Cinema* relies only partially on Deleuzian scholars like Massumi and Bennett. Although I find some of their basic premises fruitful, especially with respect to the historicity of feelings, others—with particular emphasis on prioperception and sense memory—strike me as fascinating but ultimately impossible to substantiate. Lisa Cartwright has proposed a model that combines theories of affect (particularly as practiced by Silvan Tomkins) with representation. She claims that "moral spectatorship" (empathetic identification) works at the intersection of the subjects represented on screen and the audience (41). This type of empathy recognizes otherness and culminates in critical awareness. While I agree with the need for a combined model, and I return to her concept in the first chapter, I believe that the intersection between affect and representation goes beyond empathy and beyond the representation of subjects, which is why I do not opt for this model as my primary framework.

36. I say "especially" because both documentary and fiction genres include symbolic, iconic, and indexical signs: All cinematic images (whether documentary or fictional) establish real, visual, and conventional associations with their referents. However, as Chanan has compellingly argued, indexicality is more emphatic in documentary because the viewer is aware that the images are drawn from the outside world (*The Politics of Documentary* 4); further, iconicity is more emphatic in fiction because the viewer expects the fictional world to visually resemble the afilmic world.

37. Outside of the postdictatorship context, "testimonial cinema" has usually been used to refer to Third Cinema, following Solanas and Getino's characterization: *"cine panfleto, cine didáctico, cine informe, cine ensayo, cine testimonial"* (pamphlet cinema, educational cinema, report cinema, essay cinema, testimonial cinema) (39). In Argentina, it can also refer to the films produced by Grupo Cine Testimonial, a group formed in 1982 by Marcelo Céspedes, Laura Bua, Tristán Bauer, Silvia Chanvillard, and Alberto Giudici, among others. Until its dissolution around 1985, the group produced a number of documentaries that included testimonies from marginalized social and ethnic communities. Beyond the Argentine context, "testimonial cinema" has also been used to refer to films, mostly documentaries, which include testimonies (i.e., first-person interviews/accounts, often in the form of talking heads). The latter definition usually emerges when referring to films on the Holocaust, on indigenous peoples, or on marginalized communities in general. See, for example, Burton; Feder; Friedman; Goldberg and Hazan; Hart; Kohen-Raz; Sarkar and Walker; Signer; Torchin. Although the context is obviously different, I believe that the enunciation-based redefinition as proposed in *Rethinking Testimonial Cinema* could serve these fields as well, since it paves the way for a more encompassing categorization that includes both documentary and fiction, considers the ideological implications of the different uses of the two genres, and helps perceive the historicity of testimonial films.

1 Knowledge and Feeling

Testimonial Documentary and Fiction in the 1980s

On December 10, 1983, President Raúl Alfonsín took office, surrounded by an ecstatic crowd of Argentines from all social classes and political backgrounds. He was the first democratically elected president of Argentina after seven long years of dictatorial rule. Alfonsín's primary goals had been clear since the beginning of the electoral campaign: to promote democracy and to rebuild a public sphere that had been broken by a near decade of forced exile, torture, death, censorship, and economic depression.[1] Departing from a national history of impunity, his first measure was to prosecute state-sponsored human rights violations. Thus, after repealing a military self-amnesty law, he appointed an independent organization, the National Commission on the Disappearance of Persons (CONADEP, its acronym in Spanish), to collect information on people who had gone missing during the dictatorship. *Nunca más*, CONADEP's final report compiling testimonies of survivors and relatives, sold out in forty-eight hours and has remained Argentina's top bestseller ever since. Thousands of witnesses exposed the existence of clandestine detention centers and gave detailed accounts of how military officers had tortured, raped, and killed political prisoners—in many cases also stealing babies born in captivity. As Hugo Vezzetti suggests, *Nunca más* marked a turning point in Argentine history (*Pasado* 107): The book's testimonies laid the groundwork for a new discourse on memory and ushered in an irreversible condemnation of state terrorism.

Such revelations paved the way, too, for a unique legal procedure. Between April and December 1985, the nine chief military officers who had ruled Argentina during the dictatorship were brought before a civilian court for an oral and public trial, best known as the *juicio a las juntas* (trial of the juntas). Eight hundred thirty witnesses, mostly camp survivors and relatives of missing people, testified before an audience that included judges, lawyers, journalists, members of human rights organizations, and ordinary people interested in the legal process. As a result, two officers were sentenced to life imprisonment, three were sentenced to several years behind bars, and the remaining four were absolved.[2] Both *Nunca más* and the *juicio a las juntas* were major steps toward achieving the new administration's goal of reconstructing the broken public sphere; they fostered democratic values, encouraged trust in government institutions, and filled gaps in historical knowledge that had been left by the military's intentional destruction of documents.

In this context of political turmoil and hope, the film industry became a key pillar of the incipient democracy. While maintaining Law No. 17,741, through which the Instituto Nacional de Cinematografía (then INC, now INCAA) controlled exhibition and production, Alfonsín sanctioned Law No. 23,052, abolishing censorship. Manuel Antín, the INC's new director, actively sought to reconcile entertainment with political commitment, in large part because a portion of the institute's funding came from a 10 percent sales tax. The 1960s-era movement Third Cinema—which, as stated in its foundational manifesto, was "independent in production, militant in politics, and experimental in language" (Stam 253)—was no longer an option. Its anticommercial stance did not suit the new scenario. Furthermore, following the defeat of the left-leaning armed struggle, overtly political, activism-encouraging narratives seemed archaic.[3] As opposed to Third Cinema productions, Argentine films of the 1980s combined political and market demands, denouncing, especially through fiction, what had transpired during the dictatorship.[4] Usually combining two popular genres, thriller and melodrama, these fiction films led viewers through a labyrinth of clues and feelings until they reached a final revelation that uncovered previously hidden aspects of the recent past. Luis Puenzo's *La historia oficial*, which won the Academy Award for Best Foreign Language Film in 1985, was paradigmatic in this respect. The story of Alicia, a high school teacher who had unknowingly adopted a daughter born to disappeared parents and gradually discovered the secret truth, met audience expectations by way of a generic fiction that successfully fused melodrama, thriller, and politics.[5]

It is precisely for this combination of genre and politics that 1980s fictional cinema has often been criticized. According to most scholars, the thriller format provides a sanitized version of the recent past that fails to challenge the audience. Innocent protagonists, like Alicia in *La historia oficial*, enable the Argentine people to unveil the darkest facets of the previous years without truly confronting their own responsibility (Aprea, *Cine* 55; Burucúa 72; España 30; Podalsky 6). Based on transparent, linear narratives poor in aesthetic value, these simplistic stories go from the revolutionary to the revelatory. Rather than exploring the past, they merely aim for a visceral denunciation, creating an abstract consensus around democracy (Aprea, *Cine* 52; Andermann, *New Argentine* 4). Moreover, melodramatic conventions elicit empathy and unleash sensations, turning the cinematic act into a self-purging experience. Instead of appealing to the viewers' critical judgment, these fictional melodramas prompt catharsis while precluding active thought and historical examination (Amado 23; Andermann, *New*

Argentine 3). They engulf the audience and make "no attempt to question the language of representation" (King 96).[6]

This reading has also polarized the appraisal of 1980s testimonial cinema, as evidenced by the opposing reactions to Héctor Olivera's canonical *La noche de los lápices* (1986) and Carlos Echeverría's *Juan, como si nada hubiera sucedido* (1987). *La noche de los lápices* is a fictional reconfiguration of camp survivor Pablo Díaz's testimony in the *juicio a las juntas*. Based on Díaz's experience, the film tells a love story while recreating the inhuman conditions of the detention centers. Although directed by Olivera, Díaz acts both as the speaking subject and the subject of speech. The film is grounded in his juridical testimony, the script is organized according to his advice, and the narrative is structured from his point of view—the first-person perspective of a fictional character who serves as Díaz's "I." In other words, Díaz holds primary agency both on the level of enunciation and on the level of fiction. Meanwhile, Echeverría's film—which initially seems very different—is a documentary investigating the fate of Juan Marcos Herman, the only person who disappeared from the touristic city of Bariloche during the military regime. The filmic narrative mainly comprises first-person accounts by Juan's friends, relatives, and possible murderers—all real protagonists of the events described. In line with the common appraisal of 1980s cinema, the two films have prompted opposing critical reactions. While Olivera's popular fiction has been dismissed as a naïve, self-purging, and emotional narrative, *Juan* has been praised as an anomaly—an exception within the early democracy, a highly reflexive documentary far removed from the unsophisticated, sentimental generic fictions typical of its time (Amado 23; Aprea, *Cine* 39, 59; Andermann, *New Argentine* 108–109; Margulis, *De la formación* 206, "Documentaries" 326; Piedras, "La regla y la excepción: figuraciones de la subjetividad autoral en documentales argentinos de los ochenta y noventa" 44, *El cine documental en primera persona* 52).

I would like to suggest that this appraisal is somewhat anachronistic. Seen from a temporal vantage point, generic fictions certainly seem naïve, in both formal and historical terms, while reflective documentaries look more complex and sophisticated. Such an assessment, however, mainly results from a displaced, belated reception. Moreover, the negative view is based on certain dichotomies (reason/emotion, feeling/cognition, passion/knowledge) that, as affect theories show, are not as rigid as usually perceived. These dichotomies result in another static binary (testimonial fiction versus testimonial documentary) that obliterates a general, more comprehensive understanding of testimonial cinema. An analysis of specific 1980s films that resists these rigid binaries, focusing instead on the films' present of enunciation, helps us better understand how testimonial cinema accompanied official discourses of democratization.[7] Testimonial films—whether documentary or fictional—materialized and contributed to the creation of narratives that fostered democratic participation, shaped new affective configurations, and influenced a different version of history. This analysis also encourages us to rethink the reason/affect dichotomy and sheds light on its implications in the early democracy.

In order to develop these ideas, chapter 1 will primarily focus on *Juan, como si nada hubiera sucedido*. I am interested in how the film's indexical and symbolic components help us elucidate the role of testimonial cinema in the early democracy. At first glance, this may seem like a strange choice; after all, the film has usually been interpreted as an anomaly. Nonetheless, I specifically chose *Juan* both because it embodies the most relevant aspects of the incipient democracy and because its perceived exceptional status is a starting point for rethinking the way 1980s cinema has been read. Although I agree that *Juan*'s formal techniques are quite advanced and that its content alludes to waning democratic optimism—the documentary ends with President Alfonsín's announcements of the *leyes de punto final* and *obediencia debida*—I contend that what are usually seen as anomalies are actually traces of the early democracy.[8] Thus, once I have clarified, via *Juan*, the place of testimonial cinema at this historical moment, I briefly reread Olivera's *La noche de los lápices* to revise the role of fictional testimony and to reexamine the reason/affect binary.[9]

Juan, como si nada hubiera sucedido: Democracy as Work in Progress

Juan, como si nada hubiera sucedido stands out as one of the most fascinating and complex testimonial films of the postdictatorship period. Some of its intricacy is due to its collaborative origin. Echeverría, a native of Bariloche himself, created and directed the film as his university thesis project while studying in Munich. Horacio Herman, Juan's brother, was in charge of photography, lighting, and investigation. Journalist Esteban Buch appears on-screen as he interviews Juan's relatives, friends, former military officers, and public figures presumably involved in the man's kidnapping. And Osvaldo Bayer, a famous Argentine writer who was living in exile in Germany and had been the protagonist of Echeverría's previous film *Cuarentena*, wrote texts for the voiceover in which Buch analyzes the testimonies, acting as a "juxtadiegetic" narrator (i.e., a narrator whose voice runs alongside the plot) (Metz, *Impersonal* 39). In this sense, the film is a typical product of a phase in Argentine documentary history that Margulis has called "*formacional*" (formational), because it saw the emergence both of documentary filmmakers who had been professionally trained (*formados*) in the genre and of different forms of collaboration (*formaciones*) that made these films possible (*De la formación* xxiii).

Furthermore, the film is complex not only in terms of authorship and enunciation but also stylistically and formally. Far from being a straightforward staging of the results of a three-year investigation, the narrative is structured as a messy collage that leaves us with several loose ends. Ex-military officers reluctantly answer Buch's questions, often contradicting one another. Juan's friends and relatives, sometimes unidentified, confront the viewer with their own feelings and memories. Contemporary images of Bariloche and Buenos Aires are juxtaposed with older photographs and TV footage, combining different temporalities. Moreover, the documentary openly reflects on the shooting process, showing the crew as they edit filmic material and acknowledging the existence of two different cameras: the video camera that Buch uses to conduct the interviews and a hidden sixteen-millimeter camera capturing these moments. In this sense, the film becomes doubly reflective, as it exposes the apparatus that allows for an exposure of the apparatus—"a filmic operation, 'to expose the apparatus', that only rarely shows THE apparatus, that is, its own apparatus, but is usually content to display AN apparatus that belongs to some other film" (Metz, *Impersonal* 65, emphasis in the original).

It is because of this complexity that *Juan* has been read as an anomaly. Aside from interpretations grounded in trauma theory (Bekerman 159–178; Grinberg Plá 1–21), which I will revisit in the next chapter, *Juan* has usually been defined as an exception. The reflective use of filmic language has been considered an early example of post-1990s cinema. Ana Amado observes that this reflective language appeals to the spectator's critical judgment, breaking with typical 1980s affective films that work to elicit empathy (23). In the same vein, Gustavo Aprea claims that *Juan* evidences the end of 1980s cinema, as it exhibits the exhaustion of its two most popular genres: revelatory melodrama and political thriller. Unlike simplistic stories imbued with the new democracy's optimistic spirit, Echeverría's film aims to redefine realism and to question celebratory discourse (*Cine* 39). Paola Margulis, Pablo Piedras, and Carmen Guarini argue that features like the inclusion of a journalist who represents the director, a first-person voiceover narrating the investigation, and the crew at work, ultimately link the film to the documentaries of the post-1990s (Margulis, "Documentaries" 326, *De la formación* 206–210; Piedras, "La regla" 44; Guarini 355). Jens Andermann, meanwhile, goes so far as to connect its narrative procedures to the post-2000 second generation. As in *M* or *Los rubios*, the polyphonic nature of the testimonies, instead of providing a truthful representation of the past, reinforces the absences it contains— the impossibility, in other words, of a single, totalizing truthful representation (*New Argentine* 108–109). On initial review, then, *Juan* seems to be the opposite of typical 1980s cinema. Whereas generic fictions erase every trace of reflexivity in order to establish a smooth connection with the audience, the exhibition of the filmic process lies at the core of Echeverría's documentary. In the former, viewers are engulfed into the plot; in the latter, they are starkly aware of its fabrication.

Although I certainly agree with the prominence of *Juan*'s reflective language, I would suggest that, rather than setting it apart from the 1980s, it actually embodies what is happening in that decade. Reflexivity materializes social discourses of the early democracy, offering traces of the present and helping us better understand it almost three decades later. A closer look at what makes the film reflective illuminates this temporal connection. If we focus on *Juan*'s traditional readings, we could say that reflexivity is mainly caused by the emphasis on the film as a documentary. As we watch, we witness firsthand how Buch immerses himself in the real world in search of referents. We see him walking through the streets, taking a bus, knocking on doors, and entering military facilities. We become aware that the filmic image emerges through the shooting of real objects and people—an awareness that usually escapes us in conventional fiction, in which "the cinematic signifier . . . is employed entirely to remove the traces of its own steps, to open immediately to the transparency of a signified, of a story, which is in reality manufactured by it but which it pretends merely to 'illustrate,' to transmit to us after the event, as if it had existed previously" (Metz, *The Imaginary Signifier* 40).

Several scholars have already specified the difficulty of establishing definitive boundaries between documentary and fiction.[10] Michael Chanan, however, puts forth a useful distinction for reading *Juan*: documentary and fiction can be distinguished by their somewhat different approaches to the connection between the profilmic (the world that appears before the camera) and the afilmic (the world that exists independently of the camera). As Chanan puts it: "The documentary image has a quality or dimension that is different from fiction, because it carries a determinable link with the historical world. Fiction we know to be invented and set up for the camera, whereas documentary consists of scenes drawn from the social and physical world that exists independently of the camera...In semiotic terms, the afilmic world . . . The referentiality of documentary is still of another order to fiction: it has historical reference" (*Politics* 4).

In both documentary and fiction, the cinematic image captures the profilmic scene, but the quality of this profilmic scene varies. Unlike in fiction, where the scene has been imagined and arranged in a certain way in order to be shot, in documentary the scene (even when it has been selected and rearranged) has a real existence that is external to the shoot. In documentary, the profilmic bears a special attachment to the afilmic world and has historical reference. That is to say, both fiction and documentary are indexical (in both, the referent is essential to the formation of the sign; in both, too, the profilmic is essential to the formation of the image). In documentary, however, the index's historical quality becomes more emphatic because it is formed by a historical referent.[11] According to Chanan, this difference entails specific consequences that resonate on reception:

while fiction addresses the viewer primarily as a private individual, documentary addresses the viewer primarily as a citizen and is always structured in advance by the conditions governing the public sphere.

I will return later to the different ways in which documentary and fiction address the viewer. For now, I would like to consider how Echeverría's film employs documentary, as well as the implications of this choice. In *Juan*, as Chanan has observed, the use of documentary underscores indexicality; it emphasizes that the images before us have been formed by a careful selection of elements that exist, socially and historically, in the outside world. As we watch the crew setting the stage for the interviews, we realize that the interviewees have an afilmic existence. In noting the hidden camera, we acknowledge that whatever is being captured comes from an external realm unfolding alongside the filmic universe. Unlike in classical fiction, where the referent's afilmic existence is somewhat erased, the documentary images in *Juan* serve to highlight their historical reference. They emphasize that scenes are being drawn from the social and physical world that exists independently of the camera. Furthermore, in this specific film, we could describe this dimension of indexicality as a trace of the present of enunciation—rather than a trace of the past.

The emphasis on the indexical quality of what the viewer sees ultimately highlights the existence of the afilmic present more than it shows that the present is actually past—that the objects were placed in front of the camera prior to the viewing. As we see the crew immersing themselves in the present of enunciation, we become aware of its existence. As we see them editing, rewinding, and manipulating filmic material, we recognize that the present remains under construction. We get the impression that history is a work in progress and that the *récit* is still open. In *Juan*, as Doane would say, "the promise of indexicality is, in effect, the promise of the rematerialization of time—the restoration of a continuum . . . of time" (*Emergence* 10). Because, unlike icons and symbols, the index depends upon association by contiguity (for instance, temperature touches the thermometer and leaves a mark), the object is made "present." Indexical signs have a "directness and immediacy" (*Emergence* 93) that other signs lack.

Contrary to the standard interpretation, the exposure of the present-in-progress is precisely what makes *Juan* a 1980s film. Such a portrayal responds to how this present was being perceived at the time; in fact, it arguably contributed to that perception. The documentary's messy, ongoing, open-ended form is attuned to the awareness of a messy, ongoing, open-ended historical moment. In other words, the representation of the *récit* as under construction runs parallel to the openness of the *récit*. Shot between 1984 and 1987, the making of the film accompanied the early democracy's most turbulent years. It was simultaneous not only with the unprecedented paths paved by *Nunca más* and the *juicio* but also with the instability surrounding them. Tensions resulting from the trials and military budget cuts triggered two revolts, led by Aldo Rico, over Easter weekend in 1987, as well as a third led by Colonel Seineldín on December 1. Despite the sanctioning of the *leyes*, pressures from the army were a constant during Alfonsín's administration. Moreover, having inherited a US$43 billion foreign debt from the military government, Alfonsín struggled with several economic constraints: Argentina's GDP grew by a very small percentage, and inflation rose at an extraordinary scale, sometimes at an annual rate of 700 percent. Political turmoil escalated in 1989 with a left-leaning armed attack on the La Tablada barracks, riots on the urban outskirts, and an increase in poverty. In July 1989, six months prior to the official end of his term, Alfonsín decided to resign and transfer power to his newly elected successor, Carlos Menem.

This chaotic situation also affected the dissemination of *Juan*. Given its sensitive content and the fragility of the incipient democratic government, the film was not immediately released. In 1987, only Canal 10, a small TV station in the province of Tucumán, broadcast the documentary; the home of the program's host was bombed some days later. Not until the 2000s, then, did the documentary reach the Argentine public. Although it has never commercially premiered, *Juan* was screened at independent festivals and movie theaters in 2005 and aired on public television in 2007, getting, as Margulis puts it, a "belated reception" ("The Case" 4).[12]

This belated reception is what leads *Juan* to be perceived as a post-1990s film. Our current knowledge of Argentine cinema and its development has determined our interpretation. From our temporal vantage point, 1980s films are classified as emotional, naïve generic fictions, whereas post-1990s films are seen as sophisticated, highly reflexive cultural artifacts. Therefore, *Juan*'s reflective language and emphasis on indexicality—an emphasis that is actually often cited as the primary marker of the so-called new Argentine cinema—are read as anomalies.[13] However, rather than drawing from reflective language to reinforce the absences at the heart of representation (as in post-1990s cinema), this film's reflexivity underscores the existence of a messy, ongoing, unfinished present of enunciation. Moreover, instead of evidencing the exhaustion of the 1980s, the emphasis on indexicality indicates that the democratization process is hardly over, that the *récit* is still open. This gesture is made explicit in the opening captions: "*Cada día que transcurra sin justicia y sin verdadera democracia es un paso de regreso hacia el pasado de escarnio y terror del que acabamos de despertar*" (Each day without justice and true democracy is a step back to the past of terror from which we have just woken up.) Instead of pointing to the failure of democratic expectations (Aprea, *Cine* 59), the crafting of the present as a work in progress makes the film a paradigmatic product of the early democracy.

Analogous portrayals of the present as work in progress can be found in testimonial documentaries contemporaneous with *Juan*. Lourdes Portillo and

Susana Blaustein's *Las Madres: Mothers of Plaza de Mayo* (1985) begins in medias res, almost too suddenly, with testimonies from a group of women belonging to the human rights organization referenced in the title. Such an abrupt opening gives the impression that the footage is unedited, that we are hearing their stories as they unfold. After listening to the women's testimonies of disappearance and fruitless search, to a former military officer who regrets his role in the army and to a voiceover that states facts and organizes the historical sequence, we learn that the final verdict in the *juicio a las juntas* is still pending. We then see shots of people joining the Mothers of Plaza de Mayo as they rally and a closing scene that returns to the beginning, to the same testimonies that introduce the documentary. A similarly circular sequence lies at the heart of *Todo es ausencia* (Rodolfo Kuhn 1984). The film—written by Bayer, the author of *Juan*'s voiceover—begins, is intercut, and ends with traveling shots of the Mothers as they march in front of the Government House. Inserted within this circular sequence are three long testimonies: one by Marta Francese de Bettini (a woman who lost her husband, son, son-in-law, and daughter at the hands of the military); one by Bettini's daughter; and one by Hebe de Bonafini (a cofounder of the organization, who lost her two sons and daughter-in-law). In *Malvinas: historia de traiciones* (Jorge Denti 1983), the sad testimonies of the Malvinas War survivors who feel betrayed by the Argentine military government both introduce and conclude the filmic sequence. These testimonies are intercut with rallies against the dictatorship, still in power when the film was shot. In all three films, the circular sequence confronts the viewer (paradoxically) with an open present. As in *Juan*, the use of indexical images directs the audience to a present that is still under construction, still evolving—an evolution further emphasized by the abrupt opening shots in *Las Madres* and by the traveling shots in *Todo es ausencia*.[14]

Juan's opening captions allude to yet another narrative strategy through which the film conceives of the present as under construction: the creation of two separate temporalities. For the democratic present to be considered a work in progress, it must be carefully distinguished from the dictatorial past—a past that may be over but that remains latent, as the captions suggest. The distinction between these two temporal frameworks was actually of the utmost importance for the Alfonsín administration. In order to promote democracy and reconstruct the public sphere, the government needed to be clearly demarcated from the dictatorial past. The early democracy had to be perceived as a brand-new historical period, a new possible beginning for the Argentine people.[15] And yet, how is it possible to differentiate between past and present when film is incapable of capturing the latter? How can the documentary separate two successive temporalities when its scenes are always already historical? Is there any way to mark something as past when cinematic images necessarily belong to the past already?

In *Juan*, the inclusion of photographic images is most of what allows for the staging of two distinct temporalities. Aside from typical postdictatorship scenes where relatives sort through family albums in order to reconstruct the missing person's life (I will return to such scenes in the next section), the use of photographs follows a precise and definite pattern: whenever Buch interviews a former military officer, a shot of the officer's portrait on duty intercuts the dialogue— a strategy similar to the one used in *Las Madres* and *Todo es ausencia*, where archival footage clearly marked as past serves as a counterpoint to the testimonies and rallies unfolding in the present. The photograph, Marianne Hirsch argues, is "the index par excellence, pointing to the presence, the having-been-there of the past" ("Surviving" 14). Echeverría's film takes this statement at face value. On the one hand, pictures become proof of having been there: material evidence that the present-day interviewees were indeed on duty during the dictatorship. On the other hand, photos—like archival footage in the other two documentaries— spotlight the presence of the past: they attest to the existence of a temporality that precedes the interviews. The inclusion of photographs marks two subsequent timeframes: the dictatorial past, preserved in frozen portraits, and the democratic present, pure movement unfolding in parallel to the filmic world. The incorporation of television images further emphasizes this temporal contrast. If photographic images gesture to a given past, the TV pulls the ongoing present directly into the film. Via television, the audience witnesses Alfonsín declaring the *leyes de punto final* and *obediencia debida*. A live TV broadcast transmits the absolution of Alfredo Astiz, an infamous navy officer responsible for hundreds of deaths and torture cases. Appealing to a narrative strategy that would become popular in Argentine films portraying the 2001 economic crisis, the inclusion of a TV set connects the filmic and afilmic realms, highlighting their simultaneous development. Pictures are markers of the past. TV images are signs of a present in progress, evolving simultaneously with the film's making.

One central sequence is particularly revealing of the latter narrative strategy. A long low-angle shot of a TV set allows the audience to witness the public broadcasting firsthand. This TV shot is interspersed with eye-level shots of Buch organizing filmic material. At one point, Buch suddenly pauses and turns to the TV screen. The eye-level shot gives way to a close-up that immerses the viewer in the on-screen event: a military ceremony in which local officers pledge allegiance to their homeland. The TV set has disappeared, and now, via medium and long eye-level shots, the audience is joining the ceremony. Panning and tilting, the camera follows the soldiers' and commander's faces, as well as the proud faces of Bariloche neighbors attending the event. A cut introduces a scene shot with a handheld camera in which we follow Buch as he walks with the commander away from the ceremony toward the latter man's office. We then listen to the

Figure 1.1. Buch turning to the TV screen in *Juan*.

Figure 1.2. The audience about to become immersed in the onscreen event in *Juan*.

commander's vague answers, alternated with shots of his older portrait, until a phone call interrupts the interview. In the next scene, Buch is sitting in the street as Alfonsín's voice becomes increasingly audible, a shot followed by archival footage depicting the announcement of the *leyes*.

This sequence—built around an editing practice of "temporal repetition [whereby] what happens simultaneously in the narrative happens simultaneously in the image" (Doane, *Emergence* 188–189)—encapsulates the documentary's temporal logic. The associated shots of Buch organizing filmic material and of television images situate the documentary production in the present. Both the filmic and the afilmic worlds are transpiring at the same time; both are in progress, under construction. The cuts, the succession of long and medium shots, the pans and tilts, and the handheld camera all enhance the impression that this present—as opposed to the portrait's frozen past—is ongoing, pure movement, still in the making. The low-angle shot of the TV set, the close-up of the military ceremony, and the eye-level images of the oath bring the audience into the moving present. Furthermore, this immersion is doubly underscored by Buch's presence. His movements mimic the camera and thus channel the audience's own gaze, becoming its on-screen alter ego.

In this sense, Echeverría's film seems again aligned with a subgenre (addressed in chap. 3) that becomes especially prevalent in the early 2000s, the "performative documentary": a highly reflexive type of documentary in which the filmmaker is self-inscribed within the body of the film, explicitly acting as the filter through which the world enters into discourse (Chanan, *Politics* 241). In *Juan*, however, the journalist-investigator, not the director, is inscribed in the narrative. This difference reveals, in turn, the broader differences between the 2000s and the 1980s. While in performative documentaries the filmmaker's inscription has been read as a sign of disappointment regarding representation (Andermann, *New Argentine* 94) or of the shift from class politics to identity politics (Chanan, *Politics* 242), *Juan* uses a juxtadiegetic journalist-investigator's inscription as a tool for inscribing the audience itself, as I will further discuss in the next section. The viewer joins Buch within the film, becoming immersed in the present. Via both Buch and the camera, then, the spectator joins the work in progress.

The inclusion of Alfonsín's announcements should be read in this same light. More than a sign of terminated democratic expectations, the TV footage engages the audience, alluding to the still-open possibilities of the early democracy. A similar effect occurs in *Las Madres*, where the critical view of CONADEP's methodology actually alludes to a hope for different proceedings, as well as in *No al punto final*, Jorge Denti's short 1986 documentary advocating for an alternative to the *leyes*. Only a belated reception, one that enjoys the benefit of hindsight (and thus knows that the *leyes* weren't abolished until 2005), can read their filmic emergence as closure. Instead of constituting an exception, *Juan*'s reflective language is attuned to events in the 1980s. The emphasis on indexicality (on the cinematic images being formed by a real referent) brings the present into the film. More than exposing the impossibility of historical representation, it highlights the *récit*'s open and unstable condition. The inclusion of photographs and TV images establishes a contrast between a dictatorial past—over but potentially destabilizing—and a democratic present under construction. The inscription of a juxtadiegetic journalist-investigator and of the crew manipulating filmic material, rather than demanding critical distance, draws the audience into the filmic realm, immersing viewers in an ongoing, still-evolving democratic present—an immersion replicated in the indexically marked circular sequences of *Todo es ausencia*, *Malvinas*, and *Las Madres*.

Juan and the *juicio a las juntas*: Democracy as Juridical Performance

Television not only provides *Juan* with indexical images connecting the film to its present, but it also plays a key role as a model for organizing the symbolic dimension. *Juan*'s genre-based and narrative structures are shaped by television conventions. Margulis specifies this medium's influence when analyzing the role of the hidden camera—which *Juan* uses in anticipation of a technique that would become popular in 1990s TV programs such as *Edición Plus* (produced by Echeverría himself). This camera captures undisclosed statements by people who were responsible for criminal acts during the dictatorship (Margulis, "A Professional" 3–15). Once again, the use of television techniques seems to make the film an exception to 1980s cinema. Yet at that time, as Margulis has explained thoroughly, several documentary filmmakers who had studied abroad came to employ television strategies and held a fluid view of the relationship between the two media (*De la formación* 47–108). TV techniques were used in another way, too, that adheres to the present and helps us better understand the links between testimonial cinema and the early democracy: the filmic reconfiguration of the *juicio a las juntas*, arguably the most important TV event of the decade.

Following a presidential decree, Channel 7, Argentina's public TV station, recorded all five hundred hours of the *juicio a las juntas*. However, the images were not entirely available. Only three minutes of TV footage, carefully selected by the Secretaría de Cultura de la Nación, were transmitted at the end of every day. Interestingly enough, the transmission, except for the final verdict on December 9, had no sound. Moreover, because the camera was placed facing the podium, only the witnesses' backs were shown. For about eight months, this was the only image accessible at home: the back of someone testifying on mute. If people were interested in what was being said, they either had to rely on journalists' reports or read *Diario del juicio*, a journal that provided daily transcriptions of the entire hearing.[16]

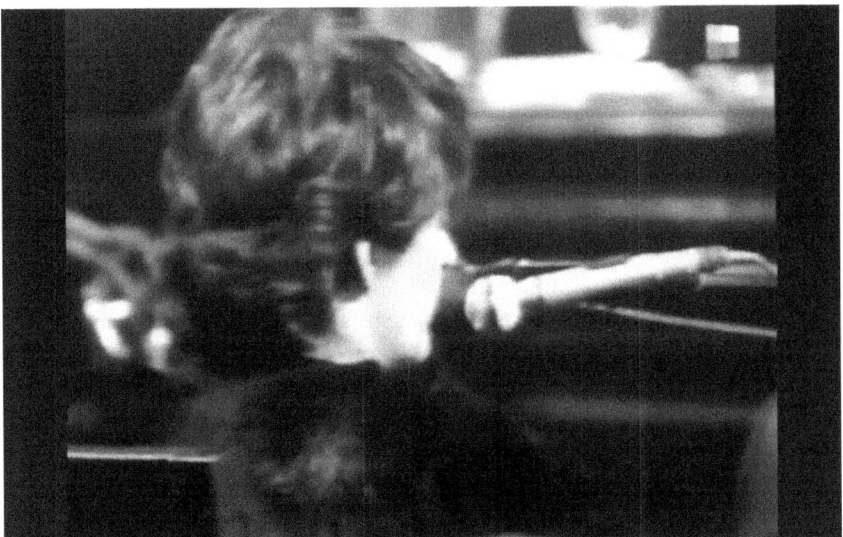

Figure 1.3. Broadcast of the testimony by Graciela Fernández Meijide during the *juicio a las juntas*.

At first glance, this is an extremely surprising way of handling a transmission. Why would the government decide to carry out public oral trials if they were going to stipulate a soundless broadcast? Why would the Alfonsín administration demand five hundred hours of recording but only allow three minutes of transmission per day? What was the point of giving a voice to survivors and victims' relatives if their stories remained silent and their faces hidden? After interviewing judges, TV producers, and government officials, Claudia Feld has concluded that the specific means of televising the *juicio a las juntas* responded to two interrelated official concerns: reconfiguring democracy while simultaneously eluding a spectacle of horror like the one that had followed the initial discovery of unidentified corpses in 1984.[17] The silent, abridged TV images were proof that the trials were being conducted, a guarantee that democratic institutions were working, and a defense against sensationalism. As Feld observes, this decision implied a partial disavowal of television strategies and language ("Aquellos ojos que contemplaron el límite" 91). The indexical quality of the medium was retained, but its potential diminished as a vehicle for feeling. What was important was the images' referential and thus performative nature; by displaying the court, the testifying witnesses, and the listening jury, the Argentine government took an important step toward reconstructing the public sphere.

Although *Juan* may seem to stand in opposition to the Argentine government, especially because of its critical view on the *leyes*, its recasting of television strategies actually complements the official transmission. As does the latter, *Juan* displays (and performs) a court scene with its suspects, witnesses, and victims. Moreover, the documentary goes a step further by incorporating what was left out of the actual legal process: time and sound. In this sense, *Juan* reinforces the official strategy, helping the government further its primary goal of reconstructing the public sphere via the criminalization of past military violence and a reconfiguration of community ties. As analyzed in the previous section, the documentary distinguishes between two temporalities: a frozen (yet latent) past represented in the military portraits and an ongoing present staged through the careful manipulation of indexicality. But a third temporality also results from the specific representation of time during the interviews: a simulation of real time. As Doane explains,

> in the technical language of filmmaking, the term *real time* refers to the duration of a single shot (assuming the shot is neither fast nor slow motion). If the physical film is not cut and its projection speed equals its shooting speed . . . the movement on the screen will unfold in a time that is isomorphic with real time, or what is generally thought to be our everyday lived experience of time—hence the term *real*. The time of the apparatus matches, is married to, the time of the action or the scene. . . . But this temporal continuity is in fact haunted by absence, by the lost time represented in the division between frames. . . . The cinema presents us with a simulacrum of time. Nevertheless, knowledge of the indexicality of the cinematic image sustains a belief that something of time, something of movement or its imprint, or, at the very least, its adequate representation, is there. (*Emergence* 172, emphasis in the original)

Unlike with the three condensed minutes of on-air TV, *Juan* manipulates indexicality to provide us with a simulacrum of real time. The single shot's projection speed makes us feel as if the interviews in the documentary were playing out as they happened. We see military officers hesitate, answer the phone, and roll their eyes. We accompany Juan's family members as they pause to remember, hold back their tears, and stare silently at the camera, trying to compose themselves. Rather than receiving an edited version of the most relevant content, we are confronted with a filmic rendition of real time—a strategy also noticeable in *Todo es ausencia*, where Marta Bettini's testimony occupies forty-five long minutes, and which we do not encounter again after the 1980s. We could say about Echeverría's film, in fact, that conveying the sense and pulse of time is the most important part of the interviews. As is especially evident in the military officers' accounts, content is sometimes sparse. More pertinent, though, is that viewers are made privy to what they cannot observe at home. Real-time interviews allow them to observe what they would see in court, as if they were actually taking part in the legal process. Such participation does not only mean experiencing real court time, but it also compensates for what the official transmission had omitted: we can now listen to all the parties involved. Via Buch, we hear suspects (former military officers, local civil authorities, and entrepreneurs who collaborated with the regime), victims (survivors of state violence), and witnesses (Juan's friends, neighbors, and relatives). Accompanying official discourse, then, this juridical performance fosters democratic participation, shapes new affective configurations, and offers a different version of history.

Of the three types of interviews, those conducted with suspects are arguably the most significant—in part because convincing the military to talk has proved almost impossible in the postdictatorship, but also because the staging completely breaks with interviews' genre conventions. To begin with, as mentioned earlier, the suspects' accounts essentially lack content. In fact, it would be quite difficult to summarize their version of what happened to Juan (Buch's primary question). What we see are fragmented answers and uncomfortable gestures. Former officers nervously touch their faces and unknot their ties. They look away, lower their voices, talk in circles. The interview with Castelli, the officer who was in charge of Bariloche when Juan was kidnapped, is a good example. At Buch's request, he first defines "subversion" ("La subversión busca la conquista del poder para imponer sus propias reglas y no trepida en cualquiera sea los procedimientos para alcanzar el poder") (Subversives want to conquer power to impose their own rules and do not hesitate, regardless of the means employed to achieve power.) He then spends the next eleven minutes arguing with Buch about whether or not to discuss the "topic" (Juan's disappearance). Reproducing a meaningful statement would be quite difficult. For those eleven minutes (a long time relative to the documentary's total length), he insists that he only faintly recalls what Buch is referring to, claims that he supposes the case might involve the "war against subversives," and complains about having to answer. The interview turns out to be an anti-interview: pure, contentless metalanguage. (Why I should I give you an interview? What is the point of talking about this?) Ultimately, it is also an anti-testimony: The connection between protagonist and event, between witness and narration, is broken. As Margulis observes,

> The place of testimony is, to a large extent, represented by Juan's private circle, his friends, and relatives, with whom the film creates strong bonds. . . . In turn, far from providing support to the testimonies by adding information about their key subjects, interviews [to public figures and military officers] turn out to function as a space in which conflicts are developed and through which action further progresses. In contrast to testimonies, most interviews are conducted with public figures with whom the film establishes a distance; they are addressed as *others* with whom it is impossible to have an affinity. This ideological distance is continually emphasized in the film. . . . The unexpected

question triggers spontaneous reactions, generating unplanned actions that create a dramatic reality effect. ("Documentaries" 333)

Unlike what happens with friends and relatives, these interviews—instead of elucidating history, giving voice to a specific social group, or eliciting solidarity—bring about consensus against the interviewee. Former officers and public figures are, as Margulis states, othered: portrayed as unreliable, distant, and speechless. Their gestures, sometimes hesitant and sometimes aggressive, override their narratives. In this sense, the documentary inverts former military strategies. As has been broadly analyzed, dictatorial power was based to a large extent on the dehumanization of its victims (Vezzetti, *Pasado* 177–190; Calveiro). For the concentration camps to work, prisoners had to be deprived of their subjectivity, so that violence could be unleashed without moral inhibitions. Negating victims' human features was a necessary condition for exercising torture—which is why dehumanizing techniques were included as a primary component in US training of Argentine military and paramilitary officers. Extreme violence is only possible, as Giorgio Agamben has famously claimed, when people turn into "bare life"; when, excluded from society, all of their attributes as citizens are revoked, permitting them to be killed (though not to be sacrificed). And while, according to Agamben, this mechanism lies at the core of sovereignty in general and enables society to function on an everyday basis, it is exacerbated in the camp until it becomes the rule. Camp conditions are literally inhuman: The incarcerated dwell outside the boundaries of humanity. As evidenced by survivor testimonies, they have no language, no name, and no history. Transformed into mere bodies, prisoners are perceived as inhuman others at the service of a ruling power.[18]

Tweaking dictatorial logic, Echeverría's film dehumanizes military interviewees, depicting them as others, stripping them of their subjectivity, and depriving them of their own narratives. Whenever we hear officers talking, they either say nothing of substance or stick to empty concepts such as the "war against subversion," a justification that, as Vezzetti has compellingly shown, turned out to be an origin myth with no authentic counterpart (*Pasado* 70).[19] No experience, no narrative, and no history can be extracted from these interviews. Instead of seeing human beings giving testimony on camera, we see a collection of voiceless, uncomfortable bodies. This particular representation complements the official position. By incorporating time and sound, the documentary opens the doors to the courtroom, encouraging its viewers to see military officers as inhuman perpetrators.

Not surprisingly, these interviews have the opposite effect as survivor testimonies, such as the one provided by Miguel D'Agostino, Juan's cellmate at the Club Atlético in Buenos Aires. Rather than eluding Buch's questions, D'Agostino tries hard to remember every detail and explain where he got his information. Without interrupting him or marking an ideological distance, Buch lets the interview develop into a testimony, veering away from Juan several times to describe the harsh conditions at the detention center. D'Agostino describes the camp and recalls the prisoners' daily routines, including torture. While he talks, his words are accompanied not by a military portrait but by images of the site where El Atlético was built. As opposed to the interviews with suspects, D'Agostino's testimony—which is structured, like the interviews in Nunca más, according to kidnapping, life at the center, and disappearance—is treated as a piece of historical evidence, an essential component of what Shoshana Felman has called the "juridical unconscious" (2): a body of evidence that might have juridical resonance in the future.

Filling the gap caused by the lack of reliable documents, his testimony, like other survivor accounts in the early democracy, such as those by Pino and Lili Cuesta in A los compañeros la libertad (Marcelo Céspedes and Carmen Guarini, 1987), allows a new official history of what happened during the dictatorship to be forged. Indeed, a similar combination of testimony and mapping can be found not only in Nunca más, where survivor testimonies are followed by an entire section dedicated to geophysical descriptions of detention centers, but also in Alicia Partnoy's The Little School (1986), which ends with an appendix that includes Partnoy's map of the camp where she was held captive. Confronted with the ethical imperative of their own survival (and of giving voice to those who have not), survivors' memories become alternative narratives that contest the military version by unveiling a calculated extermination plan, criminalizing state violence, and portraying political prisoners as victims. Defined by the challenges inherent to discussing a limit experience that resists representation, these early testimonies, as trauma scholars put it, convey a past truth that cries out and is not otherwise available. To paraphrase what Primo Levi observed, testimonial subjects do not want to forget and do not want the world to forget (195).[20]

Moreover, the meaning of these testimonies exceeds their purpose in the juridical unconscious—a purpose literally served in 2012, when Juan was used as evidence in a trial against officers responsible for El Atlético. The ethical and political value of such testimonies surpasses historical and legal signification and has a direct impact on the present. As Vezzetti claims, aside from acting as pieces of historical and juridical evidence, early testimonies become social practices that reconstruct broken community bonds (Pasado 117). In this sense, they are vehicles of social and communal memory. If one of the dictatorship's overarching goals was to shatter collective affiliations and privatize the public sphere, survivor testimonies invert the equation: Drawing from private, individual experience—from what René Jara calls a "public intimacy" (quoted in Beverley, Testimonio 42)—they reconfigure collectivity.

For one thing, testimonies restore citizenship. By making their atrocious experiences public, testimonial subjects not only return to being citizens themselves but also confront regular citizens with their own civic duties and community histories. In other words, survivor testimonies engage civilians as citizens, facing them with a shared past and demanding that they take an active stance. They foster what Lisa Cartwright calls "empathetic identification" or "moral spectatorship" (41) and what Dominick LaCapra calls "empathic unsettlement" (*Writing* 78): an intersubjective connection between the subjects represented on screen and the audience through which each responds emotionally to the other while also becoming more aware of their differences. For another, testimony helps testimonial subjects build a new collective identity. If political prisoners, as subaltern studies scholars would say, were voiceless, oppressed, and anonymous in the past, they are now able to speak for themselves. If they were dehumanized and rendered helpless victims, their own voices now restore their subjectivities and histories.

Furthermore, the polyphonic nature of these voices creates a new, eloquent collectivity. In symmetrical opposition to the interviews, survivor testimonies in *Juan* are historically, legally, ethically, and politically meaningful. This many-voiced eloquence is hardly exclusive to cinema, of course. *The Little School* once again stands out as another cogent example of the multiple meanings yielded by polyphony and symmetrical opposition. Partnoy's book is organized as a collection of short stories about everyday life at a clandestine center. The stories alternate between the first and the third person, creating a collective, polyphonic subjectivity. Moreover, these stories are often preceded by epigraphs quoting fragments of military narratives, creating a symmetrical opposition in which the latter are deprived of content and context, whereas the former are laden with historical, ethical, legal, and political meaning.

In *Juan*, the inclusion of relatives' voices adds to this multiplicity of meaning. The documentary incorporates a series of interviews, mainly devoted to reconstructing Juan as a person. Although some of these accounts provide details on the kidnapping and failed search, reconfiguring Juan (bringing him back to life) seems to be their main purpose. Friends and family depict Juan as a sensitive twenty-two-year-old law student interested in social justice. Challenging military accounts of him as a subversive combatant, Juan's loved ones offer a soft, almost naïve version of militancy. As the father puts it when Buch asks about his son's political commitments, Juan "*había ido a villas miserias. Le interesaba la justicia social, como a cualquier joven.*" (He had been to shantytowns. He was interested in social justice, just like any young person.) In this sense, the documentary's representation is certainly attuned to what Emilio Crenzel has called the figure of the "innocent victim" (*Los desaparecidos* 21), the most common portrayal of disappeared persons in the early democracy. This depiction is also prevalent in *Todo es ausencia* and *Las Madres*, where participating in literacy programs in poor neighborhoods is consistently quoted as the only example of political involvement.

As Crenzel explains, the image of the innocent victim emerged from both local and global factors: legal discourse, the protocols of international organizations, and family representation. First, the figure of the victim was at the center of the juridical process. Factors like political affiliation were irrelevant when determining victimhood and elucidating criminal responsibility. In other words, as seen in *Nunca más* and the *juicio*, only the description of what prisoners had suffered at the hands of the military was legally meaningful, precisely because the issue at stake was the latter's criminal behavior.[21] Second, organizations such as Amnesty International and the Red Cross provided standard claim forms requesting detailed accounts of human rights violations. These forms only demanded sociodemographic information and excluded political affiliation. Moreover, the erasure of militancy was a common reaction, both in opposing the military's insistence that missing people were guerrillas and in resisting the so-called *teoría de los dos demonios* (theory of the two evils). On December 10, 1983, as soon as he took office, Alfonsín decided that both military and guerrilla leaders be put on trial. The perspective driving this decision—the idea that both parties were responsible for political violence—is usually referred to as the *teoría de los dos demonios*, even though the notion of a war between two groups, misleading as it was, had been sustained long before 1983 and had in fact been embraced by both military and revolutionary organizations (Vezzetti, *Pasado* 123–128). Yet, Alfonsín's intention was less to allocate historical responsibility than to avoid future political violence. Adhering to the concept of retroactive limited justice, he believed that an exemplary trial was necessary to prevent repetition and that armed civilian action, though qualitatively different from state action, should also be prosecuted. As shown in Crenzel's study, largely based on conversations with CONADEP interviewees, survivors and relatives often decided to omit the subject of political affiliation, either for fear of being prosecuted or to avoid stigmatization (Crenzel, *Los desaparecidos* 80). Resorting to legal discourse as a safe representational strategy, family members usually began their narratives with the kidnapping and then only described their missing relative's physical characteristics, basic demographic information, and moral virtues.

Photographs played a key role in this early representation, as exemplified by Echeverría's documentary. Like Juan's sister in the film, relatives used the family album as a narrative tool. Photos allowed them to talk about the missing person's biography and private life, challenging their image as terrorists while inverting basic military ideologemes such as "family," "home," and "domesticity." Whereas military propaganda had been based on preserving family and moral values supposedly jeopardized by communist ideologies, relatives focused their own representations on family ties and ethical virtues and thus relegitimized their loved ones. Juan's father (always elegantly dressed and constantly emphasizing his medical credentials) highlights his son's morality, vaguely alluding to his political commitments. Juan's sister uses family albums to reconstruct her brother's personal life and portray him as a good citizen who led a perfectly normal existence—a scene that recalls a nearly identical one in which Marta Bettini shares photographs while emphasizing her family's religious virtues and respectability. In Echeverría's film, we even hear Juan himself; his voice has been preserved on a tape that he sent his parents before his kidnapping, casually describing university life in Buenos Aires and eagerly awaiting the family reunion. Besides serving as an index of having been there and constructing a previous temporality, photos in *Juan* serve various purposes in line with their historical moment. They are proof that the missing person existed prior to being kidnapped, help establish his or her image as an innocent victim, and act as a vehicle of memory and mourning, ultimately becoming a collective sign that alludes to a multiplicity of similar cases.[22]

Attuned to the demands of democratization, *Juan* performs a juridical process. As in the *juicio*, witnesses, victims, and perpetrators are carefully portrayed and distinguished from each other. Compensating for what the public transmission had lacked, the film opens the courtroom door, allowing the viewer to observe three different types of subjects of speech and to actually engage in the process. As Aprea has observed, this is a dialogue that the conventional use of testimonies in audiovisual documentary seeks to enable (*Filmar* 125). One actor is missing from the juridical performance, however: the prosecutor. Instead of this figure, the film incorporates a fourth subject of speech: a journalist—Buch himself—who is more like a detective. Buch interrogates suspects, searches for clues, puts pieces together, and exposes contradictions. He is an example of what Fredric Jameson calls a "social detective" (*Geopolitical* 37). In the classical detective story, an individual detective confronts a crime of an individual nature, one involving an individual perpetrator and an individual victim. The social detective typically emerges in stories involving groups of murderers and victims—an assassination plot, for example. Endowed with collective resonance, the latter unites everyone against the criminals, articulating a generalized desire and vouchsafing "a glimpse into a Utopian public sphere of the future" (47). Moreover, while the classical detective seems to be ideologically neutral, the social detective's position is overtly ideological. The social detective takes a political stance and makes a social judgment, as expressed in Buch's voiceover:

> ¿Juan fue víctima de una equivocación o un "subversivo," como se llamaba en esos años a los que se atrevían a poner en duda los fundamentos de la sociedad? . . . Juan hoy tendría 32 años. Hoy todos saben que se secuestró,

se torturó y se asesinó. ¿Cuánta gente más tiene que morir para que se hable de "crímenes," de "genocidio"? Todos estamos en contra de la violencia pero jamás reaccionamos ante la violencia de arriba. Seguimos utilizando el lenguaje de la dictadura: "excesos," "secuelas". "Desaparecido" es palabra borrada del diccionario. . . . La ciudad ha abandonado a su hijo desaparecido. ¿No le importa? ¿No teme que esto les ocurra a sus hijos? ¿No le importa que los asesinos de Juan convivan con ellos? ¿Qué van a pensar las nuevas generaciones ¿Que somos encubridores del crimen? ¿La sangre de Juan no manchará para siempre la idílica postal de mi ciudad natal? (Was Juan the victim of a mistake or a "subversive," like those who dared to criticize society's foundations were called at that time? . . . Today, Juan would have turned thirty-two years old. Everybody knows today that people were kidnapped, tortured, and murdered. How many more people need to die so that we can talk about "crime" and "genocide"? We are all against violence but we never react against top-down violence. We still use dictatorial vocabulary: "excesses," "sequels." "Disappeared" is a word that has been erased from our dictionary. . . . Our city has abandoned its missing child. Don't we care? Aren't we afraid that this might happen to our own children? Aren't we bothered by the fact that Juan's murderers live among us? What are the next generations going to think? That we are covering up a crime? Won't Juan's blood stain forever the idyllic postcard of my native city?)

Like a social detective, Buch both unites the community and becomes a vehicle for judgments and revelations on society as a whole. He simultaneously personifies a collective desire for reunification and underscores civil society's flaws in realizing this goal. Yet, the voiceover also points to a divergence in genre. As Jameson observes, nowhere does the canonical distinction between *story* and *fable* find more concrete embodiment than in the detective story (*Geopolitical* 36). For the genre to exist, the story, materialized in the detective's quest, should not coincide with the *fable*; rather, it should lead to its reconstruction, in a move that depends on the existence of a finished narrative or *récit*. In other words, because there is a finished *récit*, a closed and already-given narrative, it is possible to organize a story that tracks that narrative backward. This has important implications for viewers: as they become immersed in the story, they are confronted with a closed narrative in which conflicts are displayed but have actually already been solved. Thus, detective stories engage viewers' private subjectivities (their emotions and feelings), but since the *récit* entails closure, these stories do not require reviewers to actively strive for social resolution. In this sense, Echeverría's film deviates from the genre. As implied in the voiceover, the documentary alludes to an open *récit*. This openness is further emphasized, as I have discussed, through the manipulation of indexicality. Here, unlike in detective stories, we get the impression that the afilmic present is a work in progress. Hence, if the use of the detective story engages the viewer's private subjectivity, the genre deviation highlights the nonclosure of the afilmic realm, encouraging the audience to seek out social resolution on their own. Embodying a collective desire for democracy and justice, *Juan* strengthens community ties, symbolically rebuilds a broken public sphere, and engages civil society—an engagement further emphasized through the camera, which ties Buch to the audience, and through the nature of the documentary as a collective creation.

La noche de los lápices: Democracy as Affective Fiction

Let us revisit the popular interpretation of *Juan* as an anomaly. Unlike canonical 1980s cinema, Echeverría's film has been read in large part as a highly reflexive product that evidences the exhaustion of generic fictions. This interpretation maintains that the documentary, far from being a revelatory melodrama and relying on a transparent, linear version of history, ultimately exposes the complexities of historical representation. Rather than appealing to emotion and plunging the audience into the film, it encourages critical judgment and cognitive distance. Although I partially agree with this assessment—there is a stark and obvious difference between *Juan* and, say, *La historia oficial*—a close analysis has invited us to relativize such statements. Not only is the film marked by its present (and what are perceived as anomalies are actually traces of the early democracy), but it also challenges the binary rigidity at the center of its status as an exception. *Juan*'s indexical and symbolic components help us analyze social discourses of the early democracy, understand the role of testimonial film in this historical moment, and rethink—my primary focus in this section—the dichotomies that have traditionally sustained readings of films from the 1980s: reflexivity/genre, reason/affect, feeling/knowledge, etc. As seen in the previous sections, these binaries are ultimately hazy. While the film appeals to reflective language (emphasizing indexicality and openly exhibiting the shooting process), it also resorts to genre conventions, especially the oft-criticized thriller. Further, while the documentary encourages critical judgment and fills gaps in historical knowledge, it also elicits feelings. The juridical performance is probably the best example of this double appeal. On the one hand, the inclusion of testimonies defies military discourse and reconstructs history. On the other, testimonies engender (new) affects. Sentimental representations make us perceive officers as inhuman perpetrators and missing people as innocent victims, thus resignifying previous official narratives. Taking *Juan* as a starting point, we could in fact say that what defines 1980s cinema is precisely this mixture of feeling and knowledge—a mixture that is utterly essential to the democratization process. In the open, turbulent 1980s, reason alone cannot solidify democracy and rebuild the public sphere. Indeed, in a context of total reconfiguration, emotion and cognition must be blended together; it is necessary both to build historical knowledge and to mobilize feeling against the military past and toward the new democracy.

This combination is by no means exclusive to Echeverría's film. As I remarked in the introduction, the interrelatedness of feelings and cognition is among the basic premises of affect theory. Relying on Spinoza and Deleuze, most scholars define "affect" as "the augmentation or diminution of the body's capacity to act, to engage, and to connect" (Ticineto Clough 2). Rather than denoting a personal feeling, *affect*, as the word suggests, denotes an ability to affect and be affected. It is a sensorial intensity corresponding to the shift from one experiential state of the body to another and implying a transformation in that body's power to act. This transition between experiential states necessarily entails a change in knowledge too. As Michael Hardt puts it, "Affects refer equally to the body and the mind . . . they involve both reason and the passions. . . . They illuminate, in other words, both our power to affect the world around us and our power to be affected by it, along with the relationship between these two powers" (9). Thus, contrary to what is commonly thought, affect becomes intertwined with reason and is fundamental to cognition. Affect is a "different kind of intelligence about the world" (Thrift 175).

In Alison Jaggar's words, "Emotions are neither more basic than observation, reason, or action in building theory, nor are they secondary to them. Each of these human faculties reflects an aspect of human knowing inseparable from other aspects. . . . The development of each of these faculties is a necessary condition for the development of all" (64). Unlike the cognitivist approach, which sees cognition as an autonomous level and feelings as universal attributes located within the individual, affect scholars emphasize that feelings and cognition are actually dependent on each other rather than existing as two independent spheres.[23] "Feeling," Michelle Rosaldo observes, "is forever given shape through thought and thought is laden with emotional meaning" (88). We feel anger, for example, because we understand that a particular situation is wrong according to our social beliefs. Concomitantly, the feeling of anger helps us distinguish, perpetuate, or even challenge our social beliefs.

In *The Politics of Affect and Emotion*, Laura Podalsky builds on these affect theories to offer a more complex account of the Latin American cinematic field. Podalsky observes that many scholars (such as Nelly Richard, Beatriz Sarlo, and Jean Franco) have criticized post-1990s films for being depoliticized and usually cite their appeal to feelings as an indicator of this depoliticizing slant. Genre films addressing the 1960s and '70s are especially criticized for erasing historical specificity in favor of narrative or character development and for relegating the past to what is already known. That said, this widespread critique necessarily relies on the assumption that only cognition can provide a proper representation of history; it neglects to examine the interconnection between the two realms and ignores the historicity of feelings. In other words, this critique disregards the reality that film can shape affect and unsettle already-given emotions—not only reflect them. Amid the hyper-rationalization of politics, with truth commissions effectively doing away with the dictatorship's legacy, certain political thrillers (Podalsky argues) can probe the past in new ways. Their appeal to feelings can impart a sense of urgency that allows for radical interrogation by shaping new types of affect, disturbing existing emotions, and encouraging "alternative ways of knowing (about) the recent traumatic past" (8). Although Podalsky refers to post-1990s films explicitly marked by neoliberal sensibilities, her arguments also apply to the typical interpretation of 1980s films—which, as evidenced by *Juan*, are grounded in a rigid opposition between reflexivity and genre, knowledge and emotion, feeling and reason. If, however, we resist this binary thinking and view film from the standpoint of recent affect theories, we can better understand 1980s cinema and reexamine the role of fictional testimony in the early democracy. It is with this goal in mind that I would like to turn to the much-criticized *La noche de los lápices* and briefly review it from an affect-based perspective.

Héctor Olivera's *La noche de los lápices* is usually considered the first visual testimony of a clandestine detention center in Argentina. Unlike the proliferation of audiovisual material documenting life at the Nazi camps, there is no visual documentation of the more than three hundred camps located across Argentina—except for some portraits of officers and prisoners smuggled out of the ESMA by Víctor Basterra.[24] In order to overcome this lack, Olivera recreated a detention center in a 1986 fiction film based on survivor Pablo Díaz's testimony during the *juicio a las juntas*. The film, advised by Díaz himself, narrates how a group of high school students were kidnapped and later disappeared in an operation commonly referred to as *la noche de los lápices* (night of the pencils).[25] As mentioned earlier, Díaz acts both as the main speaking subject and as the primary subject of speech. Adopting his viewpoint, the plot is divided into two fairly symmetrical parts. The first recreates the students' struggle for a free bus pass; it depicts their political discussions, meetings, demonstrations, and, above all, their friendship and joyful everyday lives. The second part chronicles their atrocious treatment at an underground camp. In line with the genre conventions of 1980s cinema, the plot is structured as a melodramatic thriller, intensified by a love story between Díaz and Claudia Falcone, a student who remains missing.

Attuned to the dominant reading, *La noche de los lápices* has been criticized for its melodramatic appeal to emotions, linear narrative, and simplification of history (Aprea, *Cine* 59; España 30; Raggio, "La noche de los lápices" 45–74; Ros 19). Even Sandra Raggio, a historian who has worked extensively on this particular film, acknowledges the story's lack of subtlety and accuses Olivera of facilely explaining complex questions. According to Raggio, this naiveté stems from an ingenuous conception of history as conspiracy that results in Manichaeism ("La noche" 60–62). Echoing a common critique, which has actually been raised by survivors and relatives themselves, she observes that students are portrayed as pure and innocent victims, whereas perpetrators are artlessly represented as beasts: "La apelación a *imágenes icónicas muy difundidas* para dar cuenta de la dictadura, como las tomas de las botas militares pateando una puerta o los Ford Falcon verde sin patente en plena noche, busca una lectura rápida y clara acerca de los represores" (The appeal to *widespread iconic images* portraying the dictatorship, such as shots of military boots kicking a door or green Ford Falcons without license plates in the middle of the night, aims at a quick and clear reading regarding repression) (67, my emphasis).

While I agree with most of this reading, I also find it somewhat oblivious to the film's historicity. The idea that the representation is based on widespread iconic images of the dictatorship is caused, as with *Juan*, by its belated reception. Only from a temporal vantage point (as we will see in chap. 4) can we call these images "iconic."[26] Several more years had passed—not as early as 1986—before these images became widespread. A similar belatedness underlies the interpretation of the appeal to emotion; years had to elapse in order for most of the feelings mobilized by the film to be classified as emotions (as already-codified feelings). In 1986, Olivera's melodrama is still configuring new affects. The sentimental representation of students and officers, now perceived as cliché, was quite original and stirred up what were then registered as fairly new sensations. Moreover, criticism of the film's simplistic conception of history considers its role as a historical document but overlooks its role as a historical agent. Such an assessment neglects the fact that—as Massumi and Bennett would say (25; 153)—the film shapes alternative sensibilities and thus generates new knowledge. This second stance toward history (creation rather than documentation) explains the directorial choice to simplify the representation of the military years and the role of the fictional testimony, especially in the 1980s—and I say "especially" because, while generative qualities apply to the cinematic field in general, I argue throughout this book that testimonial films increasingly lose their capacity to create new affects.

A brief look into the film's representation of historical events confirms its narrative preferences. The opening credits explicitly emphasize the historical nature of what is about to be shown. Aside from listing the crew's names, the two opening captions explain that the film was influenced by a journalistic monograph and Pablo Díaz's testimonial counsel.[27] A third caption clarifies the plot's stance toward reality: "*Esta película está basada en personajes y hechos reales. Por razones argumentales se han introducido algunos cambios que no alteran el espíritu ni la veracidad de lo acontecido.*" (This film is based on real characters and facts. For the sake of the plot, we have incorporated some changes that do not alter the true spirit of what happened.) Then, after a fourth caption explaining that the opening scenes take place in the city of La Plata in September 1975 (*La Plata, septiembre de 1975*), we see a group of students running toward a public-school building. These first images condense what happens in the film as a whole: historical events are at the service of fiction.[28] The appeal to real facts, to an existing investigation, to an authentic testimony, and to specific dates and places establishes the background and validates the narrative. Yet, as the third caption suggests, the film's primary component is this very narrative. Its main goal is to create a compelling story, even if it must alter facts in the process.

This same premise dominates the film's treatment of indexicality. Here, unlike documentaries, the afilmic existence of the cinematic images is effectively erased. Only after reading about the film do we discover that it was shot on location and that extras were actually real Argentine students. Except for the easily recognizable façade of the Casa Rosada, Argentina's presidential building, the other public places (the Ministerio de Obras Públicas, the Escuela de Bellas Artes, etc.) are not immediately noticeable as real referents—in large part because the city of La Plata is fairly peripheral in the Argentine imaginary. Contrary to what happens in *Juan*, indexical images are blurred and submerged into the film. In *La noche de los lápices*, then, indexicality is at the service of the symbolic dimension.

We could thus say that the film explicitly distances itself from the mandate to exist as a historical document—a requirement that the readings seem to take for granted. From the opening credits onward, the film emphasizes that the fictional story is what matters most. The clearest proof of this priority is the deliberate simplification of Pablo Díaz's testimony. In her excellent study of how the night of the pencils was conceptualized as an event, Raggio meticulously analyzes Díaz's testimony as transcribed in *Diario del juicio* ("Narrar" 111–123). As she explains, multiple narratives and temporalities are intertwined in this account. First, Díaz associates his kidnapping with those that occurred on September 16, 1976, even though he was kidnapped on September 21. He then juxtaposes different temporalities to explain how he knew the other kidnapped students: although he initially says that they had seen each other before because they were all fighting for the bus pass, he then tells the judge that they actually met afterward. Once in the detention camp, and based on what the officers ask him, Díaz comes to believe that the members of this group are affiliated through the student struggle and hence assumes that they had met earlier: "*De vista no nos conocíamos en sí, yo después, cuando me encuentro con ellos, en distintos campos donde estuve, voy relacionando todo esto y después por los interrogatorios que me hacen a mí*" (We did not really know each other in person. But, then, as we met at different concentration camps, I started putting the pieces together, also based on the questions I was being asked) (quoted in Raggio, "Narrar" 112).

As Raggio points out, Díaz is not merely describing what he faced there but also trying to assign meaning to his experience. This process of meaning-making—toggling back and forth in time, incorporating other narratives—is quite complex. Raggio shows, for example, how Díaz's testimony in the *juicio* draws from other testimonies and is in fact more coherent than his own previous version in *Nunca más*. Moreover, as Raggio observes, Díaz's identification as a teenage student who was kidnapped because of the bus pass incident occurs as a result of other narratives, such as the way his case had been classified in the CONADEP report.

Despite the complexity of this testimony, the film opts for a simplified version, one that erases the myriad temporalities and narratives intertwined in the historical account. Instead of taking up the contradictory nature of Díaz's memory, the intricacies of the events he tries to conceptualize, and translating them into cinematic language, the film offers the simplest possible rendition through a straightforward plot. Furthermore, this simplification increases with the moments when the plot deviates from the testimony. While Díaz says at the *juicio* that he fell in love with Claudia at the detention camp, in the film their (impossible) romance begins prior to their kidnapping and serves as a leitmotif for the overall narrative structure. At the *juicio*, too, Díaz recalls having been transferred to two different camps before being regularized as a legal prisoner; there is only one camp in the film, however.

As the opening caption warns, the film was inspired by real events, but the logic of the script is more important than historical logic. In *La noche de los lápices*, historical facts serve as a background sustaining the fictional plot. Contrary to standard expectations, the film is less concerned with divulging real-life events than with employing them as markers of credibility. We could indeed say that, rather than portraying new information, the film includes a checklist of all the most important facts revealed in *Nunca más* and the *juicio*: kidnappings, tortures, fake firing squads, underground baby deliveries, and rapes. Interestingly enough, there is only one example of each, as if the narrative were designed to avoid overwhelming the viewer with information; it simply provides those elements necessary to historically situate the film. Nonetheless, this approach need not be considered the film's main flaw. In fact, the simplified representation of history can be seen as a strategy to enhance the symbolic dimension. In other words, it can be read as a tactic used to spotlight fiction: to shift the audience's focus from history to affect (and, thus, to a new type of knowledge altogether).

A closer look at the opening scenes can help us better understand the nature and consequences of such a strategy. The credits give way to a low-angle shot of two pairs of feet, followed by a long eye-level shot revealing two teenagers in school uniforms as they run happily toward a public-school building. The sequence is accompanied by an upbeat folk song for children.[29] The next scene

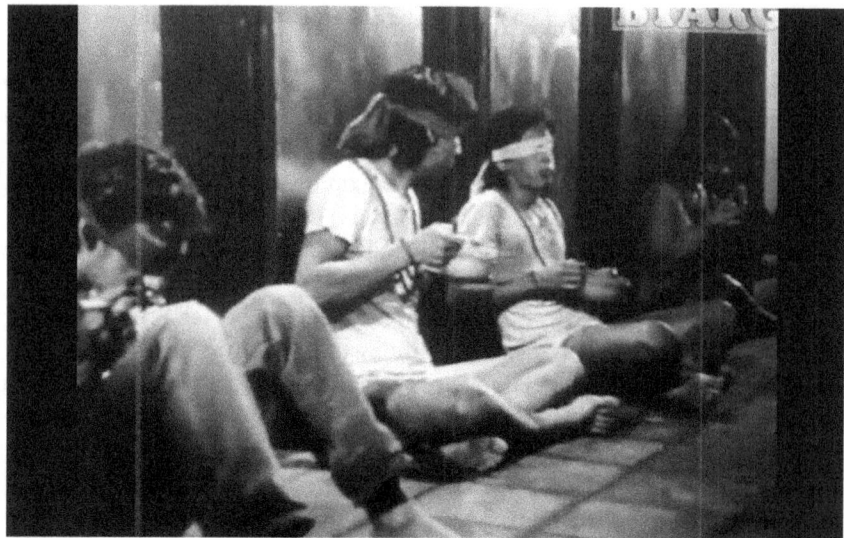

Figure 1.4. Theatricality at the detention center in *La noche de los lápices*.

mostly comprises close-ups of a group of adolescents in their school uniforms as they debate whether or not to march for the free bus pass. Several of these close-ups explore the fictional Pablo's face as his adoring eyes linger on Claudia, who is delivering a speech to the class. Even though the opening credits have reminded us that these scenes do have a real-life counterpart, the atmosphere is overtly fictional. The teenagers' gestures, voices, and even hairstyles plainly show that they are acting. Their carefully sequenced dialogues evidence an organized script. The exaggeratedly explicit eye contact between Claudia and Pablo anticipates a sentimental melodrama. And, above all, the children's folk song—composed for the film by José Luis Castiñeira de Dios and repeated throughout the entire film—creates a fairy-tale environment. As is usually the case in cinema, "music produces affect" (Metz, *Impersonal* 44). Setting the tone for the rest of the narrative, the first scenes are markedly fictional; sometimes they feel more like theater than cinema. Although this fictional tone is slightly more prevalent in the first part of the film (during the celebratory portrayal of student activism), it holds steady in the second portion, too, which depicts life at the camp. At the detention center, dialogues are clearly scripted, actors are evidently wearing make-up and have their hair done, and the children's folk song recurs in scene transitions, adding a hint of theatricality once again.

Breaking with the common perception of its purpose, *La noche de los lápices* is less concerned with unveiling historical facts than with creating affect. Everything is oriented toward portraying the protagonists as what Inés González

Bombal has called *"hipervíctimas"* (hypervictims): archetypes of victimhood (206). The sweet young students tortured, raped, and killed for an (almost naïve) utopia are rendered the very model of innocence. As opposed to the military discourse, which depicts its opponents as dangerous guerrillas—a discourse explicitly mimicked in the film via fictional television news—Pablo and his friends embody the guilelessness of political commitment. For them, activism merely entails requesting a free bus pass, having a poster of Che Guevara on their bedroom wall, and falling in love. Their most extreme form of militancy involves visiting slums to teach children how to read, handing out flyers, and painting street graffiti. These peaceful, innocent features are even recognized by the filmic military officers, who complain more than once about not having caught "real guerrillas."

We could indeed say that this representation is ideologically problematic. Not only, as Raggio has already noted ("La noche" 54), does it erase some of these students' affiliation with Montoneros, but it also comes close to legitimizing military discourse.[30] As Falcone's brother suggests—himself a former Montonero—the emphasis on the students' childish innocence ends up paradoxically justifying the military slaughter of adult activists (see Raggio, "La noche" 62, for further details on his critique). The idea that the students did not deserve torture and death because they were not guerrillas implies that the "real" guerrillas did—an implication that inadvertently endorses the military's own rhetoric. Still, ideological limitations aside, the film's treatment of history highlights the role of fictional testimony as historical agent. The creation of hipervíctimas, the humanization of political prisoners, and the contrasting dehumanization of military officers configure sensibilities that are quite new for the 1980s. More than unveiling unknown facts or reflecting codified emotions, *La noche de los lápices* sparks new affects that are of the utmost importance to democratization. Through its specific use of fiction, the film shapes sensorial intensities that affect our bodies and minds and thus foster new knowledge. Mobilizing noncodified feelings, it begins to establish sensations, to create affects that only later will become emotions: qualified, recognizable, ownable. To put it in Sara Ahmed's words, "Emotions [i.e., feelings] may not have a referent, but naming an emotion has effects that we can describe as referential" (*Cultural* 14).

A brief reconsideration of *La noche de los lápices* from an affect-based standpoint helps us dismantle not only the feeling/cognition binary that sustains typical appraisals of 1980s cinema but also the documentary/fiction dichotomy at the core of the traditional characterization of testimonial cinema as a genre. Although, as evidenced by Olivera and Echeverría's films, the choice of documentary over fiction—or of fiction over documentary—entails specific ideological consequences, it does not play any role in the definition of testimonial cinema. Both testimonial documentary and testimonial fiction adhere to the official administration's main goals: to promote democracy and to rebuild a public sphere that was broken by a near decade of forced exile, torture, death, censorship, and economic depression. Both of them resignify military discourse, strengthen community ties, fill gaps in historical knowledge, and create affective images that will later become iconic (the activist as innocent victim, the officer as perpetrator, the survivor as witness). Hence, instead of seeing them as two opposing strands, we should see them as two complementary elements of a broader, more comprehensive phenomenon. As Chanan would say, while fiction addresses the viewer as a private individual, documentary, structured by the conditions governing the public sphere, appeals to his or her role as a citizen. Instead of representing two antithetical components, they are actually two complementary (and inseparable) sides of a more encompassing genre: testimonial cinema.[31] Embodying a collective desire for history, democracy, and justice, 1980s testimonial films—whether documentary or fictional—begin to create that referent that, as I analyze in detail throughout the book, we still call "the military dictatorship."

Notes

1. Argentina had already experienced military dictatorships prior to 1976. Unlike Uruguay and Chile, the country was marked by frequent coups d'état, starting in 1930. Thus, I deliberately refer to Alfonsín as "promoting" democracy, as opposed to "restoring" it, both to avoid the impression that the last dictatorship was a parenthesis within a strong democratic tradition and to highlight the fact that the concept was actually new to the Argentine mentality in several ways. See Romero, *Breve historia contemporánea de la Argentina* for an overview of Argentine history. See Trímboli for further insight on how the notion of democracy was perceived (and neglected) before the 1976–1983 dictatorship.

2. Mostly advised by philosopher Carlos Nino, Alfonsín conceptualized the transition to democracy in terms of a retroactive limited justice—that is, the idea that justice should be implemented in order to avoid future crimes of the same nature. This approach explains why only those responsible for planning and ordering executions were put on trial (as opposed to all responsible actors, regardless of their level of responsibility). The procedure was unique both locally and globally. In Argentina, it was the first time that the state was held accountable for human rights violations against its own citizens. In Latin America, it was the only example of such a procedure by a democratic government against a former dictatorial government of the same country. Internationally, it was the first major trial held for war crimes since the Nuremberg Trials in Germany and the first to be conducted by a civilian court. See Nino for further details on the philosophical, historical, and legal framework that enabled the *juicio* and for a comparative analysis with respect to other international cases. See Balderston; Garretón, Sosnowski, and Subercaseux; O'Donnell, Schmitter, and Whitehead for a comparative view of democratic transitions in the Southern Cone. For further details on Alfonsín's presidency, *Nunca más*, and the *juicio a las juntas*, see Nino; Vezzetti, *Pasado y presente: Guerra, dictadura y sociedad en la Argentina*; Feld, *Del estrado a la pantalla: Las*

imágenes del juicio a los ex comandantes en Argentina; Crenzel, *La historia política del Nunca más: La memoria de las desapariciones en la Argentina*.

3. For further details on Third Cinema's aesthetics and politics, see Burton, ed.; Chanan, *Twenty-Five Years of the New Latin American Cinema*; Downing; Gabriel; Guneratne and Dissanayake; Lusnich and Piedras; Mestman, "Postales del cine militante argentino en el mundo" and *Las rupturas del 68 en el cine de América Latina*; Pick; Pines and Willemen; Solanas and Getino.

4. Although fiction was more popular in this period, Paola Margulis claims that documentaries shot between 1982 and 1990 also sought a reconciliation of market, industry, and political demands (*De la formación a la institución: El documental audiovisual en la transición democrática (1982–1990)* xvi–xxxii). Her claim further supports the argument that I develop in this chapter: that testimonial documentary and fiction should be seen as part of a more comprehensive phenomenon.

5. See Aguilar, *Otros mundos*; Amado; Andermann, *New Argentine Cinema*; Aprea, *Cine y políticas*; Falicov; Page for a comparative characterization of Argentine cinema in the 1960s and 1970s, in the 1980s and early 1990s, and since the mid-1990s. See Burucúa; España for in-depth studies of how 1980s cinema represented the dictatorship. See Margulis, *De la formación* for a comprehensive study of Argentine documentary between 1982 and 1990.

6. Aside from *La historia oficial*, fiction films read from this critical perspective include María Luisa Bemberg's *Camila* and *Miss Mary*, Alejandro Doria's *Darse cuenta*, Eliseo Subiela's *Hombre mirando al sudeste*, Jeanine Meerapfel's *La amiga*, and Fernando Solanas's *Sur* and *Tangos: el exilio de Gardel*. See Burucúa 72–154 for further details on the general reception of thrillers and melodramas both in 1980s Argentine cinema and abroad.

7. In this chapter, I use the term "official" (instead of "hegemonic") because I refer to discourses by the government in office that are not yet hegemonic. I return to this distinction in the next chapter.

8. The *ley de punto final* (Full Stop Law), passed by the National Congress in 1986, mandated an end to the prosecution of people accused of crimes during the dictatorship—except for those charged with the disappearance of prisoners' babies or of having stolen private property. The *ley de obediencia debida* (Law of Due Obedience), passed in 1987, exempted subordinates who had carried out orders from their superiors. Both laws, commonly referred to as "the impunity laws," were sanctioned following the original idea of retroactive limited justice and in response to military pressure after two attempted coups. They were declared unconstitutional and repealed under President Néstor Kirchner's administration in 2005. See Nino for an in-depth explanation of the political, historical, and moral reasons for sanctioning the two laws in 1986–1987.

9. Although, as mentioned in the introduction, 1982 saw the emergence of Grupo Cine Testimonio, a group of documentary filmmakers whose main goal was to give voice to marginalized people via the testimonial documentary format, I do not focus on these films because they are not concerned with representations of the dictatorship. The emergence of the group, however, attests to the importance and optimistic view of the testimonial documentary format in the early democracy. See Margulis, *De la formación* 144–156 for more details on this group's conditions of emergence.

10. Bill Nichols, for example, claims that the difference can only be established by considering the viewer's expectations; in particular, the search for realism in documentary (*La representación de la realidad* 50–60). This approach is partially shared by Roger Odin, who

prefers to shift away from the problems entailed by the notion of realism and proposes that what defines "documentary" is a specific "reading mode" (286) dictated by a set of institutions and paratextual codes. Carl Plantinga thinks that documentary and fiction can be distinguished in the way the filmic narration conceives of reality: in the case of documentary, the narration asserts the existence of what is being told (20–35). David Bordwell and Kristin Thompson argue that the documentary should be considered a genre, like the film noir or the western, with specific formal characteristics such as the use of handheld camera and visible montage, among others (323). Although I find their readings compelling, in this book I follow Chanan's distinction, as it takes a more nuanced stance toward the historical and ideological connotations of the difference between the two genres, which is key to my own analysis of testimonial films.

11. In this sense, Chanan's account seems to differ from others, such as Philip Rosen's, with respect to the indexical status of the cinematic image. As I mentioned in the introduction, according to Rosen, any image is historical, regardless of its fictional or documentary status, because it points to the past. Given that the profilmic—irrespective of its category in the afilmic world—was placed before the camera prior to the viewing of the image, then filmic images become indexical traces. While these seemingly divergent accounts could probably be reconciled through a redefinition of the "historical" (Rosen seems to emphasize temporality, whereas Chanan seems to focus on social existence), we could temporarily resolve this discrepancy by saying that, for Chanan, documentary images are doubly historical: they belong to the past, and they have a real connection to a social and historical referent in the afilmic world. It is this latter meaning that will be of special interest for *Juan*, and this is how the "historical" should be read in my interpretation of this specific film.

12. See Margulis, "Documentaries and Politics in Postdictatorship Argentina: *Cuarentena: Exilio y regreso* and *Juan, como si nada hubiera sucedido* by Carlos Echeverría" for further details on production and circulation.

13. As has already been observed, the notion of new Argentine cinema, typically applied to films produced after 1995, is far from homogeneous or transparent. If, however, we follow Andermann's provocative suggestion and understand the category in descriptive, as opposed to normative, terms (*New Argentine* xii–xiii), we can observe some constant features. Among others, and in line with *Juan*, we find the emphasis on documentary, the use of indexicality as a means of staging the present, and the inclusion of neorealist techniques and nonstudio locations (Aguilar, *Otros mundos* 176; Andermann, *New Argentine* xii; Aprea, *Cine* 41; Page 34–42). For scholarly studies on new Argentine cinema and on the controversies surrounding the category, see Aguilar, *Otros mundos*; Andermann, *New Argentine*; Aprea, *Cine*; Bernardes, Lerer, and Wolf; Page.

14. In spite of obvious formal differences, these testimonial documentaries resemble other 1980s nontestimonial documentaries, such as the canonical *La República perdida I* and *II* (Pérez 1983, 1986), where the revisionist approach to Argentine history and the celebratory portrayal of *yrigoyenismo* (the political movement seen as an antecedent to Raúl Alfonsín's *radicalismo*) suggest that the filmmaker perceives the present as a work in progress.

15. See Richard, *Cultural Residues: Chile in Transition* for an in-depth study of discourses of novelty in early postdictatorship periods. Although Richard's findings better fit the Chilean case, in which this discourse of novelty was the primary trademark of the *concertación* (the newly elected democratic government), her main hypotheses help elucidate the underlying needs of every incipient democracy, including Argentina's.

16. See Feld, *Del estrado* for an in-depth study of the history of these television images. As she explains, three stages in the trial corresponded to three different views on transmission: a testimonial phase (April–August) in which the 830 witnesses testified, a second phase (September–October) in which prosecutors and defense attorneys provided their statements, and the verdict. Although only the verdict was broadcast live and with sound, human rights organizations and journalists started to complain during the second phase about the official no-sound transmission policy. In 1986, the government authorized the production of a twelve-hour documentary based on the five hundred-hour footage, but its release was cancelled due to the 1987 Easter uprisings. The documentary was finally shown on TV in 1998. See Forcinito 42–52 for a comparison between the testimonies in *Nunca más* and in *Diario del juicio*.

17. In 1984, the discovery of unidentified corpses in local cemeteries was the object of sensationalist media coverage usually known as *show del horror* (horror show). For further references on this early coverage, see Vezzetti, *Pasado* 22; Lorenz; Nino.

18. See Vezzetti, *Pasado*; Calveiro for further details on Argentine concentration camps. See Agamben, *Homo Sacer: Sovereign Power and Bare Life*; *Remnants of Auschwitz: The Witness and the Archive*; Levi; Bauman; Scarry for in-depth studies on the logic of dehumanization.

19. The military junta resorted to several strategies in order to dismiss accusations of forced disappearance. They first denied the fact, then relativized its importance, and finally claimed that disappearances were a side effect of the war between "Argentines" and "subversive guerrillas" (Crenzel, *Los desaparecidos* 65–70). Yet, as Vezzetti argues (*Pasado* 55–95), left-leaning armed groups were not only much smaller in size than what the military claimed, but also mostly dismantled by 1979. This early defeat is often quoted as proof that the military's justification of a dictatorship that lasted until 1983 was (at least partially) false. This is why I consciously refrain from using the term "dirty war," which has become an international trademark in spite of its ideological connotations. Coined by the military junta to justify their clandestine actions (a "dirty enemy" allowed for "dirty methods" and for a "dirty war"), the use of the concept is therefore problematic. It actually echoes the military's justifications and helps establish the idea that the dictatorship was a war, thus assigning equal status to government officials and to civilian militants while blotting out the responsibilities of Argentine society. For a detailed explanation of the use and misuse of the notion of war in the Argentine case, see Vezzetti, *Pasado* 55–108. Moreover, although *genocide* is often used as an equivalent for *crime against humanity*, its specific origin should not go unnoted. The term *genocide* was coined at the United Nations General Assembly in 1948 to refer to the use of state violence against ethnic, racial, national, or religious groups; it did not contemplate the use of violence for political or economic purposes. I thus avoid using the term for the Argentine case, as I am particularly interested in highlighting its historical and political dimensions.

20. As Longoni argues in *Traiciones*, this past truth was often uncomfortable, even for relatives of missing people. Survivors were the living proof that the disappeared people had actually died. I return to this topic in the next chapter, when analyzing betrayal in *Montoneros, una historia*.

21. For an account of the public discussion on revolutionary violence between the late 1960s and 1983, see Franco; Vezzetti, *Sobre la violencia revolucionaria* 61–129. See Crenzel, *Los desaparecidos*; *La historia política* for in-depth studies on the representation of the disappeared in the postdictatorship.

22. See Jelin and Longoni; Da Silva Catela "Lo invisible revelado" for further reflections on the role of photography in the postdictatorship.

23. See Ahmed, *The Cultural Politics of Emotion* 1–17; Harding and Pribram 4–20; Podalsky 8–15 for a comparison between affectivist and cognitivist approaches.

24. Víctor Basterra was a graphic designer held captive between 1979 and 1983 at the Escuela Superior de Mecánica de la Armada (ESMA), the largest clandestine detention center during the last dictatorship. While in captivity, military officers had him forge identification documents. Basterra took advantage of this assignment: he managed to photograph officers and prisoners and smuggle the pictures out of the center during home visits. These pictures were used as legal evidence during the *juicio*. See Forcinito 73–100 for further details on the different representations of the ESMA throughout the postdictatorship.

25. See Raggio, "Narrar el terrorismo de estado: De los hechos a la denuncia pública: El caso de *La noche de los lápices*" for a detailed analysis of how this episode was conceptualized as an event and of the different versions (and origins) of its title.

26. The green Ford Falcon was the most common vehicle used by the military to kidnap people and transport them to clandestine detention centers. See Reati for an interesting analysis of why this specific vehicle was used and of how its image became the most canonical icon of the Argentine dictatorship.

27. Earlier in 1986, María Seoane and Héctor Ruiz Nuñez, two Argentine journalists, published a book also entitled *La noche de los lápices* and likewise inspired by Pablo Díaz's testimony.

28. The events narrated in the film do not take place in 1975 as the fourth caption states, but in 1976. This mistake can be read as further proof that historical events are at the service of fiction and that the film is more interested in creation rather than documentation.

29. I am indebted to Pete Walker for helping me identify the song's genre.

30. The Movimiento Peronista Montoneros was formed around 1970 as an urban guerrilla movement mostly composed of left-leaning Peronists and Roman Catholics. It was completely dismantled by 1979. As the group itself has claimed, some of the students associated with *La noche de los lápices* (for example, Claudia Falcone and María Clara Ciocchini, the other female protagonist in the film) were affiliated with this political organization. For further information on Montoneros, see Donatello; Gillespie; Vezzetti, *Pasado*; *Sobre la violencia*.

31. In this sense, I partially disagree with Blejmar when she claims that, unlike what happens in post-2003 autofictions in which documentary and fiction converge, during the 1980s and 1990s the two genres circulated in different spheres, used a dissimilar language, and established opposite reading pacts (16). As I analyze in the last two chapters, I believe that, while it is true that documentary and fiction converge more prominently in post-2000 cultural production, the different uses of the two genres also entail strong ideological differences. Furthermore, as I have argued in this chapter, I contend that documentary and fiction should be seen in the 1980s as two complementary components of a more encompassing genre.

2 Indexicality and Counterhegemony
Testimonial Documentary in the 1990s

IF THE OPTIMISTIC spirit of the early democracy started to vanish with the sanctioning of the *ley de punto final* and the *ley de obediencia debida* in 1986–87, it definitely came to a halt two years later. Between October 1989 and December 1990, the newly elected president, Carlos Menem, signed ten decrees pardoning military and guerrilla leaders who were in prison as a result of the 1985 trials. Unlike the *leyes*, approved in congress and in line with Alfonsín's explicitly advocated idea of retroactive limited justice, Menem's absolutions not only were unilaterally decided but also came as a surprise. Arguing that it was necessary to unify the nation, Menem claimed that the general amnesty, which favored emblematic military officers like Jorge Rafael Videla and Emilio Massera, was a means to reconciliation. Although quite unexpected, Menem's decision was attuned to his main purpose: to continue a deep neoliberal reform that included the privatization of public industries, the dismantling of labor organizations, and a convertibility plan that controlled the printing of money and pegged the Argentine peso to the dollar.

Inspired by the ideology of the so-called Washington Consensus and aided by Harvard-educated minister Domingo Cavallo, Menem saw in globalization, foreign investment, free trade, and deregulation of market and workplace the keys to modernity and economic growth—a view that eventually resulted in the largest economic crisis in the country's history. Argentina's dark past was an obstacle to this discourse of neoliberal optimism. It was necessary to smooth tensions and work toward forgetting. The result, however, was quite the opposite. As Alejandro Grimson and Gabriel Kessler have observed, "A pardon supposedly based on 'national reconciliation' only reinforced the image that Argentina was not a society that followed the rule of the law" (68). Arguably, Menem's decrees marked a second turning point within the postdictatorship. They put an end to the democratization process and inaugurated what we could call the "postdemocratization": a period marked by disenchantment toward government institutions and civic participation that lasted until the advent of the Kirchner administration in 2003. Indeed, although Menem's two terms in government ended in 1999, we could say that the postdemocratization includes Fernando De la Rúa's administration (1999–2001) and the turbulent years between 2001 and 2003, which saw the taking office and almost immediate resignation of four more presidents. The type of sensibility that I call "postdemocratization" is also prevalent in this four-year period and only ends with *kirchnerismo*.[1]

Yet *menemismo* was not as straightforward as it might seem. Proof of its complexity is the contradictory affiliation with *peronismo*, which—regardless of all its ambiguities and changes over time—had always relied on a strong nationalist, anticapitalist, and populist rhetoric.[2] Or the fact that Menem had appealed to his former condition as 1970s political prisoner to legitimize his electoral campaign yet released convicted members of the military almost as soon as taking office. Another major paradox was the film industry. In 1994, despite the official discourse against state intervention and the overall budget cuts in education and culture, a new law for film development, which had originated as a cross-party project but was especially supported by the ruling administration, was sanctioned. The law increased taxes on screenings, video rentals, and television broadcasts of domestic films, allowing the National Cinema Institute (now INCAA) a fivefold increase in revenues. Moreover, in order to encourage the privatization of public television, the government subsidized media conglomerates such as Grupo Clarín. Several of these groups partnered with foreign corporations, creating transnational companies that coproduced Argentine feature films—for example, Patagonik, which financed blockbusters *Evita* (1996), *Cenizas del paraíso* (1997), and *Nueve reinas* (2000). In addition, cheaper technologies like digital video—which surged due to economic policies favoring importation—triggered a significant rise in film production. This rise went parallel to an unprecedented professionalization of the domestic film scene: the establishment of private schools like Universidad del Cine, the opening or reopening of festivals such as the Festival de Mar del Plata, and the creation of specialized magazines like *El amante*. As a result, in spite of the rampant crisis and the general budget cuts, the film scene grew on an impressive scale during the Menem era, allowing for the emergence of the so-called new Argentine cinema. Interestingly enough, this emergence made the overall picture even more paradoxical. As Andermann observes, "The devastating social consequences [of Menem's terms in government] would become one of the new cinema's central topics" (*New Argentine* 1). On the one hand, the neoliberal '90s were in large part behind the success of Argentine cinema. On the other, they were these films' main target.[3]

The paradoxical nature of the film industry in the Menem era is also apparent in the specific case of testimonial cinema. After an initial "memory eclipse" (Crenzel, *Los desaparecidos* 28) between 1990 and 1995, there was an explosion of testimonial films on the military dictatorship—an explosion that on the one side aimed to contest the official amnesia while on the other was possible thanks to the new economic landscape.[4] Although many of these films, like Marco Bechis's *Garage Olimpo* (1999), still focused on the fate of disappeared people and on the atrocities that happened in clandestine detention centers, there was a major shift when compared to the 1980s. The 1990s witnessed the appearance of two main trends that would dominate postdictatorship cinema onward: the reconstruction of 1970s left-leaning activism and the representation of second-generation survival.

Andermann claims that these two trends correspond to two actual generations with different views: a first generation interested in exploring their former political beliefs, as in David Blaustein's *Cazadores de utopías* (1996), and a second generation more interested in reflecting on the act of remembrance, as in Roqué's *Papá Iván* or in the paradigmatic *Los rubios* (New Argentine 107). Amado states that these two strands emerged due to the combination of a strong reaction against the amnesty and the centrality of the organization H.I.J.O.S., which became a leading voice since the mid-1990s (15–17).[5] Carmen Guarini adds that, while focusing on different subjectivities, both trends mark a radical shift from the explicatory, didactic cinema of previous decades. For her, films like Blaustein's *Botín de guerra* (1999) are emblematic of a post-1990s tendency in Argentine cinema: the *"documental de creación"* (creative documentary), a highly subjective and reflexive type of documentary (362). Guarini's reading is in line with Aprea's, who agrees that after the mid-'90s, the representation of the dictatorship has been displaced onto the documentary. Both first- and second-generation survivors have chosen to tell their traumatic stories via interviews and direct testimonies (*Cine* 80–82).[6]

Although I certainly agree that the appearance of these two trends marked a shift in cultural production that continues well beyond the year 2000, I believe that in order to better understand testimonial cinema, we need to make a difference, albeit somewhat arbitrary, between two separate periods: 1990–2000 and 2000 onward—a distinction that is erased under the common "post-1990s" label. As opposed to what will happen in the 2000s and contrary to what happened in the 1980s, the testimonial films of the 1990s play a counterhegemonic and antiofficial role. This becomes apparent when looking at how they stage their present of enunciation. Counterhegemony is further emphasized by the choice of the documentary genre. In stark opposition to the fictional testimonies of the 1980s—a trend that will resurface in several second-generation films during *kirchnerismo*—1990s testimonial cinema opts primarily for the documentary. I find this preference to be indicative of Argentina's particular historical juncture. At a moment when the official national discourse aims to push forward and erase the recent past, the documentary, as Chanan puts it, "mobilises the viewer as a social subject, situated in history" (*Politics* 16). Paying special attention to the connections between documentary and history, in this chapter I focus mainly on three paradigmatic films: Andrés Di Tella's *Montoneros: una historia* (1994) and David Blaustein's *Cazadores de utopías*, which explore first-generation political activism, and Blaustein's *Botín de guerra*, which gives voice to the experiences of the second generation. I analyze how these documentaries' staging of the present shows their antiofficial and counterhegemonic stance within the 1990s.

Before beginning this analysis, however, I would like to clarify terminology. What definition of hegemony have I chosen? What do I mean by "counterhegemony" and why not opt for the most conventional "antihegemony" or the most up-to-date "posthegemony"? As anticipated in the introduction, in this book I follow Ernesto Laclau and Chantal Mouffe's concept of hegemony as the operation in which "a *particular* social force assumes the representation of a *totality* that is radically incommensurable with it" (Laclau and Mouffe x, emphasis in the original). Based on the premise that the social order is structured like discourse (i.e., it is a complex of elements in which differential relations play a constitutive role), Laclau and Mouffe claim that in any given society there are a number of particular demands that establish an equivalent relation with other unfulfilled demands. At some point, some of these various demands form an antagonistic frontier and unify into a stable system of signification. Eventually, one of these particularities articulates the other heterogeneous elements and fixes this unity, taking up an incommensurable universal signification and thus becoming hegemonic. The universal signification is "incommensurable" both because its bearer, though assuming the representation of a totality, continues to be a particularity and because, given that there is no outside of the relational logic, the embodied universality is an impossible object. Hence, the hegemonic identity "becomes something of the order of an *empty* signifier, its own particularity embodying an unachievable fullness" (Laclau 71, emphasis in the original). In other words, this particular element assumes a universal structuring function, acting as a *point de capiton*: a master-signifier, a nodal point, "a privileged signifier that fixes the meaning of a signifying chain" (Laclau and Mouffe 99). Furthermore, because the totality cannot be directly represented at the strictly conceptual level, the process of hegemony requires a radical investment in which affect plays a central role (Laclau 72, 111).[7]

Although Laclau and Mouffe appeal to this model to explain the emergence of collective actors, as seen in Laclau's analysis of "the people" in populism, it is useful for understanding the links between hegemony and representation more broadly. Indeed, my book, to put it in Laclau and Mouffe's terms, traces testimonial films' trajectory from counterhegemony to hegemony, the role that affect plays in this trajectory, and the process whereby "military dictatorship" becomes the empty signifier—the nodal point—articulating testimonial films' hegemonic identity. If the latter two are the central themes of the next chapters, this one deals with testimonial cinema's counterhegemonic role in the 1990s. I refer to "counterhegemony" rather than "antihegemony" to account for the fact that, even though 1990s testimonial films oppose hegemonic narratives of the dictatorship, they also aim to become hegemonic themselves—they counter the existing hegemony but not hegemony per se. As is the case with subaltern identities, they "bid for hegemony, aspire to moral and intellectual leadership of the nation, and to an alternative way of identity" (Beverley, *Testimonio*, xvii).

Moreover, the prefix "counter"—as opposed to the more unifying "anti"—better captures the plurality of antagonistic positions within a discursive formation prior to the stabilization of one antagonistic frontier. In the Argentina of the 1990s, these counterhegemonic positions often go together with an antiofficial stance. In other words, being counterhegemonic often involves going against the discourses of the government in office. Yet the two do not always necessarily coincide and certainly differ at the conceptual level. In the 1980s, for example, testimonial films staged a counterhegemonic narrative of the dictatorship that was actually attuned to the official narrative of the Alfonsín administration. During *kirchnerismo* many testimonial films, especially fiction, were in line with both official and hegemonic narratives. During *macrismo* (at least until I write this book in 2017), most testimonial narratives certainly differ from the official rhetoric yet continue to be hegemonic.

By the same token, I sheer away from the most popular "posthegemony," a term used to capture the rise of the multitude as a social force which, unlike the people, cannot be captured by hegemony. Scholars such as Jon Beasley-Murray and Alberto Moreiras argue that, in a postmodern world marked by the deterritorialization of the economy, supra- and infranational forces have rendered obsolete national forms of coercion and that ideology is no longer a political driving force in mechanisms of social control. Hence, the notion of hegemony, which depends on ideology, can no longer make sense of the social order. Yet, as I acknowledged in the book's introduction, I believe that, even when supra- and infranational forces drive testimonial narrative, the nation and ideology are still the primary driving forces in this particular case—and the best antidotes against a globalized, dehistoricized perspective of the genre. "Counterhegemonic" and "antiofficial" thus best describe what is at stake in the testimonial documentaries addressed in this chapter.[8]

Montoneros and *Cazadores*: Reconstructing 1970s Activism

In the mid-1990s, two very similar films on 1970s left-leaning militancy appeared almost simultaneously: Andrés Di Tella's *Montoneros: una historia* and David Blaustein's *Cazadores de utopías*. Both are organized around the same structure: a series of testimonies from former activists interspersed by archival footage covering key events in recent Argentine history. This footage is sometimes identical in both films, probably because of the precarious condition of Argentine archives which, as Paola Margulis has already observed, offers a limited pool of images for local documentarists ("Imágenes" 118). Yet, despite the similarity of filmic material, the directors' different ideological and generational perspectives can be noted within the narratives. Di Tella, mostly known from being the founder of the Buenos Aires Independent Film Festival (BAFICI) in 1999, is a member of that "in-between" generation (Andermann, *New Argentine* 113) that is too young to be affiliated with the first (i.e., the 1970s activists) and too old to be part of the second (i.e., their children). Since the 1960s, he has been living intermittently in Buenos Aires, London, and the United States. A pioneer of professional filmmaking in Argentina, in 1988 he directed his first documentary on disappearances for Amnesty International. It was over the course of this documentary that he came up with the idea of *Montoneros:* "*En ese momento podía hablar de la experiencia de los desaparecidos, conversaba con sobrevivientes de campos de concentración, me atrevía a preguntar detalles sobre la tortura . . . pero nunca me animé a preguntarle a ninguno de ellos si había estado en la guerrilla: era una especie de tabú muy fuerte, no personal sino social. Y por eso mismo quise hacer* Montoneros." (At that time I was able to talk about the experience of the disappeared, I was able to talk with camp survivors, I was even able to ask them details about torture . . . but I never had the courage to ask any of them whether they had taken part in a guerrilla movement: It was sort of a strong taboo, not a personal but a social one. And that's exactly why I decided to make *Montoneros*) (Firbas and Meira Monteiro 43–44).

David Blaustein, on the contrary, was a member of Montoneros. So were Ernesto Jauretche and Mercedes Depino, who, as stated in the film's credits, collaborated with the script and historical investigation. Since the 1990s, Blaustein has either directed or produced a number of documentaries related to Argentine history, including the well-known *Botín de guerra*, on the organization Abuelas de Plaza de Mayo; *Hacer patria*, an autobiographical film on his family's exile; and the already mentioned *Papá Iván*, María Inés Roqué's reconstruction of her late father's biography. An advocate for the political beliefs of first-generation activists, Blaustein conceived *Cazadores* as, in Miguel Bonasso's words, "*una epopeya montonera*" [a Montonero epic] (quoted in Sondereguer 6). This epic tone, heightened by the film's release for the twentieth anniversary of the military coup at a central movie theater, permeates the narrative since the opening credits: "*La recuperación de nuestra memoria no podría ser desapasionada ni imparcial. A los 30.000 desaparecidos y a los que todavía creen que se puede vivir la historia con un poco más de dignidad.*" (The recovery of our memory cannot be either dispassionate or impartial. To the thirty thousand disappeared and to all those who still believe that history can be lived with a bit more dignity.)[9]

Montoneros and *Cazadores* are frequently read together. They are usually seen as two films that originated in a similar desire (bringing to the fore 1970s militancy at a moment when the topic was still a social taboo) yet yielded opposite results. In one of the most detailed analyses of this contrast, Gonzalo Aguilar claims that while *Montoneros* is grounded in an external point of view that opens the space for exploration and doubt, *Cazadores* is an internal act of grieving that romanticizes the past, deliberately ignoring the present ("Maravillosa" 21–32). According to Aguilar, this difference is apparent in the choice of testimonial subjects. Di Tella interviews a number of militants with diverse perspectives, including regret and uncertainty. In Blaustein's film, the interviewees are proudly stuck in the 1970s; they repeat the same discourse and appeal to the same narrative that can be found in the original documents of the guerrilla organization. This monolithic, frozen discourse also dominates the filmic structure. Archival footage is organized around the same historical events that the group used to highlight two decades earlier, and testimonies are carefully intercalated so as to form a choral, homogenous narrative—an observation also made by Aprea (*Filmar* 131). The idealized, frozen past impacts the representation of the present. In *Cazadores* the 1990s have been suspended. They have been bracketed away from the filmic texture. Yet, Aguilar argues, it is precisely this absence that calls attention to the documentary's status within its present of enunciation. As mentioned earlier, Menem's amnesty also favored guerrilla leaders. Moreover, former members of Montoneros—precisely those who have been carefully omitted in *Cazadores*—played an important role in the 1990s' disenchantment toward politics. Mario Firmenich, for example, was exorbitantly paid for television interviews, and Rodolfo Galimberti threw a luxurious wedding party in Uruguay's high-class vacation spot Punta del Este, was appointed as consultant of Argentina's Secret Intelligence Agency (SIDE), and commercially partnered with multimillionaire Jorge Born, whom he had kidnapped on behalf of Montoneros. Thus, in eluding direct references to what was happening at the moment of the film's shooting and avoiding mentions to controversial members of the organization, Blaustein ends up legitimizing *menemismo*. Jens Andermann mostly agrees with Aguilar's assessment, especially with the idea that the two films offer contrasting views of the 1970s. Whereas *Cazadores* remains trapped in melancholy—as evidenced by the word "utopia" in the title, by the unified narrative, and by the omission of controversial leaders—*Montoneros* "refuses to provide the narrative closure which, by way of omission, allows Blaustein to recompose the group, if only as a community of mourners" (*New Argentine* 113). This difference results mainly from Di Tella's choice of structuring his film around Ana Testa, a former low-ranking militant with a peripheral view of activism. Testa's leading voice makes the documentary closer to personal quest than to collective reassertion. It makes the film a historical exploration of militancy rather than, like *Cazadores*, a "eulogy to the 1970s" (*New Argentine* 111).[10]

Although I certainly agree that the films should be read as two contrasting representations of the 1970s, I believe that they can also be seen as two parallel examples of how testimonial cinema works in the 1990s, in the midst of the postdemocratization. *Cazadores* and *Montoneros* are emblematic of how testimonial films play a counterhegemonic and antiofficial role at this particular historical moment—even when, as in Blaustein's documentary, they deliberately omit direct references. An analysis of how the two films portray testimonial subjects, organize historical sequences, and stage temporality shows that these features, which have been called upon to distinguish the films ideologically, also bring them together.

Let us first take a look at how the two films portray testimonial subjects. As previously noted, there are two juxtaposed narratives in *Montoneros*: Testa's leading narrative, organized around her personal history as a political militant, and a collective narrative built around testimonies of her fellow activists. Unlike what happened in 1980s cinema, these testimonies emphasize the political, radical edge of 1970s-era activism. Far from the innocent victims in *La noche de los lápices*, the interviewees explicitly recognize their previous engagement in the armed struggle. Yet this recognition does not necessarily lead to current endorsement. For a group of former militants, it actually leads to either uncertainty or disappointment. Ignacio Vélez, one of the founding members of the organization, makes his doubts quite explicit: *"A nosotros nos costó mucho asumir la violencia. . . . La primera vez que hubo un enfrentamiento y que se dispararon armas, que yo disparé un arma, esta sensación de horror, de poder haber herido a un semejante, a una persona. . . . ¿Habremos hecho lo correcto? ¿No nos habremos equivocado?"* (For us, taking on violence was very difficult. . . . The first time that there was a confrontation and that weapons were fired, that I fired a weapon, this sense of horror, of having possibly hurt a peer, a person. . . . Did we do the right thing? Is it possible that we were mistaken?) Silvina Walger, identified as an ex-supporter in the film's captions, is even more vehement: *"Yo nunca estaba de acuerdo. Me parecía monstruoso. Fue una de las cosas que me hizo dejar de simpatizar. Porque matar a un cana que está ahí solo en la calle no tiene. . . . Es un crimen bastante aberrante."* (I have always disagreed. I thought it was monstrous. That was one of the things that made me stop being sympathetic. Because to kill a police officer that is there on the street by himself, it's not. . . . It is a quite aberrant crime.)

Furthermore, Testa's leading voice demythologizes radical activism, when noting, for example, that she mainly became interested in politics because she had fallen in love with a militant or when she mentions in passing that she might have chosen Montoneros because the male members were more handsome than the pimply-faced members of other movements. Yet a second group of activists, like Chiqui Falcone or Roberto Perdía, proudly ascribe to 1970s-era discourse, emphatically defending their previous choices. And a third group seems to defend Montonero ideology but blames leaders like Firmenich and Galimberti, depicting them as spurious, opportunistic commanders who sent their subalterns to death while saving themselves. Breaking with the monolithic representation of the innocent victim typical of 1980s cinema, Di Tella's film offers a complex account of radical politics. As Victoria Álvarez has extensively analyzed, activism is portrayed as a gray zone where boundaries such as victims/perpetrators and martyrs/heroes are constantly blurred ("Habremos" n.p.). Not only does this gray zone become apparent in the testimonies but also in the varying affiliations with which captions identify the interviewees: "Ignacio Vélez, *fundador montoneros*; Roberto Perdía, *comandante montonero*; Graciela Daleo, *ex montonera*; Silvina Walger, *ex simpatizante*." (Ignacio Vélez, Montonero founder; Roberto Perdía, Montonero commander; Graciela Daleo, ex-Montonero; Silvina Walger, ex-supporter.) The term "montoneros" does not point to a homogeneous, given referent but to a multiplicity of options: supporters, ex-supporters, proud commanders, hesitant founders, etc. Instead of providing a totalizing discourse based on a single "true" story, the film emphasizes the existence of a plurality of narratives (Ranalletti 86)—an emphasis already evident in the title (*a* story/history, as opposed to *the* story/history).

Contrary to the two juxtaposed narratives in *Montoneros*, *Cazadores* confronts us with a choral set of testimonies that, as Aguilar noted, build a more monolithic discourse—a discourse that also includes the filmmaker and the viewer. As opposed to Testa's pedagogical explanations, speakers in *Cazadores* constantly use the second person (*"vos viste"; "entendés"*) (you know; you understand) and appeal to shared knowledge, taking historical information for granted. *Cazadores* is, to put it in Carlos Altamirano's words, "*una película de duelo hecha por ex-montoneros para ex-montoneros*" (a mourning film made by ex-Montoneros for ex-Montoneros) (1). Except in a few cases, testimonial subjects show no doubts regarding radical activism and, as Andermann observed, eulogize the 1970s. They praise the armed struggle, emphasize how common people used to support their project, and highlight the purity of their collective ideals. The sense of collectivity comes both from a homogenous discourse and from how speakers are portrayed. The film presents its more than twenty-five interviewees the same way. On the one hand, captions highlight name, earlier party affiliation, and location (for example, "María Luisa Montaldo, Juventud Peronista-Córdoba"; "Antonio Riestra, Montoneros-Santa Fe"; "Eduardo Seminaria, Juventud Universitaria Peronista-Rosario"; "Martín Caparrós, MAS-capital"). On the other, the mise-en-scene emphasizes their workplace: Eduardo Jozami and Nilda Garré are interviewed at the National Congress; Manuel Cannizzo, Juan José Salinas, and Francisco Blecho at the schools where they teach; Caparrós and Gerardo Banio at their studios; Gonzalo Chaves at a printing factory; Ricardo Velasco at his carpentry workshop; etc. If Di Tella's speakers varied in terms of their ideological stance regarding Montoneros, Blaustein's vary in terms of affiliation, geography, and occupation. This variety creates the impression that radical activism was truly a collective endeavor. Moreover, if the speakers in *Montoneros* belonged mostly to the middle-high class (as evident in their last names and accents), the interviewees in *Cazadores* include a much broader spectrum: workers, intellectuals, artists, public officers, the Argentine elite, etc.

In other words, regardless of their evident ideological differences, the two films offer a multilayered representation of activists that not only breaks with the innocent victim of the 1980s but is also at odds with the hegemonic discourse in the 1990s where, as Jesús Martín Barbero observed, economics—as opposed to politics—was the one and undisputed protagonist (6). Attuned to what was happening in the rest of Latin America, in Menemist Argentina "every corner of social life [was] commodified" (Avelar, *Untimely* 1); the "numbing logic" (Masiello 3) of neoliberalism erased political density; the rhetoric of the market obliterated the discourse of politics. This obliteration reached the notion of militancy. As Palermo and Novaro have claimed, free enterprise and the market supplanted the Peronist ideals of organized community and the welfare state (493). In the 1990s, the radical militant was perceived as anachronistic, inexistent, or a sellout. Menem's amnesty to Montonero leaders, followed by their above-mentioned public behavior, contributed to these images. Breaking with the general skepticism that followed the leaders' conversion, the films show the persistence of political passion and offer a multifaceted portrayal of activism, which in the case of Di Tella includes Montoneros's disavowal of Firmenich and Galimberti and in the case of Blaustein includes a sense of widespread social, political, and geographical collectivity.

As Alejandra Oberti and Roberto Pittaluga have pointed out, this representation of activism establishes a clear confrontation with the dominant narratives in the 1990s. It confronts the idea that the 1970s activist was an apolitical, innocent victim and defies the dirty image of the former revolutionary as a sellout to neoliberal *menemismo* (121–122). In other words, regardless of their ideological stance, these documentaries stage new affects around militancy. If the innocent victim and the sellout are part of the emotional hegemony sustaining the 1990s, these films portray what Jaggar calls "outlaw emotions": emotions—that is, affects—distinguished by their incompatibility with the dominant perception, feelings, and values (61). Far from an innocent victim, an inexistent myth, or a sellout, the documentaries' political activist goes against the grain of the neoliberal present, acting as *"elemento de contraste de las memorias hegemónicas en la inmediata postdictadura"* (a counterpoint to the hegemonic memories in the early postdictatorship) (Oberti and Pittaluga 127).

Counterhegemony also becomes apparent in the films' organization of their historical sequences and in their staging of temporality, two components that are best read together. As it has consistently been claimed since early theorizations on the documentary, the creative treatment of the document is one of the genre's salient traits. Instead of aspiring to offer a complete record of actuality—like the newsreel, the travelogue, or the television broadcast—the documentary film finds its distinctive edge in the selection, manipulation, and crafting of the document. The organization of a historical sequence is arguably the most important phase in this creative process. As Rosen puts it, the document becomes especially meaningful when placed within a concrete historical sequence "that makes it part of an assertion of meaning from the real" (247). The historical sequence thus offers a privileged lens for an ideological reading of documentary films; a reading necessarily related to the staging of temporality. "Sequences," Rosen indeed observes, "organize temporality, providing endings that confer retrospective significance on shots" (246). Moreover, as Chanan has brilliantly analyzed, in documentary the temporality of the document becomes especially emphatic: "When you stage a fiction, in the studio or on location, you are suspending time and day and entering a temporality belonging to the narrative to which the scene belongs. When you film a documentary, what you capture in the camera is a moment grabbed from the day and time given by the calendar and the clock" (*Politics* 4).

Montoneros and *Cazadores* are no exception to the close-knit link among historical sequence, temporality, and ideological meaning in documentary. Di Tella's opening scene is, in fact, emblematic of how they cannot be disentangled. In this scene, we see Testa sitting in a car at a gas station while she recalls her personal history of militancy. Her recollection goes back and forth, combining allusions to her own trajectory during the 1970s with memories of her daughter Paula's questions in the 1990s:

> *Esto empieza cuando yo tenía dieciséis años, la misma edad que Paula, en San Jorge. San Jorge es un pequeño pueblito en Santa Fe, donde nací. Paula, que estaba preparando su examen de historia de cuarto año para dar en el colegio, me pregunta qué pasó en los setenta. Ellos son jóvenes del noventa. ¿Qué pasó? ¿Por qué, si Perón los quería tanto, los echó después? Y justo el día del examen de mi hija me llama una persona que yo no veía de aquella época y que creía desaparecida* (emphasis in the original). (It all starts when I was sixteen, the same age as Paula, in San Jorge. San Jorge is a small town in Santa Fe, where I was born. Paula, who was preparing for a history exam in fourth year high school, asks me what happened in the seventies. They are the youth of the 1990s. What *happened*? Why, if Perón loved you that much, did he kick you out later? And, right on my daughter's exam day, I get a phone call from a person that I had not seen since that time and that I thought was missing.)

Ana's recollection inaugurates two intertwined sequences that guide the filmic narrative. On the one hand, the film is structured around significant events in her personal history of militancy: the discovery of a more open version of Catholicism while attending a conservative school in San Jorge, the university years in Chaco, a poor province in northeast Argentina, the relationship with Paula's father, a left-leaning activist who gets her interested in politics, their joint years of radical militancy, her pregnancy, her ideological crisis once the baby is born, her decision to separate, abandon activism, and move to Buenos Aires, her kidnapping, the horrific life at ESMA, the release, and her ex-partner's suspicions about her having survived. It is this suspicion that puts an end to both the sequence and the film. Repeating her ex-partner's words to one of their common friends, Testa says, *"Ana salió con vida de ese lugar. Ana es una traidora. Ana... ¿qué puede ser Ana?"* (Ana came out of that place alive. Ana is a traitor. Ana... what else could she be?)

On the other hand, archival footage builds another sequence structured around significant events in collective history. This sequence is not as chronologically organized. Following Paula's question (Why, if Perón loved you that much, did he kick you out later?), the sequence starts in 1973 with Perón's return from exile and the massacre at Ezeiza airport, where snipers affiliated with right-wing Peronism killed at least thirteen people. Footage then goes back in time, to previous images of left-leaning activism: sermons by Padre Mugica, a famous third world priest killed by the Argentine Anticommunist Alliance (AAA), news reports on Montoneros's actions, their kidnapping and execution of Aramburu, Fidel Castro's visit to Argentina in 1959, and finally Onganía's taking office in 1966. After this long, forty-minute flashback, the sequence returns to Perón's arrival and the Ezeiza massacre and then follows a strict chronological order: members of Montoneros kill Rucci, Perón's right-wing ally, in retaliation for Ezeiza; Perón becomes increasingly distant from the organization; he dies; the AAA gains power; violence escalates; the 1976 dictatorship starts; and democracy returns in 1983, ending the collective sequence.

Examined closely, Testa's personal history and the one built in the archival footage not only span similar years but are also organized around a parallel leitmotif: betrayal and ideological change. The turning points in both narratives make this leitmotif quite explicit: the Ezeiza massacre marked the end of the alliance between left- and right-wing Peronism and Perón's disavowal of the former, especially of Montoneros. The turning points in Testa's story also mark her ideological transformation, from radical activism to uncertainty and desertion. In fact, it is right after the second filmic appearance of the Ezeiza massacre that the documentary begins its latter half and that Testa's doubts emerge: *"Yo ya no daba más. Yo ya quería entregarme."* (I could not take it any longer. I wanted to turn myself in.) Moreover, if, as some of the interviewees suggest, Perón could be perceived as a traitor, Testa is faced with a similar accusation throughout the film, as highlighted in the closing remarks: (Ana is a traitor. What else could she be?)

It is not hard to imagine that, especially for a contemporaneous viewer, this leitmotif evokes the present. It recalls the ideological transformation of *peronismo* via *menemismo*, a hot topic in the mid-1990s. Should the latter be explained as a right-wing development of the former? Has this oscillation between left and right been present since Peronism's origins? Is Menem a traitor to the cause or a logical offspring of a contradictory political movement? And, more importantly, are Montoneros part of the same phenomenon, as the recent conversion of Firmenich and Galimberti seems to imply? Or are they a complex, multifaceted organization which, just like Testa, is open to ideological transformation, uncertainty, and historical change? I am less interested in answering these questions one way or the other (a task that would not do justice to the careful staging of Di Tella's documentary) than in noting that the film's narrative brings the past into the present, destabilizing certainty and inviting a political reading of a moment that seems to have suspended politics.[11]

Montoneros and *Cazadores*: Disclosing Modernity in the Present

The temporal connection between the 1970s and the 1990s is actually what sustains *Montoneros*, as condensed in Testa's use of verb tenses in the opening scene that I have just quoted: "*Esto* empieza *cuando yo tenía dieciséis años*. . . . *Paula, que* estaba *preparando su examen de historia* . . . *me* pregunta *qué pasó en los setenta. Ellos* son *jóvenes del noventa* . . . *Y justo el día del examen de mi hija me* llama *una persona que yo no* veía *de aquella época*" (my emphasis). (It all *starts* when I *was* sixteen. . . . Paula, who *was preparing* for a history exam in fourth-year high school, *asks* me what *happened* in the seventies. They *are* the youth of the 1990s. And, right on my daughter's exam day, I *get* a phone call from a person that I *had not seen* since that time.) Past and present intertwine. The 1970s cannot be disengaged from the 1990s. Testa mixes with Paula. Paula's history, which is the history of the 1990s youth, cannot be separated from Testa's itinerary, the political itinerary of the 1970s radical youth. Although it might seem at first sight that Testa is about to tell a remote, distant story (a sensation emphasized by the sound of an old film projector accompanying the first archival images), she progressively brings that story into the present, interweaving temporalities.

Contrary to what one might expect, this interweaving of temporalities does not result in the representation of a dynamic, open present. In *Montoneros*, the 1990s are portrayed as already-given, static, and closed. The stasis is apparent in some of Testa's pessimistic assertions (for example, that there is no longer room for idealism and hope) and in the film's treatment of indexicality, which comes to the forefront over the course of a road trip to the specific sites where Testa's history took place. The documentary's temporal journey runs parallel to a spatial journey. As Testa talks, the camera follows her to San Jorge, Chaco, and Buenos Aires. Real images of streets and highways can be seen through the car window, and real sites act as backdrop for her memories. While walking in a school backyard, Testa recalls her years at that school. She tells us how her fellow activist was kidnapped, while pointing to the real corner where this happened. She shows the viewer the exact fence that she had to jump over to escape from the military. In other words, she also connects the two historical moments via her 1990s visit to those 1970s places.

In this sense, Di Tella's film is attuned to a broader tendency in Latin American documentary since the 1990s that Piedras describes as "documentary road movie:" that is, "a progressive permeation of the generic codes of the road movie that connect with its emphasis on mobility and displacement. . . . Films which explore both intimate and public history, assembling narratives that engage with the multiple forms of the trips through spaces that are significant to both personal and collective memory" ("Contemporary" 219). In these documentary road movies, Piedras observes, mobility and displacement in the form of road trips to specific sites of memory not only allow for historical reconstruction but also enable a reconfiguration of bonds of solidarity among people. Instead of the desire for individual liberation typically propelling US road films (Laderman 2; Cohan and Hark 1), the Latin American road trip becomes a basis from which to rethink individual and collective identities.

Piedras's observations perfectly match what happens in Testa's journey. The 1990s visit to 1970s places unleashes recollections and, at the same time, rebuilds a collective and deeply affective notion of militancy. The road trip charts an "emotional [i.e., affective] geography" in which feelings are shaped in their "socio-spatial mediation and articulation rather than as entirely interiorized subjective mental states" (Davidson, Bondi, and Smith 3). Yet, what I find most disturbing—and what interests me most—is the road trip's paradoxical revelation: nothing has changed. Testa verbalizes this stasis when looking at the corner where her friend was kidnapped: *"Es increíble. Esto está exactamente igual."* (It's incredible. This looks exactly the same.) The nun at her previous school transmits a similar static feeling when she interrupts Testa's recollection of how they used to sing the anthem in the backyard and proudly claims that they are still doing the same. Moreover, the real places to which Testa points look exactly like several of the places in the archival footage. The house and the fence that she jumped over, for example, are identical to a house and a fence from a news report on Montoneros escaping in the 1970s. A garage where, according to one of these reports, a guerrilla used to hide looks like a replica of the one at Testa's parents' in the 1990s. While Testa talks, there is even a green Ford Falcon parked in front of the house from where she managed to run away during her 1970s escape. In *Montoneros*, indexicality sends an uneasy message: everything remains the same. Contrary to what happened in *Juan*, where Buch's road trip disclosed a present in progress, in Di Tella's documentary, the spatial journey unveils a static afilmic realm. In fact, had they been in black and white, the city images of the 1990s would have been

Figure 2.1. YPF logo during Ana Testa's road trip in *Montoneros*.

indistinguishable from those in the footage—an impression further emphasized in an interview shot at a 1990s slum that looks as precarious as the slums in the 1970s footage.

The disclosure of a static referent establishes a sharp contrast with the neoliberal discourse of progress, modernity, and success—and interrupts its necessarily teleological, forward-looking temporality. As opposed to what is being stressed in the optimistic rhetoric of *menemismo*, the documentary stages an Argentina that is still the same as in the 1970s—if not ideologically, at least economically. Instead of a modern, hypertechnological present that, as Menem infamously promised, would make it possible for Argentines to travel through the stratosphere and arrive in Japan in one hour, the film exposes a "backward" present that looks like the 1970s.[12] The gas station where Testa begins her testimony is paradigmatic of this contrast. As the camera pans out, it reveals a deserted station that is almost in ruins. On the back of the scene, old pumps are marked with blurry logos of YPF, Argentina's national oil company privatized by the Menem administration. Shot in 1993, the images thus correspond to a YPF gas station right after privatization, unveiling the emptiness behind the promise of progress and modernization.[13] If, as Aguilar observes, the documentary's camera is always in motion in its exploration of the past ("Maravillosa" 28), this constant movement reveals a present which, instead of advancing toward global capitalism, remains at a standstill.

The permeation of the generic codes of the road movie becomes more relevant here. As several scholars have noticed, the genre has had from its inception a close connection with modernity (Laderman 13; Cohan and Hark 3). Road movies rely on a modern artistic medium, the cinema, which is "crucial to modernity's reconceptualization of time and its representability" (Doane, *Emergence* 4). They are also built around modern means of transportation: car and motorcycle. Additionally, road movies stage forward movement, thus "arous[ing] our desire for modernity" (Orgeron 2). Part of this desire also stems from the display of iconography composed of what we could call, following Sara Ahmed, the "happy objects" of modernity: objects that promise happiness, in this case associated with feeling modern, and that circulate as social goods, accumulating positive affective value (*Promise* 22). Cars, highways, expanding horizons, diners, and gas stations—usually portrayed in impressive aerial and traveling shots—transmit the feeling that achieving modernity means being independent, accomplished, and happy. This longing for modernity serves, as it has already been observed, to articulate the values of individual freedom and mobility at the core of US national mythology (Cohan and Hark 1; Orgeron 3).

By contrast, one of the distinctive features of the Latin American road movie, also prominent in *Montoneros*, is "the tense relationship of Latin American countries with modernity as epitomized by the precarious infrastructures and the uneven access to motorized vehicles and other modern technological advances" (Garibotto and Pérez 2). If the US road movie is vital to mapping national mythologies and advancing modern ideals through the display of the happy objects of modernity, the Latin American road movie turns these happy objects into "affect aliens" (Ahmed, *Promise* 49) that refuse to share the orientation toward these objects as being good, playing up the dark side of modernity in the wake of the neoliberal crisis. Di Tella's documentary is a case in point. From the rear window, Testa's spatial journey becomes a journey that traces the failed landscape of Argentine modernity. The car passes abandoned highways, unexploited land, deserted gas stations, and side streets, unveiling the objects of modernity as affect aliens and arriving to stagnant cities that look exactly like they did in the 1970s.

The notion of the 1970s and the 1990s as static temporal continuum is also at the heart of Di Tella's *Prohibido* (1997), a documentary on how intellectuals and artists responded to the dictatorship. Thematically rather than chronologically organized, the film features footage of the 1970s with 1990s testimonies from radio hosts, musicians, writers, plastic artists, and thinkers who cover topics such as censorship, exile, and fear. Like in *Montoneros*, a broad range of voices, including those belonging to military historians and to officers and censors in favor of the regime, provides a widespread view of the 1970s that mixes with the 1990s, establishing a tight connection between the present of enunciation and the military past. The staging of this connection is, however, not so much built upon the generic codes of the road movie but mostly on what could be described as "archival footage reenactment"; after each 1990s testimony—always shot in color—the speaking subject is portrayed in black and white, at a setting that seems anchored in the 1970s (trying to hide on a street that looks dangerous, walking through a deserted area as if trying not to call attention, etc.). The final scenes make this temporal continuum quite clear. Closing credits offering information on the number of artists and intellectuals still missing combine with footage reenactment showing flooded and empty streets. Shots of 1990s demonstrations organized by H.I.J.O.S. and Madres de Plaza de Mayo intersperse with footage of TV programs from 1995 and 1996 in which right-wing journalists Marcelo Hadad and Mariano Grondona interview former military leaders, defending their past actions. First differentiating and then mixing the two historical moments, *Prohibido* implies that they should be seen as one moment—an implication further emphasized in the film's closing dedication to photographer José Luis Cabezas, the victim of a historic death that epitomizes 1990s-era corruption and violence.[14] Challenging the official discourse of national reconciliation and progress, Di Tella's documentaries unveil a backward 1990s that got stuck two decades earlier.

At first sight, *Cazadores*'s staging of the present is quite the opposite. Contrary to the abundance of historically marked indexical signs in *Montoneros* and *Prohibido*, Blaustein's documentary seems to have deliberately erased every trace of historicity. Interviews are shot at working sites that have been emptied out of people and movement. Only those minimum objects that are needed in order to situate the workplace have been included in the mise-en-scene. We know, for example, that Francisco Blecho is a teacher because he is sitting in front of a blackboard, wearing his white uniform, or that Gonzalo Chaves works at a printing factory because we see the rotary press standing still behind his back. None of these objects, however, points to a specific historical juncture—in fact, it is hard to tell, at least until the closing scenes, whether these workplaces refer to the militants' jobs in the 1970s or at the time of shooting. Throughout the entire film, in fact, only two objects allude to the 1990s: a sign advertising books at 1 peso in Elvio Vitale's bookstore (a price that was only possible during the convertibility plan that pegged the Argentine currency to the dollar) and the word "*Divididos*" written on the board at Juan José Salinas's high school—a reference to an iconic rock band from the 1990s. As Aguilar claimed, in *Cazadores* the 1990s have been suspended. Allusions to controversial Montonero leaders have been erased. Indexicality has been manipulated so as to remove historical markers. Blaustein's documentary seems exclusively concerned with the past, with eulogizing and repeating the radical '70s, with restoring history as if time had not gone by (Altamirano 2), with repeating an anachronistic discourse as if the present did not exist (Beceyro 11). Indeed, Andermann claims that, rather than being a typical documentary of its epoch, the film "pays homage to 1960s cinema" (*New Argentine* 111)—an observation shared by Aprea, who argues that the movie is closer to Third Cinema than to the social documentaries of the 1990s (*Cine* 80).

Yet, if we take a close look at the organization of the historical sequence, we notice that there is a radical difference with Third Cinema, precisely regarding the conceptualization of past and present. As in *Montoneros*, in Blaustein's documentary, testimonial narratives accompany a historical sequence built around archival footage. This sequence is chronologically organized: it starts with images of Evita and Perón's popularity, followed by their overthrow in 1955, Frondizi and Onganía's governments, the surge of left-leaning militancy, Aramburu's execution, Perón's return from exile, Ezeiza, the leader's death, and ends with the 1976 coup. Part of this sequence connects the documentary with Third Cinema: the collective narrative, several images which, as acknowledged in the credits, come directly from *La hora de los hornos*, and the inclusion of some of the latter's most canonical techniques, such as long close-ups of Che Guevara. The film's conceptualization of temporality is, however, quite the opposite. Suspending the present and building a narrative that is exclusively concerned with the past—with a past that, according to the sequence, ends in 1976—is at odds with Third Cinema's aesthetic and political project: merging temporalities in order to impact the present. As opposed to what happens in *Cazadores*, in classical militant cinema, the past becomes only relevant when dialectically linked to an open, ongoing present.

La hora de los hornos (1968), the most paradigmatic product of the genre and the one that has repeatedly been compared to *Cazadores*, is a good example of this temporal interdependency. On the one hand, relying on the idea that history is the basis for understanding Latin America's present, the film is structured diachronically. Historical events build a chronology that goes from the colonial era to the death of Che Guevara, which occurred only a few months prior to the documentary's release. On the other, because the documentary's main goal is to intervene in the present, the historical sequence is open, unfinished, and incomplete. As Solanas and Getino later theorized in their manifesto, *La hora de los hornos* is structured as "film act" (*cine-acto, película-acto*), that is, the ultimate form of the documentary cannot be found in the filmic texture but in the screening (*Cine* 35). It is in the process of showing, watching, and discussing that the final product is formed.

The most well-known, visible example is the projection's momentary interruption, when the narrative comes to halt and a voiceover invites an outside moderator to guide a discussion with viewers. In light of this project, the film is deliberately conceived to trigger the emergence of a particular, different event in each screening, depending on viewers' needs. The organization of the historical sequence and the staging of the past are geared toward achieving this goal. Hence the chronological events included in the sequence are organized as fractal monads that repeat themselves over and over again: colonization, colonial exploitation, underdevelopment, and the wish for liberation. The repetition of this monadic sequence renders all parts of the film equally effective and allows for different, socially specific screenings—that is, the viewer is confronted with the connections among colonization, underdevelopment, and the wish for liberation, regardless of the section shown. In these fractal monads, images of the past merge with images of the present. For example, nineteenth-century civil wars are mixed with twentieth-century US military interventions. As Paul Willemen, influenced by Walter Benjamin suggests, rather than only organizing past and present sequentially, the film merges them in "dialectical images that stress the relations with the viewer as being the productive site of cinematic signification" (Pines and Willemen 11). This monadic, fractal structure serves a purpose that is of the utmost importance for Third Cinema's political project: It holds back a closure of the historical sequence, leaving the audience in charge of this closure and therefore conceiving of the present as a work in progress.[15]

While in *La hora de los hornos* the historical sequence remains open to include the present, relying on the spectator for comprehension and coherence, in *Cazadores* the historical sequence is organized around a narrative of closure that suspends the present and marks the past as history. As opposed to what happened in canonical militant cinema, in *Cazadores* the filmmaker acts as historian:

> For the historian's account is always produced from a point in time after the sequence is completed; otherwise the end of the sequence could not be securely identified and its integrity would therefore be in doubt. This historiography therefore assumes a disjunction in knowledge between actual historical agents and historians, and the possibility of a convincingly secure narrative ending is the site of this disjunction. The historian always locates a beginning and an ending that anchor the sequence as a sequence, but the historical agent would have to know his or her future with absolute certainty in order to construct a correct integral sequence. (Rosen 238)

The construction of a closed historical sequence ends up, as opposed to what happened in *La hora de los hornos*, freezing the present by way of exclusion. As suggested in the erasure of historically marked indexical signs during the interviews and contrary to what happens with the representation of the 1970s in the archival sequence, the 1990s are perceived as already given, closed, and devoid of movement. Taking into account that, as I have recently analyzed, this perception contrasts with the official discourse of neoliberal progress, I would like to argue that, rather than legitimizing the 1990s, *Cazadores*'s conceptualization of temporality joins *Montoneros* in its antiofficial stance. Although they appeal to opposite representational strategies (*Montoneros* stages a historically marked present interwoven with the past, while *Cazadores* removes historical markers to suspend the present and delve into the past), they both unveil a static present of enunciation at odds both with the cinema's "illusion of continuous time and movement" (Doane, *Emergence* 9) and with the official rhetoric of neoliberal modernization.

Cazadores's epilogue, which surprisingly enough has rarely been analyzed, condenses the ideological implications of this temporal construction. At the end of the film, once the collective sequence is over, the present emerges explicitly for the first time in the interviewees' narratives. Portrayed in extreme close-ups and sometimes looking directly at the camera—two techniques that successfully create a simultaneity effect, as if there had been a flash-forward and viewers were finally witnessing the present—the speakers contrast the 1990s with the past period of radical activism. They seem to answer the question, "In light of this neoliberal present, do you think that 1970s militancy was worth it?"

Answers vary, but most of them establish a sharp contrast between the two periods that replicates the temporal closure achieved in the narrative sequence. They contrast the image of an idealized, frozen past with the image of a stagnant present in which activism has vanished and there is no room for utopia: "*una época intensa, con ética, con moral, con sentido de la lealtad . . . una época maravillosa. . . . No como ahora donde todo pasa por una comercialización de la vida. . . . En este presente, y con estas cualidades, lo que querría es recomponer un espacio de utopía.*" (an intense epoch, filled with ethics, with morality, with a sense of loyalty. . . a wonderful epoch. . . . It's not like today, when everything is related to a commodification of life. . . . In this present moment, with these characteristics, what I would like is to recompose a space of utopia.) As in the historical sequence, past and present are carefully separated. Whereas the 1970s were the moment of revolutionary upsurge and historical change, the 1990s are static and empty.

Making the contrast even more emphatic, the film ends with an overview of what former activists are doing in the 1990s, framed by footage of uprisings from the 1970s (for example, "Francisco Blecho, *preso durante la dictadura. Hoy es maestro rural en una escuelita de Tucumán*"; "María Luisa Montaldo *pasó seis años en diferentes cárceles de la dictadura por ejercer su profesión de abogada. Hoy sigue asesorando las luchas por la tierra urbana.*") (Francisco Blecho, imprisoned during the dictatorship. Today he is a rural teacher in a little school in Tucumán; María Luisa Montaldo spent six years in different dictatorship jails for being a lawyer. Today she is a counselor for people fighting for land.) Although it might seem at first sight that the film is suggesting that activism is still viable in the neoliberal present, the message is quite clear: radical activism is closed and frozen in the archival footage; today there is only, at best, room for individual work ethics—a message also at odds with Menem's deregulation of the workplace.

We could indeed say that the documentary shows how, in the 1990s, radical activism has turned into "affective labor"—labor where "value is an investment of desire" (Negri 87), labor that "produces first and foremost a social relationship"

(Lazzarato 142). In the documentary, this transformation can be read in two rather opposite ways. On the one hand, as Negri and Lazzarato have analyzed, this type of labor is always embedded within capitalist relations of production. Desire is channeled into valuable circuits that serve capitalism. In this case, then, the individual work ethics proposed in the film is at the service of neoliberal Argentina. Put simply, regardless of how precarious your working conditions are, you invest in your work because it is meaningful. On the other, the idea that militancy has been converted into affective labor infuses both 1970s militancy and 1990s labor with affect, doubly challenging Menemist discourse. As Mora González Canosa and Luciana Sotelo notice, *"el tipo de coherencia que el film propone entre el pasado y el presente no se sitúa tanto en el nivel de la política como en el de la ética. Ambos tiempos se superponen en el final . . . [remitiendo a un presente que] si bien ya no está mayormente signado por un proyecto colectivo, evoca la 'dignidad' a la que alude la dedicatoria."* [The type of cohesion between past and present that the film proposes is not really to be found on the level of politics but on that of ethics. Both periods juxtapose at the end . . . [pointing to a present that], even when not really marked by a collective project, evokes the "dignity" alluded to in the dedication] ("Futuros" n.p.).

Botín de guerra: Temporal Constellations in the Midst of Neoliberalism

David Blaustein's antiofficial and counterhegemonic stance is emphasized a few years later in *Botín de guerra*, a 1999 documentary on Abuelas de Plaza de Mayo and the search for their missing grandchildren—children of disappeared parents who were born in captivity and were stolen by the military, becoming "a nodal point around which reconstruction efforts have hinged in the aftermath of state violence" (Lazzara 320).[16] The film juxtaposes testimonies of grandmothers and recovered grandchildren (now young adults able to tell their own stories) with archival footage reconstructing recent Argentine history. A symmetrical balance guides the organization of testimonies. Grandmothers evoke domestic scenes interrupted by the violent kidnapping of their children, recreate the search for their missing grandchildren, and narrate their later recovery. Grandchildren rely on a parallel structure: they talk about their life without the biological family, recall nightmares, doubts, and uncertainties, and remember how they discovered their real identity and happily reunited with their real grandmothers. The historical account conveyed by each individual testimony, then, always repeats the same structure: the kidnapping, the life without the biological family, and the final recovery and reunion. The symmetrical balance becomes even more emphatic because each of the testimonies is interrupted by archival footage in black and white. In line with what happened in *Cazadores*, this black-and-white sequence is chronologically organized. Moreover, it begins at the exact point where the earlier film ended: the military seizure of power in 1976. This opening event is followed by images of the first demonstrations against the regime, the later collapse and the trials of its members in the early democracy, and Menem's decrees releasing those members in 1989–1990.

If in *Cazadores* the organizing event was the surge of left-leaning militancy, especially *peronismo*, in *Botín de guerra* it is the decrees. Menem's pardons establish a temporal hinge that points in two different directions. Backward, the documentary can be read as the prehistory leading to this event. Forward, the film can be read as the point of departure seeking a response to that event. In other words, *Botín de guerra* traces the chronology leading to an unfair present that should be rectified. It is the documentary that places itself at the beginning of that reversion, for it confers legitimacy to the only claim that could initiate a legal process after the decrees: the theft of babies. Because the appropriation of minors is a continuing crime, the military theft of babies has no statute of limitations. Therefore, this criminal act did not fall within the scope of the amnesties. Relying on this particularity, in 1997, only two years prior to the film's release, Abuelas de Plaza de Mayo initiated a legal claim on the fate of 194 children. If we pay attention to the careful organization of the historical sequence, we could say that from the big screen Blaustein accompanies the claim. As Betina Kaplan has already observed, the film encourages a sense of justice while reinforcing Abuelas' strategies (151). During the dictatorship, the military justification for stealing babies was that they wanted them to be raised among well-bred families. In the 1990s, the documentary presents a counterargument: it creates a new affective image of the grandmothers as sophisticated, articulate, and respectable women giving their testimonies while sitting in their comfortable, cozy, middle-class houses. This portrayal matches the grandchildren's testimonies, which always contrast their prior sense of loneliness with the warm, homey feeling of coming back to their biological family.

Resorting to a strategy already employed in *Cazadores*, the epilogue condenses the film's overall stance. The earlier documentary ended with images of 1990s workplaces that were suddenly set in motion to suggest a new form of individual ethics. *Botín de guerra* ends with the grandmothers in motion, alluding to the legitimacy of their claim. The women walk, rally, and comfort one another, accompanied by the upbeat rhythm of "Sin cadenas," a song specially composed for the film by *Los Pericos*—a band whose bass player is the brother of one of the recovered grandchildren. They dance to the song's lyrics at a 1999 concert that celebrates their tireless search. They participate in national politics, protesting the assassination of Cabezas. Once the song is over, lyrics give way to a crane shot of a crowded Plaza de Mayo. The shot is juxtaposed with an overwhelming sound produced by the concert audience chanting "*Ya van a ver, ya van a ver, van a tener que aparecer.*" (You will see, you will see, they will have to appear.) This juxtaposition not only suggests that the grandmothers' purity contrasts with the

Figure 2.2. Urban shots belonging to the 1990s in *Botín de guerra*.

corrupt deeds of *menemismo* but also gives the impression that their search is widely and collectively supported.

The present of enunciation also penetrates the film's representational strategies. Four types of images intertwine within the documentary: the black-and-white footage that builds the chronological sequence, color images that capture grandmothers' and grandchildren's testimonies, color paintings depicting the nineteenth-century massacre of indigenous populations, and color urban shots of 1990s Argentina. It is in the careful mixture of these images that the documentary stages temporality. Testimonies are always shot in comfortable, domestic interiors that, as Moira O'Keeffe observes, "create an interview environment that seems to be part of the day-to-day existence of the interviewee" (525). They contrast with exterior shots of urban landscapes that transmit an uneasy feeling. The contrast is made explicit because these exterior shots, combined with all kinds of unnerving sounds (sirens, chains, screams), always follow the individual accounts. Chicha Mariani's recollection of the silent afternoon when her son and daughter-in-law were kidnapped is, for example, followed by silent images of a desolated, creepy afternoon in the 1990s. Her memories of loneliness and despair are visualized in contemporary images of empty buildings and threatening streets. The 1990s urban images are thus visual counterparts of the testimonial narratives, allegorizing the horrors of the recent past. More than this allegorization, however, these scenes also establish another contrast that alludes to the temporal constellation at the core of the documentary: their color contrasts with the black and white of the footage, differentiating past from present. The horror of the past, the film then suggests, is not over. The horror both surrounds the 1990s domestic interiors and unfolds parallel to the interviews. The shots of marginal, 1990s urban landscapes not only allegorize the past but also the present. The use of colors and filters, as well as the careful juxtaposition of different types of images, produces two interrelated effects: it differentiates the 1970s dictatorship from the 1990s present and, at the same time, alludes to their continuity.

Furthermore, the juxtaposition of different types of images leads the spectator to a historical sequence that goes beyond the one proposed by the black-and-white footage or the testimonial accounts. The paintings of slaughtered and torn indigenous families portray the horrific results of General Roca's "Conquest of the Desert," a military campaign between 1878 and 1885. Continuing with the invasions started by General Rosas in 1833, the Conquest of the Desert aimed to control native populations, especially *araucanos* and *tehuelches*, and to seize their lands for the Argentine state.[17] These paintings, prepared for the film by Enrique Breccia, are part of a prologue preceding the opening credits that provides a broader interpretive framework for what the viewer is about to see. The voiceover accompanying the paintings—based, like in *Juan*, on texts selected by Osvaldo Bayer for the documentary—makes this interpretive framework quite explicit:

> *El diario La Tribuna de Buenos Aires el primero de julio de 1879 informa:* "*Llegan los indios prisioneros con sus familias. La desesperación, el llanto no cesan. Se les quitan a las madres sus hijos para en su presencia regalarlos a pesar de los gritos, los alaridos y las súplicas que hincadas y con los brazos al cielo dirigen las mujeres indias. En aquel marco humano, unos se tapan la cara, otros miran resignadamente al suelo, la madre aprieta contra el seno al hijo de sus entrañas.*" *[El General Roca dice:]* "*La ola de bárbaros que ha inundado por espacio de siglos las fértiles llanuras ha sido por fin destruida, dejando así libres para siempre del dominio del indio esos vastísimos territorios que se presentan ahora llenos de deslumbradoras promesas al capital extranjero.*" (On July 1, 1879 *La Tribuna* of Buenos Aires advised: "Captive Indian families arrive. Desperation, tears. Children are torn from their mothers' arms to give them away, amid screams, and the pleas the mothers utter on their knees, arms raised to the sky. In that human picture, some cover their faces, others look down with resignation. The mother hugs the child of her womb to her bosom. A pitiless war against the savages." [General Roca wrote:] "The wave of barbarians that has swept our fertile plains for centuries has been wiped out, releasing from the Indians vast territories that are now available and full of sparkling promise for foreign capital.") (English translation from the film's subtitles)

Betina Kaplan argues that these paintings form an isolated prologue that is not connected to the rest of the narrative (152). I contend, however, that the prologue establishes a parallel between the stolen indigenous children and the stolen children during the last military dictatorship—a parallel that is at the core of the film's ideological content. Both criminal acts, the film suggests, respond to a national project of modernization based on foreign investment. In other words, what the native populations and the 1970s political activists have in common is that they had to be eliminated for being internal obstacles to entrance into the global market (the former because they owned exploitable land and the latter because they fought against capitalism). In this sense, *Botín de guerra* is attuned to a larger discourse arguably inaugurated in 1982 by David Viñas's *Indios, ejército y frontera*. Disgusted by the military celebrations marking the centennial of the Conquest of the Desert in 1978, Viñas argued that the dictatorship was a historical continuation of the nineteenth-century extermination of indigenous populations and that these native communities had to be seen as the precursors of the 1970s disappeared. "Western civilization," "modernity," and "progress" were in fact invoked in both historical moments in order to justify exterminations. At the exact same time of the documentary's shooting and release, Viñas expanded these ideas in a series of articles compiled in his 2000 *Menemato y otros suburbios*. According to Viñas, *menemismo* had to be seen as the culmination of the two earlier historical moments—a view that has since then been prevalent in the left-leaning intellectual discourse and that became especially prominent in uprisings protesting the 2001 Argentine crisis.[18] Like in the nineteenth century and in the last military dictatorship, the neoliberal 1990s aimed to open Argentina to the international market at the expense of marginalization and social exclusion. The 50 percent of Argentines below the poverty line were in this sense the offspring of the disappeared and of the native communities.

If we return once again to the juxtaposition of different types of images in Blaustein's film, we can see that this temporal constellation lies at the very heart of the documentary. The use of color and camera filters stages a present that connects the nineteenth century, the military dictatorship, and the 1990s. A second prologue made of black-and-white footage that precedes the testimonial accounts further emphasizes this temporal connection. Images of the most iconic, modern parts of Buenos Aires in the 1970s (the Obelisco, Florida Street, and Santa Fe Avenue) are intercalated with images of people standing in line to buy US dollars, counting bills, and making calculations. The images in this second prologue do not really play any role in the construction of the clear-cut, straightforward chronological sequence built in the archival footage (i.e., coup, demonstrations, collapse, trials, and decrees). Inserted in the documentary right after the paintings, these images of a 1970s modern, dollar-oriented Buenos Aires—a Buenos Aires that, if it were not for the black and white, one would immediately associate with the 1990s—tie the three historical moments together, turning once again the happy objects of modernity into affect aliens and thus alluding to the film's critical stance in the midst of neoliberal Argentina.

Shot at roughly the same time as *Botín de guerra*, Andrés Habegger's *(h)istorias cotidianas* (1998–2000) and Carmen Guarini and Marcelo Céspedes's *H.I.J.O.S., el alma en dos* (2000) also refer to the 1970s yet stage a counterhegemonic view of their neoliberal present.[19] *(h)istorias cotidianas*, directed by the son of a missing political activist and produced by Blaustein, is organized around a quite conventional format. Following a set of opening credits offering standard contextualization (after the 1976 coup, dissidents were prosecuted, which resulted in thirty thousand disappeared people), the testimonies of six children of missing parents mix with archival footage of the dictatorship and with shots of 1990s Buenos Aires. The testimonies are arranged according to a combination of *Botín de guerra* and *Montoneros*'s strategies. Some of the interviews are shot in comfortable interiors and others on the streets, at significant places in the interviewees' personal histories: a building where the parents were abducted, a house where the family lived prior to the kidnapping, their favorite park, etc. *H.I.J.O.S., el alma en dos*, directed by two members of the first generation, includes a wide range of interviews with young adults who belong to the human rights organization referenced in the title, both across Argentina and in France. Unlike the other documentaries explored in this chapter, there is no archival footage of the dictatorship and there are no captions identifying the speaking subjects. We are only confronted with testimonies shot at domestic settings and with "present" footage of H.I.J.O.S.'s activities, such as *escraches*, meetings, and camps.

Similar to what happened in *Botín de guerra*, in these documentaries the children's testimonies aim to narrate their own experiences as orphans and to reconstruct an integral image of their missing parents. Appealing to family photographs, they rebuild their parents' histories as family members, activists, and victims of the military. Past and present intertwine, in a temporal constellation that criticizes the present of enunciation on multiple fronts. First, like in *Cazadores* and *Montoneros*, the children's memories confront the audience with a multifaceted, affective portrayal of 1970s-era activism that counters the official and hegemonic view. In *H.I.J.O.S*, this portrayal reaches the present. When emphasizing the political activities and views of H.I.J.O.S. and its transgeographical ties, the documentary implies that activism is still widespread and alive. The idea of not identifying the interviewees, though paradoxical with the film's insistence on identity, serves to reinforce this sense of collectivity. Regardless of your name or the details in your personal history, the documentary suggests, you are part of a collective group, marked by a shared past and by a common present militancy.

Second, like in *Botín de guerra*, the narratives establish a link between the 1970s dictatorship and the neoliberal present. In Habegger's film, it is again the use of colors that helps build this connection. The shots of 1990s Buenos Aires appear in black and white after the scenes that include photographs or archival footage, thus suggesting continuity with the past. The urban shots appear in color after the testimonies, thus marking the present. In Guarini and Céspedes's documentary, it is the testimonies' content that establishes this link. Several speaking subjects claim that the De la Rúa's administration has, like the previous Menemist government, economic and historical ties with the dictatorship—a claim that is also made explicit in the long scenes showing an *escrache* to De la Rúa's brother-in-law. Finally, in *(h)istorias cotidianas*, the urban shots symmetrically stage those significant places that serve as sites of family memory and the most modern parts in the city such as new bridges, huge highways, and tall skyscrapers. The symmetry suggests that loss and death have been the high price paid for (an uneven and failed) modernization.

"The creation and mobilization of affect," Nigel Thrift argues, "have become an integral part of the everyday urban landscape. Affect has become a part of how cities are understood" (172). The statement perfectly condenses what these documentaries show. In 1990s Buenos Aires, loss and grief intermingle in the city's landscape, creating a complex image of modernity as negative affect and transforming urban streets in "allegorical ruins" (Avelar, *Untimely* 10) that point to a dark past. In Habegger's documentary, the codes inherent to the road movie provide again an indispensable tool for staging these ruins—as epitomized in Victoria Ginzberg's testimony, which is shot while she walks the city, photographs in hand, searching for the places where the pictures were taken. Instead of arousing our desire for modernity, here mobility and displacement confront us, as they did in *Montoneros*, with its affect aliens. Rather than making tolerable "the incessant rationalization of time . . . necessary to the ideologies of capitalist modernization" (Doane, *Emergence* 11), here the mobile images expose us with the evil side of such ideologies. Yet, as Andermann points out, this movement in space also becomes a work of mourning. In postdictatorship Argentina, "the absence of *places* for mourning can be both drawn out and counteracted in an opening toward *space*" ("Expanded" 166, emphasis in the original). In a city marked by disappearances, and thus by the absence of mnemonic places, "[landscape] functions as a domain of unfastening from place, of an errant, itinerary memory which holds a possibility of overcoming melancholy and eternal repetition" ("Expanded" 166). This errant act of memory enables, in Piedras's words, "social reconstruction after the multiple social traumas suffered in Latin America over the last few decades" ("Contemporary" 221).[20]

The documentaries' closing scenes bear these double marks of mourning and social reconstruction. After traversing the city, the six testimonial subjects in *(h)istorias cotidianas* find a specific place that allows them to put an end to their grief and parents' histories. Úrsula Méndez chooses the building from where her mother was kidnapped and where she actually organized a memorial to, in her own expression, "be at peace" with her mother's image. Cristian Czainick opts for the riverside, since he believes that his father was thrown to the River Plate.

Claudio Novoa highlights the meaning of having a tomb to visit his father's remains, which have been recently found and buried. Victoria Ginzberg finally finds the right park and spot in which the last photo of her family was taken. Florencia Gemetro decides to reunite with her parents through her militancy in H.I.J.O.S. and chooses the organization's *escraches*. And Martín Mórtola Oesterheld returns to his childhood house in the outskirts. These sites of memory allow them to work through the past and to close their parents' history, albeit symbolically. A set of captions accompanies the final shots and aids in this symbolic closure, providing biographical details for each testimonial subject, the exact date when their parents disappeared, and, in the case of Novoa, the date when their bodies were recovered. The closing captions thus invert the opening set alluding to the thirty thousand disappearances and put an end to their family itineraries, "recovering" their missing histories.[21]

Moreover, the choice of these sites of memory also serves to construct a bond of solidarity as second-generation survivors, as illustrated by the closing scene in which they share their family photographs with one another. *H.I.J.O.S., el alma en dos* comes to an end with a parallel realization. A sequence of photographs of the *escraches* is accompanied by an upbeat, festive song that refers the viewer back to the opening scene, in which members of the organization celebrate a (minor) legal conviction to Alfredo Astiz, the military officer whose 1986 absolution had been documented in *Juan*.[22] Attuned to what happened in *Botín de guerra*, the reconfiguration of the social bond is proposed in these two contemporaneous documentaries as a means to counteract the officially driven amnesia. Gemetro's closing words in *(h)istorias cotidianas*, which precede the final set of captions, put it quite explicitly: Since in 1990s Argentina there is no hope for legal conviction, the duty of second-generation survivors is to fight for social condemnation—a duty that these testimonial documentaries take at face value.

Given that these films deal with the representation of second-generation survival, it is not surprising that, as implied in Andermann and Piedras's readings, they have mostly been interpreted from the standpoint of trauma. Drawing on Freud's distinction between "melancholy" and "mourning," Ana Amado observes that *Botín de guerra* and *H.I.J.O.S., el alma en dos* join other testimonial narratives by relatives of the disappeared such as *Encontrando a Víctor, Papá Iván*, and *Los rubios*: "*poéticas testimoniales [que] eludieron el pliegue melancólico de un proceso privado de elaboración del duelo e integraron sus acciones a una estrategia activa—en tanto política y colectiva—de relación del presente con aquel pasado traumático*" (testimonial works that have shifted away from a melancholic and private process of mourning to integrate past and present via an active, political, and collective strategy) (Amado 139). In their respective articles, Silvana Bekerman and Liliana Feierstein mention Blaustein's documentary as yet another case in which film serves as a means for staging and processing psychosocial trauma. In this sense, Bekerman suggests, the film is attuned to documentaries like Echeverría's *Juan*. Creating a common bond among missing parents, surviving children, and spectators, the film allows for the transmission of an experience that was deemed to vanish together with the dead bodies of the disappeared (Bekerman 157; Feierstein 126). Moira O'Keeffe claims that "taken as a group, these documentaries shed light on how social memory of the repression in Argentina is, in part, constructed through film. Such films can provide a foundation for healing at both the personal and cultural level without pretending that all the questions have been, or can be, answered" (535). Finally, referring equally to *Botín de guerra* and to *Televisión x la identidad*, Michael Lazzara states that "the recovery of lost children was and continues to be a vital trope deployed in the re-suturing of a posttraumatic nation and the invention of an integrated national story" (320).

Although these 1990s documentaries can certainly be read from the standpoint of trauma—a standpoint that can yield analyses as illuminating as those by Amado, Lazzara, and Andermann—I believe that this approach does not fully account for the films' historicity. The oversight is best evidenced by the established parallel between *Botín de guerra* and *Juan*, which, as we saw in the previous chapter, carries the traces of a very different political moment. The omission is also evident in the parallel between *Botín de guerra* and *Televisión x la identidad*, a series sponsored by the Kirchner administration that aired in 2007 on primetime television and that, as I examine in the next chapter, serves a very different ideological purpose. Instead, an analysis of how these 1990s testimonial documentaries organize their historical sequences, manipulate indexicality, and stage temporality helps elucidate their stance within their present of enunciation. In this sense, in spite of their choice of second-generation testimonial subjects, they are closer to *Montoneros* and *Cazadores*. They are paradigmatic products of the 1990s. Unlike what happened in 1980s cinema, where the present was conceived as a work in progress, as pure movement in the making, 1990s cinema stages a static, closed, and alien present that contrasts with the official and hegemonic view of optimistic modernity. Appealing to the political call at the heart of documentary, these films stage temporality, organize historical sequences, and represent speaking subjects in such a way that they unpack the incommensurable universal signification that "modernity" achieved as Argentina's master-signifier in the 1990s.

Notes

1. For further details on menemismo (1989–1999) and its subsequent period (1999–2003), see Grimson and Kessler; Acuña; Romero, *Breve*; *Crisis*; Martucelli and Svampa; Basualdo;

Epstein and Pion-Berlin; Fiorucci and Klein. I deliberately used the verb *continue* when referring to Menem's neoliberal reform because, as it has already been noted, Menem deepened a neoliberal reform that in reality had started during the military dictatorship. (See Lvovich and Bisquert 50–55.) The fact that Menem was reelected for a second term seems to contradict the idea that this period was marked by disenchantment toward government institutions and civic participation. As the scholars referred in this endnote point out, however, the reelection can be explained precisely as a result of disenchantment: Argentines' skepticism toward politics combined with their fascination with economic policies that gained them access to imported goods led the reelection vote. This phenomenon is sometimes referred to as *voto licuadora* (blender vote), in an allusion to people having voted for Menem because of their ability to purchase products manufactured abroad, like blenders, that made them feel modern.

2. For further details on the connections between *peronismo* and *menemismo*, see Borón; Levitsky and Wolfson; Martucelli and Svampa; Palermo and Novaro.

3. For in-depth analyses of the film industry during *menemismo*, see Falicov; Andermann, *New Argentine*; Aprea, *Cine*.

4. Other factors that made possible the explosion of testimonial films in the mid-1990s were retired naval officer Adolfo Scilingo's declarations on how the military had abducted and tortured a number of people and later thrown their bodies to the River Plate, General Martín Balza's acknowledgement of military crimes, and the continuous protests of human rights organizations. See Ros (13–22) for a condensed yet thorough summary of this period.

5. H.I.J.O.S. is an acronym for *Hijos por la Identidad y la Justicia contra el Olvido y el Silencio*. The organization, whose members are children of disappeared people, was formed in 1995 as a direct reaction against *menemismo*. At that time, they became quite famous for organizing *escraches* (outings) to raise public awareness about military officers being free on the streets in spite of their crimes. The organization became even more visible after 2003 due to the support of the Kirchner administration. For further details on their origins and ideas, see *"Quiénes somos"* on the organization's website.

6. The prominence of these two trends can also be traced to other types of narrative; 1970s-era political activism is the primary focus of Martín Caparrós and Eduardo Anguita's written compilation of testimonies *La voluntad*, Carlos Gamerro's novel *Un yuppie en la columna del Che Guevara*, Miguel Bonasso's *La memoria en donde ardía*, and Cristina Zuker's *El tren de la victoria*. Activism is also the main theme of Roberto Perdía's memories *La otra historia*, Marta Diana's *Mujeres guerrilleras*, and Ernesto Jauretche's *No dejés que te la cuenten*. The second generation is the primary focus of Félix Bruzzone's novel *Los topos* and Ernesto Semán's *Soy un bravo piloto de la nueva China*, Lola Arias's play *Mi vida después*, and the plays of the group Teatro x la identidad. This is also the main theme of Mariana Eva Perez's blog and homonymous book *Diario de una princesa montonera* and Juan Gelman and Mara La Madrid's compilation of testimonies *Ni el flaco perdón de dios*.

7. See Laclau and Mouffe 1–36 for a genealogy of the notion of hegemony and 55–78, 122–131 for an explanation of their notion's similarities and differences with the Gramscian conception of hegemony, especially regarding the primacy of the category of class and the existence of a hegemonic center in discursive formations.

8. See Beasley-Murray; Hardt and Negri; Moreiras; Williams, Gareth for paradigmatic references on posthegemony. See Beverley, *Testimonio* 1–28 for a critique to this paradigm that could be extrapolated to what happens in the case of Argentine testimonial cinema.

9. For further details on *Cazadores*'s reception at the time of its release, see Oberti and Pittaluga (119–121). Although I will not focus on the details of this contemporary reception, which mainly discusses emphases and omissions of Blaustein's particular representation of Montoneros, I agree with Oberti and Pittaluga's claim that contemporary reactions are a good indication of militancy still being a social taboo in the 1990s.

10. See Altamirano and Beceyro's articles in *Punto de vista* 55 and Piedras, *El cine* 160 for a similar critique of *Cazadores*'s frozen discourse. See Forcinito 120–126 for a reading of *Montoneros* from a gender-based perspective.

11. See Longoni for an in-depth analysis of the figure of the traitor in survivors' narratives. In the film, Ana's story is a good example of how survivors, especially women, are confronted with the difficult task of legitimizing their survival and negotiating their own meaning against the suspicions raised by them having survived. As Longoni points out, survivors' stories often allude to several issues that are difficult to digest, especially for relatives of people who died: a confirmation that other people were killed, a relativization of heroism, and a reexamination of 1970s-era revolutionary projects. All three issues are at stake in Testa's narrative.

12. I am referring to Menem's famous speech for the inauguration of the new academic year at a rural school in Salta, Argentina, when he said: *"Se va a licitar un sistema de vuelos espacial mediante el cual, desde una plataforma que quizás se instale en la provincia de Córdoba, estas naves espaciales van a salir de la atmósfera, se van a remontar a la estratósfera y desde ahí elegir el lugar a donde quieran ir. De tal forma que en una hora y media podemos estar desde Argentina en Japón, en Corea o en cualquier parte del mundo."* (We will select the best proposal for a spaceship system that allows to launch spaceships from a station, probably located in the province of Córdoba. These spaceships will leave the atmosphere, arrive to the stratosphere, and, from there, choose where to go. In this manner, we could travel in an hour and a half from Argentina to Japan, Korea, or any other part of the world.)
The complete speech is available on YouTube, https://www.youtube.com/watch?v=H1DTY2XMbzE.

13. I am indebted to Andrés Di Tella for generously answering my questions regarding the film's shooting.

14. José Luis Cabezas was a journalist assassinated in 1997, after he had taken the first public photographs of Alfredo Yabrán, a powerful man accused of drug and weapon trafficking and money laundering, who had close ties with Carlos Menem. For further details on the crime, see Balmaceda and Fernández Llorente.

15. See chapter 1 for general references on Third Cinema. See Garibotto and Gómez for a more detailed analysis of the connection between the organization of the historical sequence and Third Cinema's politics in *La hora de los hornos*.

16. Abuelas de Plaza de Mayo is a human rights organization founded in 1977 with the goal of finding children stolen and (most of the time) illegally adopted during the military dictatorship. It is estimated that around five hundred children were born to mothers in prison who were later disappeared. As of October 2016, 121 of these children have been found. For further details on the abduction and recovery of children throughout the postdictatorship, see Lazzara. For further details on Abuelas, see "Quiénes somos" on the organization's website.

17. See Andermann, *Mapas*; Montaldo; Viñas, *Indios* for classic references on these events.

18. For further examples of this view, see Avelar, *Untimely*; Colás; Grimson and Kessler.

19. Released in 2005, *H.I.J.O.S., el alma en dos* was shot in 2000. We could thus technically say that the film should be considered as a post-2000 film and thus included in the next chapter. Yet, I find that this film is a paradigmatic example, both in form and content, of the 1990s testimonial documentary and its counterhegemonic stance. It is also a good example of why, as I argued in the introduction, my periodization is meant less as a rigid classification than as a pointer to broad, progressive tendencies.

20. For general references on the connections between landscape and memory, see Assman; Huyssen; Jelin and Langland; Lefebvre; Nora; Schama; Young, James.

21. In this sense, I partially disagree with Andermann's reading, when he states that in these films, among which he includes *(h)istorias cotidianas* and *Papá Iván*, "the viewer is confronted with an errant act of memory (in the double sense of adriftness and confusion of the facts" ("Expanded" 177). As I analyze in detail in the next chapter, I believe that there is a difference between the two types of films and that, while they can both be seen as errant acts of memory, the latter meaning of *errant* (confusion of the facts) does not apply to Habegger's film, which provides a closure, albeit symbolic, of history—and, in fact, ends with a reconversion from mobile space to monumental place. By the same token, whereas Habegger's documentary could be considered a work of mourning, it could arguably be said that, precisely because of its lack of closure, Roqué's does not result in successful mourning.

22. After having been absolved in 1986, in 2000 Astiz was sentenced to serve three months in prison for telling journalist Gabriela Cerruti that he was the best-trained man in Argentina to kill journalists and politicians and for defending the actions of the past military dictatorship. Because this was considered a minor crime, he did not actually spend time in jail. In 2011, however, once the trials to military officers had been reopened by the Kirchner administration, he was sentenced to life in prison.

3 Distortion and History in Post-2000 Second-Generation Performative Documentaries

BEFORE DELVING INTO the cultural production of *kirchnerismo*, I would like to turn attention to the widely discussed *Papá Iván* (Roqué, 2000) and *Los rubios* (Carri, 2003). These two films, shot toward the end of the postdemocratization and in the midst of the political turmoil surrounding the 2001 crisis, manifest a significant change in the Argentine documentary tradition.[1] First, unlike what happened in earlier films such as *Botín de guerra*, here the second generation is both the subject of speech and the speaking subject. María Inés Roqué is the daughter of Juan Julio "Iván" Roqué, a founding member of the Fuerzas Armadas Revolucionarias and a Montonero leader who died after a confrontation with the military in 1977. In 2000, while living in Mexico, Roqué decided to travel back to Argentina and shoot a documentary about her father. *Papá Iván*, released in 2004, is a forty-five-minute film that mixes interviews with Iván Roqué's fellow activists, friends, and wife with footage of 1960s and '70s Argentina.

Throughout the documentary, we can hear María Inés Roqué's voiceover as she reflects on the shooting process and reads a letter that her father wrote to his children explaining his reasons to join the armed struggle. We can also see the director on screen as she walks through the streets, tracing Iván Roqué's biography, and talks to some of the interviewees. Albertina Carri's parents, Roberto Carri and Ana María Caruso, were upper-class members of Montoneros who were kidnapped while living in a working-class neighborhood in Buenos Aires and who have been missing since 1977. Like *Papá Iván*, *Los rubios* is a mixture of interviews with friends, relatives, neighbors, and former activists, with metacommentary on the filmic process. Albertina Carri also appears on screen in two different types of situations: as a director instructing her crew and as an interviewer/interviewee played by actress Analía Couceyro. If, in earlier documentaries, the second generation's voice began to occupy an important place in the reconstruction of the past, it now takes center stage. Second-generation members are now the filmmakers responsible for enunciation and the primary speakers within their own narratives. In this sense, the films mix the two most common I-voices identified by Metz: the extradiegetic of the external narrator and the intradiegetic of the character (*Impersonal* 39)—a mixture that, as we will see, complicates the referential nature of testimonial cinema.²

Second, the two films are indicative of the increasing presence in the Argentine cinematic scene of what Stella Bruzzi calls "performative documentary": "a mode which emphasizes the often hidden aspect of performance . . . featur[ing] the intrusive presence of the filmmaker" (185–187). As already noted, performative documentaries have been a leading trend in United States and European cinema since at least the 1980s.³ Shifting away from 1960s direct cinema and cinema vérité's desire to stage an unmediated reality, performative documentaries assert the necessarily mediated quality of the filmic image by inscribing the auteurial subject within the film. Breaking with earlier modes of political cinema more concerned with the representation of collective history, they turn to self-representation as a form of identity politics. The filmmaker's self-inscription underscores the subjective, historically specific dimension of power relations and political dynamics. As Bill Nichols puts it, "The referential quality of documentary that attests to its function as a window onto the world yields to an expressive quality that affirms the highly situated, embodied, and vividly personal perspective of specific subjects, including the filmmaker" (*Introduction* 132).

It is not until the early 2000s that this subgenre appears in the Argentine cultural scene. Although, as Pablo Piedras points out, performative documentaries began to appear in the 1990s, the epistemological break that made their centrality possible occurred a decade later.⁴ In the midst of the political unrest surrounding the 2001 crisis—at a moment when individual subjects perceived themselves as affected by and situated in history—didactic, explicitly political forms of collective documentary such as those put forward by Third Cinema seemed outdated. Following the crisis of totalizing historical explanations, documentaries have increasingly relied on subjective discourse as a means of political reconfiguration. This change in perception is best evidenced by the difference between the pedagogical intention of Fernando Solanas's voiceover in *La hora de los hornos* and his subjective presence as an interviewer in his 2004 documentary *Memoria del saqueo*. As Antonio Gómez contends, "[The] collective, militant, solidary first person [of Third Cinema] has been replaced in more recent documentaries by a singular, recognizable voice, a first person that identifies itself by its proper name . . . against the backdrop of a damaged collectivity" ("First Person" 46–47). A parallel epistemological break can be noted in films dealing with the dictatorship. The optimistic stance toward the possibility of reconstructing history in 1980s documentaries such as *Juan* or even in 1990s films such as *Montoneros*, *Cazadores*, and *Botín de guerra* gave way to performative documentaries in which the filmmaker's self-inscription invites an often-pessimistic reflection on historical representation. Several second-generation documentaries fall within this category. To the emblematic *Papá Iván* and *Los rubios* we could add Gabriela

Golder's *En memoria de los pájaros* (2000), Laura Bondarevsky's *Che vo cachai* (2003), Natalia Bruschtein's *Encontrando a Víctor* (2005) and *Tiempo suspendido* (2016), Nicolás Prividera's *M* (2007), and Carri's *Cuatreros* (2016), among many others.

In the previous chapter, I analyzed how the documentaries' staging of the present showed their antiofficial and counterhegemonic stance within the 1990s. In this chapter, I am interested in seeing how the use of documentary in second-generation performative films registers the increasing hegemonization of testimonial cinema—and, to some extent, the exhaustion of trauma theory and subaltern studies. Given the political and historical expectations at the heart of documentary (expectations that, as we have seen earlier, were crucial to mobilize the viewer in the 1990s), it is not surprising that, in the early 2000s, it is the documentary genre that first evidences testimonial films' increase in hegemony—as well as the loss of political and historical appeal associated with acquiring hegemony. It is from this perspective that I reconsider *Papá Iván* and *Los rubios*. I find the use of documentary in these films to be indicative of how testimonial cinema went from being one particularity among others to taking up an incommensurable universal signification. In the closing section, I anticipate what I examine in more depth in the next chapter: the testimonial genre's hegemony increases during *kirchnerismo*, as these narratives also become the official version of history. Via *Televisión x la identidad* (2007), a documentary-fiction hybrid, I argue that this increase is accompanied by a progressive fictionalization of the genre.

Papá Iván and *Los rubios*: Generic Deviations and Testimonial Parodies

Papá Iván's opening sequence makes us believe that we are in front of a classic testimonial documentary. Family photographs accompany María Inés Roqué's voiceover as she reads a letter that her father left before going underground: "*Agosto 26 de 1972. A mis hijos, Iván y María Inés. Les escribo esta carta por temor a no poderles explicar nunca lo que pasó conmigo. Porque los dejé de ver cuando todavía me necesitaban mucho y porque no aparecí a verlos nunca más.*" (August, 26, 1972. To my children, Iván and María Inés. I am writing this letter fearing that I will never be able to explain what happened to me. Because I stopped seeing you when you still needed me and because I did not come back to see you again.) The next scene shows the filmmaker as she sits on her desk, facing the letter. A zoom-in allows us to confirm the date and read the first paragraph. The voiceover continues: "*Aunque sé perfectamente que la mamá les habrá ido explicando la verdad, prefiero dejarles mis propias palabras para el caso en que yo muera antes de que lleguen a la edad de entender bien las cosas.*" (Although I am certain that Mom will have told you the truth, I would rather leave you my own words, in case I die before you are old enough to understand everything right.) We then see black-and-white images of a typical Argentine highway, and we hear María Inés Roqué's voiceover again, this time in a more colloquial tone, as if she was now talking instead of reading. Often pausing in the middle of a sentence, as if thinking what to say next, Roqué explains that she decided to shoot the documentary in order to come closer to his father's real image and to better understand several facts that had always been blurry in her mind. The next scene is a close-up of Pancho Rivas, a man identified in the captions as a Montonero and FAR activist. In response to María Inés Roqué's questions, he starts to recall Iván's personality as a guerrilla leader.

The opening sequence thus condenses most components of conventional testimonial documentaries—or, at least, the components found in all the testimonial documentaries analyzed in my book so far: a first-person account of history, interviews with speaking subjects who are able to both delve into private details and to offer political commentary, and indexical objects such as photos and letters that attest to the existence of the referent, replicating, as Andermann puts it, "the absent presence of Juan Julio Roqué" (*New Argentine* 116). Rivas's testimony is actually quite close to what Bhaskar Sarkar and Janet Walker identify as the "ideal type": "Framing is in close or medium shot, the interviewer . . . is off-screen, and the interviewee's glance is at an oblique angle just past the camera lens" (10). Furthermore, in *Papá Iván*, the authority of the first person is (at least in the opening sequence) overly emphasized. There are three types of personal testimony that explicitly present themselves as authorized sources of history: that by Iván Roqué in the letter, that by his daughter, and those by his fellow activists and relatives. Not only do these testimonies appeal to verbs that highlight witnessing (for example, *"recuerdo"* and *"sé"*—I remember, I know), but they also rely on discourses of truth and authenticity, thus complying with testimonial documentary's main purpose of being, in José Rabasa's words, "engaged dissemination of truth" (177). Iván Roqué underscores that his own words will allow his children to understand everything *right*. María Inés Roqué anticipates that her documentary will reconstruct her father's *real* image and will make *facts* clear—a promise that she seems to fulfill from the very beginning, as she insists on providing evidence of the letter and of her reading the letter. And the colloquial tone of the speaking subjects, including the filmmaker, gives the impression that the narratives are spontaneous, authentic, unscripted, and unfolding simultaneous to the shooting.

Yet, as the documentary develops, testimonial conventions become weaker. The aura of authenticity surrounding the speaking subjects, for example, starts to vanish after we are introduced to Miguel Lauretta, a man who—the captions tell us—has been accused of collaborating with the military while in captivity at ESMA. Miguel Bonasso, also interviewed by Roqué, claims that Lauretta was the one who betrayed Iván and even toasted to his death. When confronted with María Inés Roqué's questions, Lauretta becomes uncomfortable. He interrupts his narrative, nervously touches his face, and uses abstract vocabulary that makes it difficult to create a coherent picture. A similar attitude—an attitude, in fact, reminiscent of that shown by the military officers interviewed in *Juan*—permeates the next testimony: that of el Tío, the activist in charge of the house where Iván was ambushed. Lauretta and el Tío's unreliable narratives come to the fore. They are much longer than the other testimonies and they are introduced right at the film's climax, when Roqué is about to unveil details surrounding her father's death—the event that actually prompted the creation of the documentary. The first person is no longer deemed an authorized source of history. Indeed, the film ultimately leaves us with the impression that speaking subjects are not really qualified to talk about politics or history but can only be held accountable for their own personal feelings.

This impression is further emphasized by the contrast between the historical unreliability of Lauretta's and el Tío's accounts and the emotional authenticity of Iván Roqué's wife, Azucena. Portrayed in a series of extreme close-ups, Azucena offers a detailed description of her contradictory feelings: her doubts regarding Iván's radical activism, her admiration for his deep political convictions, her disappointment when he left the family, her pain as an abandoned romantic partner, etc. As Alejandra Oberti and Roberto Pittaluga have already noticed, her testimony becomes the leading narrative in the film, conveying all the authenticity that is missing from the narratives directly dealing with politics (113). The contrast between these two narratives (the unreliable/political and the authentic/personal) is duplicated in the contrast between the two primary testimonies in the voiceover. María Inés Roqué's narrative as she reflects on her personal reasons for shooting the documentary and on her mixed feelings toward her father sounds much more authentic than Iván Roqué's narrative in the letter. This difference is underscored by the counterpoint between the colloquial, intimate tone of María Inés Roqué's own story—which, as Piedras explains, has been recorded as a conversation with coproducer Hugo Rodríguez (*El cine* 83)—and her formal, rigid tone when reading her father's letter. We could actually say that this contrast in tone ends up creating an opposition that should be understood both in aesthetic and ideological terms: an opposition between a skeptic second generation, whose performative documentaries, as Piedras points out, usually rely on an expressive, almost poetic voice that is open to exploration (168) and a firmly radical first generation, whose documentaries are framed by seemingly neutral, normative, and didactic voiceovers (83).[5]

The representation of history follows a path similar to that of the testimonies. The first part of the documentary presents the viewer with carefully organized footage of two major events in 1960s Argentina: Onganía's *coup d'état* in 1966 and *el Cordobazo*, a 1969 student- and worker-led revolt against Onganía.

Yet, as it happened with the individual testimonies, the narration of collective history vanishes as the documentary unfolds. As Piedras notices, the film lures the viewer into thinking that she will have access to new historical knowledge but then refuses to indulge expectations (*El cine* 78). The historical sequence gets interrupted. The last piece of footage presented in the film is a loose image of Videla without further contextualization. Moreover, in spite of María Inés Roqué's stated goal at the beginning, both the personal history and the image of her father remain unclear once the film is over. Initial details on Iván's personality as a guerrilla leader, his charismatic figure as a teacher, and the experiences that drove him to militancy give way to abstract, contradictory images. Even the facts surrounding his death—precisely what María Inés Roqué wanted to definitively clarify—stay confusing. We are still not sure about the way he died and whether he had been betrayed. The director's voiceover points to this lack of general closure in the final remarks:

> *No tengo nada de él. No tengo una tumba. No existe el cuerpo. No tengo un lugar donde poner todo esto. Yo creía que esta película iba a ser una tumba pero me doy cuenta que no lo es, que nunca es suficiente. Y ya no puedo más. Ya no quiero saber más detalles. Quiero terminar con todo esto. Quiero vivir sin que esto sea una carga todos los días y parece que no puedo. . . . Hice la película para entender por qué había hecho lo que había hecho y quién era en medio de todo eso, ¿no? . . . [S]iempre me va a quedar la pregunta.* (I don't have anything from him. I don't have a tomb. There is no body. I don't have a place to put all this. I thought that this film was going to be a tomb, but I realize that it is not, that it is never enough. And I can't take it any longer. I do not want to know any further details. I want to get over with all of this. I want to live without this being a daily burden, but it seems that I can't. . . . I made this film to understand why he had done what he did and who he was in the middle of all this, right? . . . The question will always remain.)

I will return to these remarks later, when addressing possible interpretations from the standpoint of trauma. For now, I would like to underscore how these observations are indicative of the generic deviations in *Papá Iván*. Although the film is advertised as a documentary and has won a number of prizes in this category, it calls into question the genre's basic components: history is elusive, speaking subjects are unreliable, and the first person lacks authority.[6]

Not surprisingly, these deviations translate into the film's treatment of indexicality. Once the closing remarks are over, we see a series of undated black-and-white pictures: a boy playing in the sand, a boy with an older woman who looks like Azucena, a boy smiling at the camera, and a girl surrounded by ruins that could be Teotihuacán. These might as well be portraits of a young Iván Roqué, of his children while he was still with them, or—more likely—of his family's life after his death. Similar to what happened with the historical accounts, the

Distortion and History in Performative Documentaries | 111

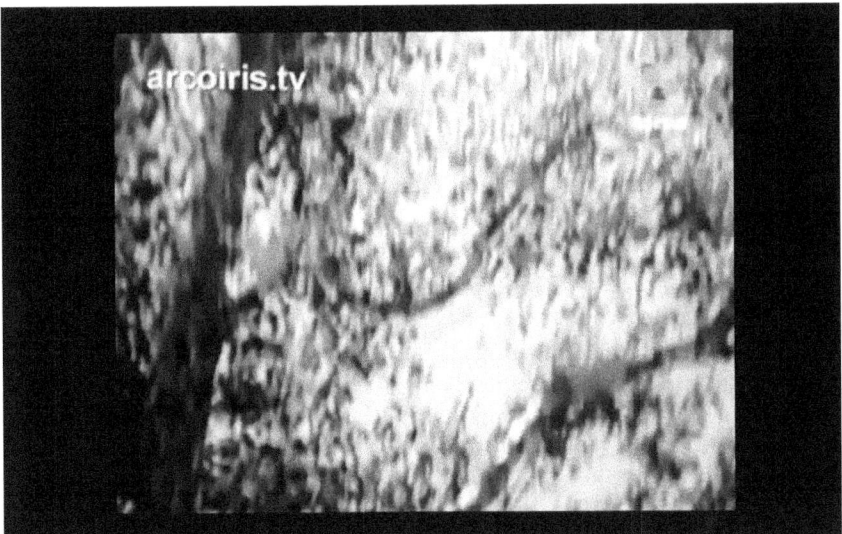

Figure 3.1. Out-of-focus foliage in *Papá Iván*.

photographs gradually lose their indexical status. If at the beginning of the documentary they accompanied the voiceover's reading of the letter, attesting to Iván Roqué's existence and family life, by the end they have become as unclear as the rest of the narrative. Instead of being, as Hirsch claimed, an index par excellence pointing to the having-been-there of the past ("Surviving" 14), they are indicative of the film's ultimate confusion. And it is indeed with a sequence of confusing images that the documentary comes to an end: shots of unidentified highways and a series of out-of-focus shots of tree foliage. Unlike what happened in 1990s films such as *Montoneros*; *H.I.J.O.S., el alma en dos*; *(h)istorias cotidianas*; and *Botín de guerra*, where street images registered the present, here they end up staging temporal and spatial imprecision. As the out-of-focus foliage suggests, *Papá Iván* has progressively lost its focus as a documentary. Rather than a testimonial film, it has become a parody—"imitation characterized by ironic inversion . . . repetition with critical distance . . . repetition with difference" (Hutcheon 6–32)—of a testimonial film.

Contrary to *Papá Iván*, *Los rubios*'s deviations from (and parody of) testimonial documentary conventions are explicit from the very beginning. There are no testimonies—not even those about personal feelings, not even Albertina Carri's—that look authentic. The dismantling of testimony's authority is achieved in at least three different ways. First, all personal content is elided from first-person narratives. In the interviews with former activists, for example, references to both their own personal histories of militancy and their feelings toward Carri's parents are scarce. As opposed to what happened in *Cazadores* and *Montoneros*, we do not know what drove these interviewees to activism. We are not told anything about their attitudes and beliefs, past or present. There is also nothing substantial that comes to light regarding the Carris, only lateral anecdotes that do not even allow for an emotional reconstruction of their images. Second, despite Albertina Carri's remarks in the voiceover ("*Los amigos de mis padres estructuran todo de manera tal que parezca un análisis político*" (My parents' friends refer everything back to politics), the interviewees offer no political commentary—or these types of commentary have been edited out of the film. As opposed to what we would expect if we took into account that these people are former militants, in their narratives there are no major references to either politics or history. Indeed, testimonies by former activists, distorted testimonies by neighbors who recall the dark-haired Carris as blonde, and testimonies by street children who had not even been born when the couple disappeared are treated as if they were equally relevant for political or historical reconstruction. In fact, we could even say that the accounts by neighbors and children are treated as more relevant because they occupy the entire mise-en-scene, whereas the former activists' talking heads always appear indirectly, on a TV screen in Carri's editing room.[7]

Third, the dismantling of testimony's authority is especially manifest in the (de)construction of Albertina Carri's subjectivity. As mentioned earlier, Carri appears on screen in two different types of situation: as a filmmaker and as an interviewer/interviewee played by Couceyro. The latter strategy illustrates Carri's parody of generic conventions. In spite of *Los rubios* being a narrative about disappeared activists created by their daughter, it is always Couceyro—that is, a fictional Albertina—who is either giving testimony or collecting testimonies. The appearance of Carri on screen as she directs the actress who is playing her giving testimony further emphasizes the inauthenticity of the situation. We are constantly reminded that the speaking subject in front of the camera is neither a survivor nor a direct witness but an actress. The guarantee of testimonial authority is manifestly broken before the audience—a break evidenced again when we see Couceyro rehearsing the script and even offering suggestions on how to modify the content. Moreover, Albertina Carri's authority as a testimonial subject is undermined in the rest of the interviews as well. When asking questions to the missing activists' neighbors, Carri does not disclose her name, thus avoiding a direct confrontation that could lead to spontaneous revelations—as it happens when María Inés Roqué challenges Lauretta on her father's death. In the interviews with the Carri's fellow activists, it is Couceyro playing Albertina the one who asks questions, forcing the interviewees to participate in a fictional scene in which they interact with a fictional character. As Carri states in *Los Rubios: cartografía de una película*, "*La actriz que representa mi papel en el documental remite constantemente a la ficción y asimismo permite un relato 'distanciado.'... Eso que la actriz ve representado en una materia lábil nunca se fija en una versión/verdad, el verosímil se arma y desarma."* (The actress who plays me in the documentary constantly points to fiction and also allows for a 'distanced' narrative.... What the actress represents is a vague matter that never gets fixed around one version/truth. Verisimilitude is constructed and destroyed) (24). Indeed, as Gómez points out, the film is the opposite of *testimonio*: it deflates the first person to emphasize an "I" who "*does not* tell his own story and tells, instead, the story of a historical subject who *cannot* tell his own story" ("Displacing" 66, emphasis in the original). The three discursive levels identified by Metz (the primary level of enunciation, the secondary that corresponds to the primary enunciator in charge of a story, and the third level including temporary diegetic enunciators) collapse into one, calling into question all types of referentiality (both deictic and anaphoric).

A parallel deconstruction occurs with respect to the Carris' subjectivity. Despite the number of objects that, according to the filmmaker in the above-mentioned book, was collected prior to the shooting, all material traces linking to the couple's existence have been erased.[8] The treatment of photographs is again a telling example. The film is full of photographs—hanging from the walls in Albertina Carri's studio, covering her desk, occupying a central place in close-ups—that, paradoxically, make it impossible to reconstruct Roberto Carri and Ana María Caruso's faces. Most pictures are portraits of babies and children. There are either no photos of adults who could have been their age at the time of the kidnapping and disappearance or, as Andermann observes, these pictures have been covered as if by accident under other photographs and papers (*New Argentine* 116). Any image that could restore their identities has been carefully omitted. In one of the closing scenes, Carri explicitly confronts the viewer with this erasing strategy as she shoots Analía Couceyro with a pair of scissors, cutting photographs and mixing the torn pieces with Playmobil toys. Challenging the usual representation of missing Argentines, in which the photographic image is on the spotlight, the pictures of the real Carris, the pictures of unidentifiable people, and the fictional Playmobil figures stand on equal footing.

Letters—which, as seen in *Papá Iván*, are another possible index attesting to the missing person's past existence—are also distorted. We can only see the mother's handwriting once on a card congratulating Albertina on her birthday. In all the other scenes, we see the camera panning over letters that, just like the photos, are not clearly linked to any real person. Martín Kohan also observes this distortion in one of the film's key moments: when Analía Couceyro, playing Albertina, reads from Roberto Carri's book *Isidro Velázquez*. Instead of having been written by Roberto Carri, the sentences read aloud belong to a quote by another author.[9] In *Los rubios*, the manipulation of material traces sends an uneasy message: those missing remain missing. Albertina Carri makes this quite clear in an interview with María Moreno:

> Quería evitar que los diversos elementos como los testimonios, las fotos y las cartas dejen esa sensación tranquilizadora, ese "ya está, conozco a Roberto y a Ana María y me voy a mi casa." Lo que yo planteo es precisamente que no los vamos a conocer, que no hay reconstrucción posible. Son inaprehensibles porque no están. Entonces no se trata de hacerlos presentes, que es lo que suele suceder. (I really wanted to prevent testimonies, photos, and letters from leaving a reassuring sensation, something like "that's it. Now I know Roberto and Ana María and I can go home." What I actually propose is that we will never get to know them. There is no possible reconstruction. They are unreachable because they are not here. So, it is not a matter of making them present, which is what generally happens.) (Moreno n.p.)

Yet *Los rubios* goes a step further from the filmmaker's words. It does not only confront the viewer with the Carris' absence. The film does not only elude representation. It also makes this elision the center of the narrative. As it happened with the testimonial accounts, the documentary makes explicit from the very beginning its deviations from generic conventions. Carri appeals to the typical elements in representations of disappeared people, such as photos and letters, to overly deviate from the genre. Thus, when seeing confusing photos, looking at unidentifiable letters, and listening to spurious sentences, the viewer both misses a definitive image of the Carris and becomes strikingly aware of what she or he is missing. As Gabriela Nouzeilles notices, "the search for the real and the authentic is always imperfect, unsatisfactory. The larger the amount of data, the more distant the object of [the] quest appears, continuously receding behind the veils of representation" (268).

Displacement and elision indeed guide *Los rubios*'s historical explanations. In spite of being a daughter's documentary on her disappeared parents, the audience achieves a minimal knowledge of the Carris' private and political trajectories. Information on their fate is limited: "*El 24 de febrero de 1977 Roberto Carri y Ana María Caruso fueron secuestrados y ese mismo año asesinados. Tuvieron tres hijas: Andrea, Paula y Albertina.*" (On February 24, 1977, Roberto Carri and Ana María Caruso were kidnapped. They were killed that same year. They had three daughters: Andrea, Paula, and Albertina.) Descriptions of their lives and ideas are absent. By the end of the film, it is not even possible to recall to what political organization they belonged. A similar confusion lies behind the narration of collective history. Captions made of phrases by military officers and by dead activists emerge together on screen. Couceyro reads aloud from *Nunca más*, but the paragraph is a marginal description of a building with no further contextualization. And it is the actress, pretending to be a young Albertina Carri, the only person who hints at a broader juncture: "*Alguien intentó explicarme algo de unos señores buenos y unos señores malos; algo de los peronistas, los descamisados, los obreros, los militares, los montoneros. No entendí nada de todo lo que me dijeron. Ni una sola palabra."* (Someone tried to explain something about good and bad people; something about Peronists, *descamisados*, workers, military officers, Montoneros. I didn't get it. Not even one single word.) Far from providing an explanation of the heterogeneous components in the sentence, the film avoids the narration of history. Facts are disorganized; there is no causality; sequences have no closure. In Gustavo Noriega's words, *"la película es el documento de una frustración."* (The film is the document of a frustration) (19). *Los rubios* shifts away from historical interpretation, becoming deliberately complicit with historical distortion—a move made evident by the insertion of fictional scenes in which Playmobil toys stage imaginary versions of the Carris' kidnapping, including an alien abduction.

This complicity with distortion is crucial to understanding the film's widely discussed ending. The crew, who is now at the countryside where Carri and her sisters grew up, walks away wearing blonde wigs, in an allusion to the distorted memories of the Carris' neighbors. In the above-mentioned interview, Moreno interprets this final gesture as some sort of poetic justice, as if the film was marking its distance from "el Negro," the nickname given to a torturer in the detention center where the couple was held. She also suggests that the blonde wigs could be seen as a solidarity symbol. When wearing the wigs, the crew is implicitly saying "We are all blondes," as in "We are all Jews" or "We are all lesbians." Nouzeilles reads the ending as a promise of a future community based on friendship and dialogue as opposed to political or biological affiliation—a reading in line with Andermann's interpretation of the closing shots as a reassertion of a self-chosen, queer, and prosthetic family beyond biological identity (*New Argentine* 119). Yet, for Kohan the ending reveals a celebration of appearances that entails a number of risks. Choosing the blonde wigs means choosing the sign that opened the path to the Carris' death—they were kidnapped when one of the neighbors pointed to their (wrong) hair color. It also means choosing the symbol of the failure of their political project—the people perceived them as blonde foreigners because they belonged to a higher class that did not really fit in the proletarian neighborhood.

While it is true that class difference is at stake in several scenes (the Carris were, like Couceyro suggests in the film, a "white dot" in a foreign environment; Albertina Carri openly shows her upper-class status when typing on a Mac computer and insisting on her technologically advanced shooting equipment), choosing the blonde wigs not only emphasizes this difference but also underscores distortion. Choosing the wigs means choosing a memory that is known to be false. It means abandoning the search for real referents and opting for a purely fictional space—as fictional as the countryside, the location where a young Albertina used to imagine her parents' impossible return. Wearing the blonde wigs also entails displacing the deictic reference that is typical of testimonial cinema (a type of cinema that depends on an "I" whose reference is to be extradiegetically found) onto an anaphoric, fictional reference. *Los rubios*'s final message is quite compelling: there is no longer room for historical reconstruction; there is only room for distortion.

Reconsidering *Papá Iván* and *Los rubios*: Performing Hegemony in Documentary

Most readings of *Papá Iván* and *Los rubios* have focused on what I have just highlighted: the films' distorting and inconclusive nature. Yet, although there is consensus around these characteristics, there is disagreement on how to interpret them. As mentioned in this book's introduction, Ana Ros sees in the lack of closure an emblematic feature of "self-aware memory" (5)—memory that is no longer perceived as static but as an open-ended, specific, and dialogic process. If the previous generation was concerned with remembering real events, the second generation is aware of the impossibility of complete reconstruction. This awareness helps in the process of active transmission and enables second-generation survivors to work through, as opposed to act out, trauma. In other words, instead of being fixated on reiterating the past, the second generation acknowledges its gaps, silences, and painful intrusions. This recognition makes mourning—active forgetting—possible. Furthermore, the recognition of these gaps and silences enlarges the construction of memory, often allowing filmmakers to question institutionalized narratives. The exposure of class difference in *Los rubios* and of the contradictory image of Juan Julio Roqué in *Papá Iván*, for example, goes against the grain of human rights organizations' narratives such as those by H.I.J.O.S., challenging the ownership of memory and highlighting its artificial essence (39–46). Jordana Blejmar examines Carri's playful use of childhood objects and argues that they help this autofiction overcome the limitations of monuments and conventional testimonies. The film's disorder, unlikeness, and constant reconversion of pieces do not aim to reveal what happened but how memory works. *Los rubios* should thus not be seen as an example of postmemory but as a memory in its own right (55–65). Oberti and Pittaluga also analyze *Papá Iván* as an act of memory in contrast to first-generation narratives. As opposed to monolithic discourses such as those found in *Cazadores*, Roqué's documentary stages a fragmentary memory that allows the viewer to relativize the notion of militancy. Like a collage, the film puts several pieces together but does not reach any definitive conclusion. It shows how a work of memory becomes an act of mourning (116–118).

Andermann, Nouzeilles, Macón, and Sosa agree that there is a link among fragmentation, mourning, and a critique of the previous generation, but rather than considering the films as works of memory, they follow Hirsch's concept and understand them as postmemory artifacts— "response[s] of the second generation to the trauma of the first [which are] mediated not through recollection but through representation, projection, and creation" (Hirsch, "Surviving" 8–9). In her groundbreaking article on *Los rubios*, Nouzeilles explains this link and claims that Carri's documentary is at odds with both the 1980s memories of the innocent victim and the 1990s Montonero memories that idealized the image of the radical militant:

> As a postmemory artefact, countering the call for total recollection that underlies the politics of memory held by the organizations of the relatives of the disappeared, *Los rubios* is the chronicle of the impossibility of reconstructing the past and of offering a complete and reliable version of it. . . . Against expectations, the realization that the past can only be recovered imperfectly, or through metaphorical displacement, does not make of *Los rubios* a melancholic project. On the contrary, the movie suggests that the process of putting together, in cinematic language, the pieces of an unworkable puzzle constitutes in itself a way of dealing with loss. (270–271)

Rather than mimetically identifying with the first generation, Nouzeilles claims that this postmemory film relies on a fragmentary narrative as a means of irreverent interrogation, which results in therapeutic liberation. Similarly, Macón argues that what makes *Los rubios* a postmemory narrative is the fact that the film modifies trauma as experienced by the first generation. Not only does the documentary alter traditional ways of representing trauma but also trauma's primary components (45). Andermann seconds these claims when, referring both to *Papá Iván* and *Los rubios*, he states that their fragmentary, adrift images point to the impossibility of fully reconstructing the missing parents as historical objects of research and to the instability of survivors' discourse. The films' use of landscape and mobile images, especially through panning and traveling shots, should thus be read as a formal counterpart to their practices of mourning ("Expanded" 177–181). "The postmemory documentary," Andermann observes, "stages this constitutive aporia of enunciation" (*New Argentine* 115), a staging that allows these films to spatialize mourning and prevents them from being trapped in melancholy. Along the same lines, Sosa sees *Los rubios* as "a sound case of postmemory" (*Queering* 54) because it challenges the compulsory demand for genealogical inscription that became mainstream in human rights discourse. Like Prividera's *M*, Carri's film refuses to reduce kinship to bloodlines and instead queers traditional victimizing narratives while bringing into light new images and landscapes (52).

Ana Amado, Joanna Page, and Antonio Gómez, however, interpret the films' inconclusive nature as a sign of the impossibility of mourning and as a critique of postmemory. The fragments and residues that in Roqué's film resist closure allude, according to Amado, to this impossibility. Successful mourning comes only as a result of successful representation (Amado 185). It is only through an organization of the fragments and residues into a coherent narrative—an organization at which *Papá Iván* clearly fails—that mourning is achieved. This failure is, Amado continues, also evident in *Los rubios*. The documentary's ambiguity and, in particular, its displaced ending in the countryside—displaced both in terms of location and in terms of subjectivity—is indicative of the lack of a space for mourning (193). Like in *Papá Iván*, in *Los rubios* there is no tomb, no monument, and no body. There is no physical space in which to anchor the work of mourning. Along the same lines, Page argues that Carri's documentary interrupts the process of active forgetting, remaining faithful to the gaps that arise from traumatic experiences: "Through a series of self-reflexive devices, the film disrupts identification, refusing to indulge in catharsis and mourning simply the impossibility of mourning, the absence of history and of experience, and the effects of these absences on identity and agency in the present" (169). Referring also to this absence of knowledge, Gómez further claims that, when Carri discloses the impossibility of understanding the stories about her parents transmitted via relatives and friends, "she seems to know for a fact that mediation was unsuccessful, which is actually an extremely straightforward enunciation (and critique) of ... 'post-memory'" ("First-person" 49).

I believe that *Papá Iván* and *Los rubios* allow for each of these readings—as well as for their exact opposite. First, it is certainly possible to interpret them from the standpoint of trauma theory and to see them as films that expose the gaps, silences, and residues inherent to traumatic memory. The narrative fragments scattered in the filmic text could be seen as symptoms of a wound caused by the inability to consciously process a catastrophic event—as thinkers such as Freud, Caruth, Laub, and Felman would say. The bits of discourses that resist closure could be cogent examples of a traumatic memory that has been overwhelmed by occurrences and that has not settled into understanding or remembrance. In this sense, each fragment encapsulates a piece of truth that would otherwise not be available, opening the path for a recuperation of the past and allowing for individual liberation. Albertina Carri seems to endorse this option in one of the film's first captions: *"Exponer a la memoria en su propio mecanismo. Al omitir recuerda."* (To expose memory in its own functioning. When we omit, we remember.) From the standpoint of trauma theory, then, these inconclusive documentaries—with their loose footage, their displaced speaking subjects, and their open endings—are doors to a repressed reality. They are thus "at once historical and clinical: a medium of historical transmission and the unsuspected medium of a healing" (Felman and Laub 9).

Yet, their inconclusive, fragmentary narratives can also be read the opposite way. They can also be seen as a manifest indication of the flawed nature of the major premises driving trauma theory. As Roqué's final remarks suggest ("I thought that this film was going to be a tomb, but I realize that it is not"), exposing the bits and pieces of traumatic memory does not result in healing.[10] The documentaries' open-ended sequences can be interpreted both as a means of working through trauma but also as an acting out that does not lead to closure. The scattered fragments of discourse and the multiple attempts at approaching the elusive figure of the missing parents can be regarded, instead of as stages toward active forgetting, as acts of compulsive repetition—as implied in the recurrent sequences of Couceyro rehearsing Carri's testimony. Moreover, the evident existence of a script, the exhibition of a shooting process, and, in Carri's case, the publication of a book explaining how she had thought of every detail challenge the notion of trauma as unwitting reenactment. Even if they carry unconscious aspects, the scripted narrative and the exposure of representation attest to careful planning and deliberate construction, calling into question the idea that traumatic memory is a spontaneous occurrence. Carri and Roqué's testimonies are not uncontrolled, unexpected utterances from which to reconstruct hidden traumatic events but discourses that are openly addressing those events and self-reflectively foregrounding their symptoms. Finally, the films' elusive, distorting histories defy trauma scholars' claim that trauma allows us to access and recover referentiality (see especially the fourth chapter of Caruth's *Unclaimed*). As the blurry photos, the Playmobil toys, and the heterogeneous explanations suggest, there is no historical truth that can be recovered from *Papá Iván* and *Los rubios*. Roqué's closing words are again indicative of this impossibility: "The question will always remain." Both private and collective history stay, as Carri observes in the film regarding her parents, inaccessible.[11]

Second, it is also possible to draw on Hirsch's theory and read these second-generation documentaries as postmemory artifacts. While observing the striking repetition over time of the same few images of the Holocaust, especially at the hands of the second generation, Hirsch ponders several options. Have these repetitive images become decontextualized clichés that shield subsequent generations from memory and mourning? Does repetition, on the contrary, retraumatize, thus enabling memory, mourning, and working through? Or is this repetition an effect of compulsive, melancholic replay ("Surviving" 8–9)? After analyzing several samples of second-generation cultural products, she chooses the second option and concludes that, by exposing themselves to repetition, postmemorial viewers engage in mourning. Yet, Hirsch warns, "it is only when [images] are redeployed, in new texts and new contexts, that they regain a capacity to enable a postmemorial working through" ("Surviving" 29). Repetition, repositioning, and reintegration are aesthetic strategies whereby the newer generations both produce and overcome trauma. *Papá Iván* and *Los rubios* can be easily read along these lines. When, in Nouzeilles's words, Carri puts together the pieces of an unworkable puzzle or when, as Andermann observes, the films appeal to mobile and adrift shots, they are repositioning traumatic fragments. Indeed, the documentaries rely on the three primary repositioning strategies that Hirsch analyzes in "Surviving Images." They creatively manipulate canonical photographs, such as the gates to Auschwitz or, in the case of our films, the portraits of the disappeared. They exhibit representation in a way that recalls Hirsch's "traumatic realism," where "the scars that mark the relationship of discourse to the real are not fetishistically denied, but exposed" (32). And they redeploy indexical images, allowing for a redirection of the look, as opposed to reinforcing an ideologically authoritative gaze.[12] Interestingly enough, in order to explain the latter strategy, Hirsch uses an example that resembles *Papá Iván*'s closing scenes: she claims that a second-generation artist has redirected her look (and successfully engaged in mourning) by juxtaposing an image of out-of-focus foliage and a photograph that should have carried referential value.

Once again, however, the films could be read in the exact opposite way: as major challenges to postmemory theory. Instead of redeploying traumatic fragments, reproducing traumatic effects, and enabling mourning, they could be examples of Hirsch's third option: compulsive, melancholic replay. As mentioned earlier, their open-ended structures could also be seen as figures for the impossibility of mourning and for the failure of mediated knowledge. Moreover, in their critique of first-generation discourse and in their ambiguity toward 1960s and '70s revolutionary projects, the documentaries distance themselves from one of the basic premises supporting Hirsch's argument: the existence of an empathic link across generations. Postmemory constitutes, for Hirsch, "an intersubjective transgenerational space of remembrance . . . defined through an identification with the [first generation]" ("Surviving" 10). Yet, far from being examples of "retrospective witnessing by adoption" (Ibid.), *Papá Iván* and *Los rubios* shift away from their parents' generation, emphasizing biological and ideological orphanhood. Indeed, the use of photographs shows how the films break with the postmemorial generation as understood by Hirsch. For Hirsch, photographs provide an integral link for the second generation, for those who, in their desire for memory and knowledge, are left to track the traces of what has been there and no longer is. Pictures "materialize" memory ("Surviving" 14). It is the photographic image's indexicality—the fact that the image testifies to the reality of the past, the fact that it has referential value—that carries the evidential force that is necessary for postmemory. Because photographs materialize memory, they provide the sense and bodily experience that connects two generations. Photographs become markers of truth-value, allowing second-generation viewers to relive and reenact the traumatic past. As already mentioned, it is the exact opposite that takes place in *Papá Iván* and *Los rubios*. Rather than a resource for examining the past or for witnessing by adoption the memories of the first generation, photographs make history even more elusive and the missing parents even more missing. They interrupt the indexical connection that is necessary for a successful process of intergenerational reenactment and postmemory.

Furthermore, as several scholars have already argued, the concept of postmemory does not quite apply to the Argentine case. In *Tiempo pasado*, Beatriz Sarlo claims that Hirsch's concept is misleading, as any type of memory is always a result of mediation, creation, and imaginative investment. The application of this concept to the Argentine context, she suggests, is most likely the result of unnecessary academic jargon (126). Noa Vaisman compellingly states that the Argentine case is unique because children of disappeared people need to construct a memory around the ghostly figures of parents who are missing. Unlike Holocaust survivors who pass on the trauma to their children through cohabitation, here the disappeared parents are absent and hence unable to transmit their traumatic experiences. Rather than postmemories, then, these children produce what Vaisman calls "dis-appeared memories"—memories constructed around an absent core, the parental figure, whose very essence is ghostly and ephemeral (185–203). Mariana Eva Perez agrees that these "orphans of spectres" ("Their lives" 7) are very different from the descendants of survivors mostly analyzed by Hirsch and highlights the need to search for new categories that can account for what this group of former child victims has lived firsthand. The latter's cultural production does not refer to the atrocities committed in the recent past but to how those who were children at the time deal with the legacy today—an observation that certainly applies to *Papá Iván* and *Los rubios* (6–16).

Third, if we take into account their present of enunciation, the films can be seen both as a typical product and as an exception. On the one hand, they are paradigmatic examples of post-2000 narratives, in which the second generation is both the primary subject of speech and the primary speaking subject. Attuned to the centrality of the children of the disappeared in the early 2000s, Carri and Roqué are not just protagonists who are interviewed to voice their own stories but filmmakers who create them, direct them, and organize their narratives from an adult's lens. Moreover, as Blejmar suggests, H.I.J.O.S.'s playful spirit, as seen in escraches, resonates in *Los rubios*'s playful aesthetics (60). On the other hand, and taking into account the present of enunciation one more time, these films go against their contemporary narratives. As most critics have observed, the documentaries' reluctant discourses regarding the previous generation's political project differ from those of the second generation's leading voice, H.I.J.O.S. The founding principles of the organization clearly condense the predominant view: "We acknowledge our parents' political struggle: because they wanted to change society, they wanted things to be different, and that is why they were taken. They were fighting so that we could all have a decent job, so that we could all study, so that we could all have access to good hospitals, they were fighting for a better life" (*HIJOS* n.p., English translation from the website). *Papá Iván* and *Los rubios* distance themselves from these assertions. In fact, Carri explicitly recognizes this distance in her interview with Moreno: "*Cuando aparecen los H.I.J.O.S. no me interesan nada. . . . No me interesaba la mirada reivindicativa y me daba impresión el nombre. Yo no quiero ser hija toda la vida.*" (As H.I.J.O.S. made their appearance, I was not interested. . . . I was not interested at all in their vindicating view and I was turned off by their name. I do not want to be a daughter my entire life) (n.p.).

Cogent incarnations of trauma theory's major premises, films that challenge the basic premises driving trauma theory, cultural artifacts that show the relevance of the notion of postmemory, critiques of postmemory, paradigmatic second-generation narratives, narratives that go against second-generation discourse; *Papá Iván* and *Los rubios* certainly allow for each of these interpretations. They can also be seen, as mentioned in the introduction, as part of a broader national and global trend that shifts away from totalizing explanations, choosing self-inscription as a form of political reconfiguration. If, however, we attend fully to the films' historicity and take into account the three interrelated levels of interpretation—the textual representation of history, the dialectical relationship between this textual representation and the narrative's present of enunciation, and its diachronic localization in history—we can also read them as signs of the increasing hegemonization of testimonial cinema in Argentina. In other words, if we place their inconclusive, distorted representations of history within the context of the development of the testimonial genre, we can see that their failed narratives document the repetition (and exhaustion) of this mode of representation. *Papá Iván* and *Los rubios*'s deviations from testimonial films' conventions are only possible because these conventions have been sedimented (and exhausted) over time. Their parodic nature comes to light because there is an original that has persisted long enough to be reiterated critically, to be ironically inverted, to be repeated with difference. The films show that, after two decades of continuous production, testimonial films have shifted from providing alternative narratives to becoming crystallized representations of recent Argentine history.

It could indeed be said that, since the 2000s, most second-generation documentaries have registered such shift in a similar fashion. *Encontrando a Víctor, Tiempo suspendido*, and *M*, for instance, closely resemble *Papá Iván* and *Los rubios*. Just like Roqué, Bruschtein opens *Encontrando a Víctor*, the documentary about her missing father, with an indexical object—in this case a photo of the late Víctor Bruschtein—that promises a pathway to unveiling his personality and history. The structure is actually organized around a format analogous to that chosen by Roqué: scenes in which the filmmaker wanders on the streets mix with interviews with several relatives and with a long interview with her mother that evidences doubts regarding revolutionary violence. As it happened in *Papá Iván*, however, the quest does not yield any original findings, a failure that also translates into the film's manipulation of indexicality. If *Papá Iván* ended with photos whose indexical markers had been removed, *Encontrando a Víctor* closes with Bruschtein projecting images of herself onto a big-size replica of the opening photo—an alteration that lays bare the subjective component of photographic evidence. Bruschtein further examines the unfeasibility of historical reconstruction in *Tiempo suspendido*, a film on the increasing memory loss of her grandmother Laura Bonaparte, one of the founders of Madres de Plaza de Mayo. The documentary combines Bonaparte's earlier testimonies (shot following the conventional talking head format, based on assertive statements, and accompanied by footage supporting those statements) with scenes in which the woman, now with progressive amnesia, revisits those earlier materials together with Bruschtein. More than a testimonial documentary, the film documents testimonial narratives' itinerary from reconstruction to distortion—an itinerary condensed in the family photographs, originally the basis of Bonaparte's memory and now a visible index of her impossibility to remember.

Prividera's *M* follows Carri's lead in exhibiting the deviation from generic conventions from the very beginning. An opening shot of a river—where, the viewer anticipates, the filmmaker's mother must have been thrown—gradually turns into an out-of-focus image of a TV screen carrying the distant sound of someone giving testimony. Just like the opening shot, the history of Prividera's disappeared mother comes out of focus as the documentary unfolds. Despite Prividera going to several institutions and meeting with a wide range of possible witnesses, none of the testimonies offers new insights. Moreover, like in *Los rubios*, the director's presence in front of the camera, rather than facilitating the speaking subject's narration, disrupts its natural development—which in the case of *M* does not happen as a result of fictionalization but of Prividera's recurrent, and quite rude, interruptions. Testimonial discourse, this documentary implies as well, does not lead to historical reconstruction but to historical distortion.

"Distortion" also accurately describes what ends up happening in Bondarevsky's *Che vo cachai*, in Golder's *En memoria de los pájaros*, and in Carri's *Cuatreros*, three documentaries seemingly aiming to explore the recent past. In *Che vo cachai*, Bondarevsky, who went into exile alongside her Montonero parents, travels back to Argentina, Chile, and Uruguay to explore how second-generation survivors have reacted to their relatives' loss in the three countries. Golder's seventeen-minute documentary explores how the filmmaker's friends and family experienced the dictatorship—an exploration stemming from Golder realizing, as an adult, that her childhood had been surrounded by inexplicable absences and mysterious phrases. *Cuatreros* has a twofold goal: to document the life of Isidro Velázquez, a mythical social bandit killed by the police in 1967, and to understand the fascination of this figure for two 1970s-era missing activists, Carri's own father and Pablo Szir. As seen in *Los rubios*, Roberto Carri made Velázquez the center of a sociological study. Szir created a film on the bandit that remains missing as well.

A set of moving captions floating around *En memoria de los pájaros* condenses the three films' resulting aesthetics: "*Un movimiento centrífugo y una sensación de mareo.*" (A centrifugal movement and a dizzying sensation.) In *Che vo cachai*, short clips of unidentified archival footage and of undiscernible radio transmissions combine with mobile images of anonymous second-generation members, creating a disorienting sensation that impedes understanding. In Golder and Carri's films, the confusion is even more prevalent, as the mise-en-scenes are always formed by split screens where two sets of images (indeed, up to four in *Cuatreros*) unfold at the same time and prevent the viewer from focusing on one distinct story. Instead of adding space, this doubling (or "double doubling") is, to borrow Metz's words, "a spatial limitation, a visual restriction . . . that enables one to pay attention to the 'apparatus' of cinema" (*Impersonal* 54–55) and move away from the narrative. In *En memoria de los pájaros*, disconnected testimonies, moving captions consisting of incomplete phrases, and loose footage further break with narrative coherence. Testimonial strategies of representation, the film suggests, result in a multiplicity of fragmentary, frozen narratives that, instead of providing new insights, numb the spectator.

Cuatreros could arguably be seen as a more extreme version of *Los rubios*. In the 2016 film, Carri's voiceover, clearly meant to be perceived as scripted, is divorced from the images on the multiple screens. The voiceover conveys a highly subjective narrative about the process leading to the documentary—a collage full of first names and cultural citations with no reference. The images are formed by footage, mostly from the 1960s and '70s, until the very end, when we see a blurry Carri playing with whom we assume to be her son. None of the initial quests finds traditional closure. As it happened in *Los rubios*, by the end of the film we do not know anything about either Velázquez or the missing activists' thought. We do not gain a clearer understanding of the historical figure nor do we learn from Szir and Roberto Carri's studies. We are left with the (quite skillfully achieved) impression that we have witnessed two parallel films: a sort of audiofilm on Albertina Carri's personal anecdotes and a collection of raw footage of the 1960s and '70s. Rather than being mere additions to testimonial cinema, then, Golder, Carri, and Bondarevsky's documentaries echo the others in this chapter in repeating, exposing, and parodying the conventions that have made testimonial cinema the most canonical genre in postdictatorship Argentina.[13]

I would thus like to suggest that, in post-2000 second-generation documentaries, "performative" carries a double meaning. On the one hand, these documentaries are performative because they feature the intrusive presence of the filmmaker—because the auteurial subject is self-inscribed in the film. Such a subject is less concerned, however, with an authentic representation of the self than with engaging in what performance studies scholar Richard Schechner has called "restored behavior": a group of rehearsed actions separated from the person doing them and as distant from the self as an actor from his or her role on stage (35–116). On the other hand, these documentaries are performative because they perform the testimonial genre—because they repeat, expose, and parody the conventions that have transformed testimonial films into a canonical genre. As Diana Taylor puts it, "Instead of the once, the act that bursts on the scene only to vanish, we can also think of performance as an ongoing repertoire of gestures and behaviors that get reenacted or reactivated again and again" (*Performance* 10). This is certainly true for the documentaries analyzed in this chapter, in which the testimonial repertoire—first-person narratives, indexical objects, road movie–style shots, and talking heads, among others—gets reenacted again and again before the audience's eyes. Yet this type of reenactment is somewhat different from the one in the testimonial documentaries such as those in the previous chapter. Here the intrusive presence of the filmmaker overly exposes the existence of an ongoing repertoire. When disrupting the talking heads, when manipulating the photos, when exhibiting the crew at work, when erasing urban markers—when "expos[ing] the apparatus" (Metz, *Impersonal* 55)—the documentarists exhibit the gestures, behaviors, and techniques that have composed this repertoire for several decades. If performance can be defined, in Marvin Carlson's words, as "the display of a recognized and culturally coded pattern" (70), then second-generation documentaries are performances in the purest expression of the term: they not only display a recognizable pattern but they also display the persistent existence of such display.[14]

Indeed, two of the most pivotal scenes in *Los rubios* explicitly bring together these two signifying dimensions of performance. In one of the scenes, Albertina Carri goes to the Centro de Antropología Forense (Center for Forensic Anthropology) to give a blood sample for a DNA test. The performative nature of this gesture is evident on multiple levels. First, Carri makes sure to let the viewer know that her visit is actually a repetition. She has already been to Antropología Forense, but she returns so that the blood extraction can be performed again, this time in front of the camera. Second, both Carri and actress Analía Couceyro give blood, emphasizing the parodic edge of the extraction. Finally, the purpose of such test lacks significance. Why would Carri, who already knows that she is the biological daughter of Roberto Carri and Ana María Caruso, be interested in a DNA test? How could the confirmation that she is the Carris' daughter—something that in her case has always been certain—add new meaning to her personal history? The DNA scene is ultimately depleted of content. It becomes pure performativity, which, according to Andrew Parker and Eve Kosofsky Sedgwick, can result in "the *dis*linkage precisely of cause and effect between the signifier and the world... in a radical estrangement [from] meaning... [in an] 'aberrant' relation to its own reference" (168, emphasis in the original).[15]

The DNA scene becomes an empty gesture whose deeply ironic nature comes to light if we take into account the importance of the DNA test as the only possible means to verify biological identity for those children of disappeared people who were adopted illegally. As Amado explains, this group, consolidated around H.I.J.O.S., makes biology the center of their social and political identity (180–195). Claiming family genealogy, for which the DNA test is absolutely necessary, is the most basic prerequisite to belong to the organization and the starting point for social and political activism. In most cases, too, activism is grounded in a vindication of the missing parents' revolutionary projects. For this group, then, biological affiliation means generational and political affirmation. More conventional documentaries featuring second-generation survivors, such as *Botín de guerra*, are a case in point; the interviewees always begin their testimonies by stating their (now fully recovered) real names and reconstructing their parents' history and ideals. In this sense, as Christian Gundermann suggests, H.I.J.O.S.'s discourses and cultural manifestations become *"actos melancólicos"* (melancholic acts) that refuse to accept the first generation's loss as well as their political project's failure (12–13). Carri's DNA performance thus entails strong ideological connotations. It is a performance of H.I.J.O.S.'s discourse, politics, and mode of representation. If, as Taylor puts it, for Madres and H.I.J.O.S. performances such as marches and escraches are "vital acts of transfer, transmitting social knowledge, memory, and a sense of identity through reiterated actions" (*Performance*, 25), for Carri the performance of the DNA test allows for an ironic inversion of knowledge, memory, and identity. If H.I.J.O.S.'s escraches prove how "performance transmits traumatic memory and political commitment" (Taylor, *Archive* 164), Carri's performance ironically questions such transmission and commitment. In Page's words, "Far from reinforcing a sense of biological continuity, the analysis of Albertina's DNA... points to the absurdity and the inevitable failure of such quests for identity" (174–175).

The other scene condenses what happens in the film as a whole. Carri and her crew read and discuss a statement whereby the INCAA rejects funding for their project:

> [*Los rubios*] *pide ser revisado con mayor rigor documental.... Requiere una búsqueda más exigente de testimonios propios que se concretarían con la participación de los compañeros de militancia de sus padres, con sus afirmaciones*

y discrepancias. Roberto Carri y Ana María Caruso fueron dos intelectuales comprometidos en los setenta, cuyo destino trágico merece que este trabajo se realice. (*Los rubios* needs to be revised with more documentary rigor.... The film requires a more thorough search for testimonies. This could be achieved by including your parents' fellow militants, their assertions and discrepancies. Roberto Carri and Ana María Caruso were two intellectuals really committed to the 1970s. Their tragic fate deserves that this type of work be done.)

Once again, the performative nature of this scene is apparent on multiple fronts. First, the crew's self-inscription allows for a performance of failure. The discussion of the rejection letter has no meaning, since it is being included in the film, which has supposedly been rejected—and which shows the INCAA as a sponsor in the credits.[16] The reading of the statement thus becomes a parodic gesture that infuses the entire documentary with irony. Second, if we take the statement at face value, we cannot help but read the film as a parody (an ironic inversion) of what the INCAA has requested—and, consequently, a parody of the normal, dominant view on what a testimonial film should be in the early 2000s. Instead of an arduous search for political testimonies by former activists, the documentary ironically deviates from these testimonies—which, as already analyzed, barely appear on TV at the back of Carri's editing room, offer no political commentary, and are as relevant as children's and neighbors' insubstantial gossip. Rather than providing "documentary rigor," the film critically exposes every possible convention at the core of the documentary genre: it makes representation mechanisms hypervisible; confronts the viewer with fictional, rehearsed, and scripted narratives; and is built on images whose referentiality remains always elusive. The determinable link to the social and historical world that was, for Chanan, a marker of documentary's indexicality disappears from Carri's narrative. Breaking with documentary's illusion of staged reality, in the film everything is known to have been set and rearranged for the camera. The historical quality of the cinematic image is, contrary to what usually happens in the genre, blurred and parodied. Indexicality, claims Doane, promises the lure of contingency and of direct access to the present. "But such a lure and such a promise," she adds, in an assertion that could easily refer to Argentine performative documentaries, "carry with them the threat of meaninglessness" (*Emergence* 107).

This type of performativity is precisely what makes post-2000 documentaries different from early-democracy documentaries such as *Juan*. When, in the latter, we saw the crew editing, rewinding, and manipulating filmic material, we recognized that the present was still under construction, that history was a work in progress, and that the *récit* was still open. Indexicality promised the lure of contingency. When, in post-2000 performative documentaries, we see similar strategies, we cannot but perceive them as meaningless, as parodies of a canonical, crystallized mode of representation. If, in the earlier case, the testimonial repertoire was still being created (and was thus an original that could not be critically repeated yet), in the later it has been ongoing for several decades (and its reenactment becomes a repetition that foregrounds such persistence). If "the cinema is perceived as both record and performance" (Doane, *Emergence* 24), it is certainly the latter aspect that describes these films.

Furthermore, the parody of documentary strategies is what makes recent performative documentaries also different from 1990s films such as *Cazadores*, *Montoneros*, and *Botín*. Rather than organizing historical sequences that mobilize the viewer as a social subject, featuring speaking subjects that foster political examination, manipulating indexicality, and staging mobility to challenge the neoliberal present, post-2000 performative documentaries confront the audience with the repetition and saturation of these strategies in contemporary Argentina. They confront the viewer with the hegemonic status—and subsequent loss of critical potential—of testimonial cinema in the early 2000s. Not surprisingly, hegemony increases during *kirchnerismo*, as testimonial discourse coincides with the official discourse of the Argentine government. When referring to *Los rubios*'s release, Carri intuitively condenses this itinerary: *"si la película se hubiese estrenado en 2001 la habrían desestimado como 'otra película sobre desaparecidos' y si se hubiese estrenado en 2005 me habrían tratado de oportunista."* (If the film had been released in 2001, it would have been set aside as "yet another film on disappeared people." If it had been released in 2005, I would have been seen as an opportunistic person) (*Los Rubios: cartografía* 110). As implied in Carri's words, by 2001, testimonial films are already regarded as a canonical (and exhausted) genre—that is why hers would have been seen as *yet another* film on the dictatorship. In 2005, in the midst of *kirchnerismo* and the official centrality of the 1970s, her film would have been considered an opportunistic endeavor. At the time of its release in 2003, however, *Los rubios* illustrates how second-generation testimonial documentaries perform (repeat, expose, and parody) hegemony—they exhibit the process by which testimonial cinema has fixed previously heterogeneous elements around a rather stable unity, around an empty signifier called "military dictatorship."

Televisión x la identidad: Enabling Hegemony in Fiction

In the next chapter, I explore in more detail how the increasing hegemonization of testimonial films runs parallel to increasing fictionalization. But before I fully examine this process and its ideological consequences, I would like to give a snapshot with an analysis of *Televisión x la identidad* that helps better understand testimonial genre's hegemony and better situate the different places of documentary and fiction within this context. Miguel Colom's *Televisión x la identidad* (2007) aired on primetime television, was sponsored by Abuelas de Plaza de Mayo, and supported by the Kirchner administration. Like *Botín de guerra*, it addresses the military's theft of babies born in captivity and tells the story of their later recovery and reunion with their biological families. The series is made of three chapters based on a mixture of fiction and documentary: "Tatiana," "Juan," and "Nietos de la esperanza." "Tatiana" is the story of the first granddaughter identified by Abuelas de Plaza de Mayo in the 1980s. The chapter is a fictional account of her parents' kidnapping, Tatiana's adoption which, in this odd case, was handled legally, her life with the adoptive family, her biological grandmother's search, and the final reunion. "Juan" is the story of Juan Cabandié, an emblematic, publicly active grandson who serves in the Frente para la Victoria (*kirchnerismo*'s political party).[17] The chapter intercalates fictional scenes showing Juan's life with an abusive adoptive father and fictional scenes depicting the steps leading to the discovery of his real identity. "Nietos de la esperanza" features an imaginary character, Lucía Galeano, built on the real experiences of various recovered grandchildren. The chapter shows the kidnapping of Lucía's mother, Lucía's childhood in an unfitting adoptive household, the biological grandparents' efforts to find her, and her restitution to the real family. Each chapter closes the fictional narrative with a (documentary) appearance of the real protagonists, who repeat and reinforce the previous historical account. The real Tatiana certifies the accuracy of the fictional reconstruction of her life while standing on a theater stage surrounded by her family. Once Juan's fictional story is over, we see the real Juan Cabandié at the ESMA giving a speech on the same events we have just witnessed. In the last chapter, several real grandchildren mix with imaginary Lucía and take turns to summarize their personal histories.

Colom's television series, then, relies on a structure that is similar to Blaustein's film. Both of them juxtapose testimonies of recovered children (now adults) with a visual reconstruction of the dictatorship. In both of them, personal histories are built around a parallel chronology: the kidnapping of the biological parents, the lives of their children with adoptive parents, and the final encounter with their real families. As a matter of fact, some of the children who were interviewed in *Botín de guerra* reappear in *Televisión x la identidad*, and their testimonies are almost identical, sometimes even literal, to those in the film. See, for example, the testimonies by Tatiana Ruarte Britos and Juliana García. Yet these seemingly identical narratives yield a very different ideological result, owing to their different uses of documentary and fiction and their different places within postdictatorship history. In spite of the similarity of the individual testimonies, *Televisión x la identidad* relies on a temporal construction that is telling of the ideological implications entailed by the fictional representation of the recent past, especially after the 2000s.

As analyzed in the previous chapter, in *Botín de guerra* the use of documentary was crucial for creating a temporal constellation with strong ideological undertones. Black-and-white footage of major events in Argentine history (coup, demonstrations, collapse, trials, and decrees) built a careful chronological sequence leading to an unfair present that had to be rectified. Color images captured grandmothers' and grandchildren's testimonies in warm, comfortable interiors that provided the necessary environment to counter Menem's decrees and legitimize Abuelas' claim. Color shots of unnerving, threatening streets in 1990s Argentina differentiated the 1970s dictatorship from the present and, at the same time, established their continuity. And color paintings depicting the massacre of indigenous populations created a link between the nineteenth-century discourse of modernity and the 1990s neoliberal rhetoric of progress. It was in the careful mixture of these sets of images that the documentary staged temporality and stated its critical, counterhegemonic, and antiofficial position within the neoliberal '90s. In *Televisión x la identidad*, the juxtaposition of images also creates a temporal constellation with strong ideological undertones. The use of fiction, however, allows for a temporal construction that, rather than criticizing the present, legitimizes its hegemonic and official discourse.

The contrasting representation of space is a case in point. In *Botín de guerra*, interior shots captured comfortable spaces supporting Abuelas' image. These spaces contrasted with exterior shots of unnerving streets in neoliberal Buenos Aires. The fact that these contrasting sets were formed by documentary images was important for historically situating the filmic narrative and creating a critical discourse. In the television series, on the contrary, adoptive households are fictionally portrayed as dark, hostile spaces. Juan's adoptive household, for example, is filled with ghostly shadows, creepy sounds, closed windows, and old furniture that contribute to creating an uncanny feeling. Interior domestic spaces provide the perfect setting for those nightmares that haunt children who are unaware of their real identities—like Juan's recurrent nightmare of a pregnant woman uttering his name. These interior spaces establish a double contrast. First, they contrast with the external spaces where the final (documentary) scenes with the real protagonists are shot. The real Tatiana appears on stage, warmly surrounded by her supporting family. Juan gives his speech at the ESMA in the open air, accompanied by a sympathetic crowd. And the grandchildren who appear at the end of the last chapter share their testimonies in a summer garden full of light, which instills in the spectator the same liberating sensation the protagonists have experienced after learning the truth. More than historically situating the narrative, then, here the contrast between interior and exterior spaces mobilizes emotions. Fictional spaces create an emotional environment built on two opposing semantic fields: dark/bright, uncanny/familiar, latent/manifest, false/true, haunting/liberating, etc.

Yet, rather than configuring new affects, as it happened with fictional testimonies in the early democracy or even with 1990s documentaries, *Televisión x la identidad* activates these semantic fields to solidify already-codified feelings. In *La noche de los lápices*, sensibilities around the figure of the innocent victim and the inhuman crime perpetrator were shaped for the first time, bringing about knowledge that was new to the early democracy. In *Botín, Cazadores*, and *Montoneros*, images of second-generation survivors and of 1970s-era activists stirred original sensations that had still not been conventionalized by the 1990s. *Televisión x la identidad*, on the contrary, builds on all these images to further crystallize naturalized feelings. The appeal to (and consolidation of) naturalized emotions certifies official discourse, granting further authority to the relatives of the disappeared, *kirchnerismo*'s symbolic pillars. As Pablo Bilyk observes, "Televisión x la identidad *intenta reconstruir en sus escenas las emociones de un periodo histórico particular . . . [pero establece] como la realidad de los años '70 en Argentina un relato construido en el presente, empapado por una serie de emociones ajenas a las complejidades históricas que regían ese momento.*" (*Television x identity* aims to reconstruct the emotions of a particular historical period . . . [yet it establishes] as a 1970s-era reality a narrative that is built in the present, touched by emotions that are foreign to the historical complexities of that time) (163).

Second, households contrast with another type of interior space: the institutional space. Courtrooms, documentation centers, orphanages, and all the public institutions staged in the television series are the exact opposite of the hostile adoptive spaces. They are portrayed as warm, familiar, and run by friendly, understanding employees. This contrast also creates emotional tension but, more importantly, builds a temporal constellation that ideologically affects the narration of history. In the television series, the representation of institutional spaces does not register any chronological differences. Although in each chapter white signs carefully indicate dates and places (for example, "Villa Ballester, 24 de octubre de 1977"; "Oficinas Conadi, febrero 2004") (Villa Ballester, October 24, 1977; Conadi offices, February 2004), there are no differences in the representation of public institutions in the military '80s, those in the neoliberal '90s, and those contemporary to the Kirchner administration after 2003. The courtroom, the orphanage, and the police station where Tatiana gets assistance in the 1980s and the public offices that allow Lucía to reunite with her biological family in the midst of *menemismo* are depicted in an equally friendly manner. This friendly depiction matches the warm portrayal of the institutions that help Juan recover his real identity in 2004, during the Kirchner administration.

In *Televisión x la identidad*, the use of fiction allows for a staging of institutions that are not historically marked; it enables representations in which the referential quality of indexicality has been wiped. Unlike what happens in documentary, where "the institution is a social microcosm that reveals an inevitable gap between aims and practices" (Chanan, *Politics* 226), fictional representation diminishes the perception of an institution's social components. Space seems to be outside of time, invariable, and untouched by history and politics. This temporal amalgam places violence outside of the public sphere. It encapsulates history within the private realm, suggesting that violence is related to particular individuals and by no means linked to the political context. Maybe this is why, oddly enough, in the entire series there are no direct references to the military, only some vague allusions to Juan's adoptive father being a retired police officer. Contrary to what one might expect—especially if we take into account that Kirchnerist discourse has always emphasized its radical break with previous political projects—the temporal amalgam, enabled by the use of fiction, ends up legitimizing the present of enunciation. The series reinforces the positive image of each of the state apparatuses (police, court, legal system) and of public institutions in general. Although it might seem paradoxical, this strategic move is crucial for securing hegemony in the wake of a 2001 crisis marked by widespread reticence against everything public, as epitomized in the famous slogan *"que se vayan todos"* (Everyone must go).

A temporal construction with similar ideological connotations lies behind the representation of the revolutionary years immediately preceding the military dictatorship. Black-and-white images fictionalizing a home movie open the first chapter. The fictional video shows Tatiana's parents staging a puppet show for the children of a poor suburban neighborhood. The voice of Tatiana's grandmother accompanies the scenes, as she explains to her granddaughter what she is watching and, by extension, her (and the television series') prehistory: *"Tus papás se conocieron en Córdoba. . . . Ellos formaban parte de un grupo de titiriteros que visitaban las villas y los barrios más pobres. Tu mamá y tu papá buscaban apasionadamente su lugar en el mundo y, como ese lugar no existía, pensaban que había llegado la hora de imaginar un mundo nuevo."* (Your parents met in Córdoba. . . . They were part of a group of puppeteers who visited slums and poor neighborhoods. Your mom and your dad were passionately searching for their place in this world. Since that place did not exist, they thought that the time had come to imagine a new world.) This romanticized explanation is the only reference to left-leaning activism in the entire series—an explanation further romanticized, as Bilyk notices, by the use of a child's perspective to frame recent history (162).

The revolutionary '70s are condensed in domestic, childish scenes outside of the main narrative in the chapters. They are represented as a romantic utopia even further removed from politics and history than what is told in the chapters. This depoliticized distance is underscored by the choice of format and costumes. The scenes in the home movie seem much older than those telling Tatiana's story, in large part because they were shot in black and white with a handheld camera and because Tatiana's parents are wearing typical '70s-era clothes, such as wide-leg flare jeans and loose shirts, that contrast with the more modern outfits in the main narrative. The fictional home movie thus gives the impression that the

Distortion and History in Performative Documentaries | 133

Figure 3.2. Fictional home movie in "Tatiana."

revolutionary '70s are an archaic, romantic utopia—even though, strictly speaking, they only took place a couple of months prior to the history represented in the central narrative. As it happened with the portrayal of institutional spaces, the use of fiction allows for a decrease in indexicality. What we are seeing in the home movie is not a documentary but something that *looks like* a documentary. The scenes we are watching do not belong to the 1970s but *resemble* the 1970s. In other words, instead of privileging an indexical image, *Televisión x la identidad* offers an iconic representation of the revolutionary years—a representation in which the sign visually resembles the referent as opposed to being materially connected to the referent.[18] And, if indexicality underscores the historical qualities of the referent, iconicity has the opposite effect: it wipes out the connection with history.

This type of iconic representation is, once again, attuned to the official discourse of *kirchnerismo*. Although I explore in depth the connections among fiction, iconicity, and (the preclusion of) historical examination during *kirchnerismo* in the next chapter, I would like to anticipate here that iconicity and romantization are inextricably linked and that this link permeates Kirchnerist discourse.[19] Indeed, Néstor Kirchner's famous speech at the ESMA for the twenty-eight anniversary of the military coup—the same event in which the real Juan Cabandié gave the speech featured in *Televisión x la identidad*—relies on a romantic image of 1970s' militants that reminds us of Tatiana's parents in the television series: "Cuando recién veía las manos, cuando cantaban el himno, veía los brazos de mis compañeros, de la generación que creyó y que sigue creyendo en los que quedamos que este país se puede cambiar. . .que ha dejado un sendero, su vida, sus madres, que ha dejado sus abuelas y que ha dejado sus hijos" (As I was just looking at the hands, as I was listening to people singing our national anthem, I saw the arms of my comrades, of the generation who believed, and still believes, that this country can change. . .a generation who has left a path, their lives, their mothers, their grandmothers, and their children) ("Discurso" n.p.).[20]

In *Testimonio: on the Politics of Truth*, Beverley points out that: "paradoxically *testimonio* does not seem particularly well suited for periods of postrevolutionary consolidation, perhaps because its very dynamics depend on the conditions of dramatic social and cultural inequality that fuel the revolutionary impulse in the first place" (61). Although ultimately referring to a very different context, this statement helps understand the main transformation that happened between *Botín de guerra* and *Televisión x la identidad*: the achievement of hegemony. The journey from Blaustein's documentary to the 2007 television series corresponds exactly with testimonial narrative's itinerary from counterhegemony to hegemony—a hegemony best evidenced by the need to include testimonies from real grandchildren to certify *Televisión*'s chapters. And I would like to highlight, following Laclau and Mouffe once again, that it is the recent past (the 1970s) the empty signifier that lies behind the articulation of hegemonic identity. The 1970s are the nodal point articulating universal signification. The loss of historical and political appeal registered in contemporary performative documentaries such as *Papá Iván* and *Los rubios* seems to be directly linked to the ideological implications of this passage from counterhegemony to hegemony as well as to the universalization and erasure that this passage necessarily entails.

It is in light of this historical transformation that I would like to reassess the different uses of documentary and fiction. "If there is an opposition between contemporary cinema's attitudes towards the past of struggle and dictatorship," observes Andermann, referring both to *Papá Iván* and *Los rubios*, "it is not one between fiction and documentary. . . . Rather, a radical break has appeared between the 'survivors' tales' of the generation of 1960s and 1970s political activists and the 'secondary witnessing' or 'postmemory' of their children" (*New Argentine* 107). Although I agree with the existence of two opposing intergenerational discourses—as seen in the contrast between María Inés Roqué's personal testimony and her father's letter, or in the ironic title and in the parodic treatment of the INCAA's statement in *Los rubios*—I actually believe that there are two additional ideological differences in post-2000 films that should not remain unnoticed: one between the uses of documentary and fiction and another (interrelated) one between two groups within the second generation. While performative documentaries register the increasing hegemonization of testimonial cinema, fiction tends to accompany this process. Whereas documentary in general evidences the passage from alternative version to official history, fiction mostly enables hegemony. As seen in *Televisión x la identidad*, the use of fiction allows for testimonial narratives legitimizing the present of enunciation. Fiction tends to create environments that solidify naturalized emotions, contribute to the erasure of the historically marked quality of indexical images, and help build a romanticized, iconic representation of the revolutionary '70s. As opposed to what happened in the early democracy, when documentary and fiction were two complementary dimensions of testimonial cinema, an ideological rift has taken place together with the hegemonization of the genre since the 2000s.

This rift is, however, far from being undisputable. As I mentioned earlier in the book, not only are documentary and fiction highly contested categories but have also, as we have just seen in *Televisión x la identidad*, become quite hybrid since the 1990s. Yet, as I have been arguing so far, the different uses of the two genres entail important ideological consequences, particularly when taking into account the impact on iconicity and indexicality. Furthermore, I contend that this clash between documentary and fiction is the formal counterpart of an ideological tension among the members of the second generation regarding recent history, especially regarding the political projects of the first generation. Whereas fiction allows for an iconic representation of the revolutionary years very much attuned to human rights organizations such as H.I.J.O.S., the manipulation of indexicality in performative documentaries often challenges such discourse. Second-generation testimonial films thus reveal the existence of two tendencies at odds in contemporary Argentina (and in contemporary representations of Argentina): a commodification of the recent past, where the 1970s are an invariable and static referent (an empty signifier) that serves as a background for cultural creation, and a politicized reading of that commodification, where the 1970s are still a terrain for examination. Thus, although I am interested in ideologically distinguishing the two genres, my intention is less to create a normative baseline for the evaluation of contemporary cultural products than to argue for a reading of post-2000 second-generation cinema as a site of political negotiation. Rather than seeing second-generation narratives as if there were no difference between documentary and fiction, between the use of a child's or an adult's perspective, or between the post-2000s and the early democracy, I think that we need to interpret them, as I aim to do in these last two chapters, as sites of ideological confrontation.[21]

Notes

1. For a detailed explanation of the 2001 economic crisis, see Epstein and Pion-Berlin; Romero, *La crisis*; Stiglitz.

2. These observations actually suggest that, as I claimed in the previous chapter, *(h)istorias cotidianas* fits better within the 1990s. Although Habegger is the son of a missing activist—and we could thus say that the second generation serves in this film as both the speaking subject and the subject of speech—he stages a typical '90s narrative in which the filmmaker shoots the interviews but is not the primary speaker within the film.

3. See Bruzzi; Chanan, *Politics*; Nichols, *Introduction*; and Renov for further details on this trend outside of Latin America.

4. See Andermann, *New Argentine* 93–130 and Piedras, *El cine documental* 63–192 for a more detailed history of this trend in Argentina. In his book, Piedras chooses the terms "first-person documentary" over Bruzzi and Nichols's "performative documentary" because he finds the latter to be too restrictive. For Piedras, first-person documentaries are films that incorporate different manifestations of the auteurial self and not only the filmmaker's body (for example, her or his voiceover). Although I find Piedras's definition compelling (and more attuned to some of the films, such as Carri's *Cuatreros*), I believe that the more broadly understood category of performative documentary accurately describes most post-2000 Argentine films where the filmmaker's body is explicitly included in the narrative—as seen in the majority of the films analyzed in this chapter. I thus choose to keep this more common category to avoid confusion. More importantly, *performative* carries additional meanings (repetitive, parodic, etc.) that, as I contend in the next paragraphs, are relevant to an understanding of these films' role after the year 2000.

5. Although it would take my argument in another direction (and I will thus not explore it here further), it would be fruitful to read this counterpoint from a perspective based on gender. The poetic, expressive, and hesitant female voices could be read, rather than as an affirmation of characteristics that have traditionally been used to define women's "essence," as a kind of "strategic essentialism" in Gayatri Spivak's sense (Ray 205)—that is, a temporary mimetic strategy used by minority groups themselves to achieve certain goals. This mimetic strategy allows women filmmakers to challenge the male-dominated, patriarchal edge of 1960s and '70s-era revolutionary projects as well as to decenter and question conventional representations of history. The other documentaries created by women filmmakers that I mention in this chapter (*Los rubios, En memoria de los pájaros, Encontrando a Víctor, Che vo cachai, Tiempo suspendido, Cuatreros, Diario argentino, El tiempo y la sangre*, and *Un tal Ragone*) are indeed cogent examples of this tendency.

6. *Papá Iván* has been awarded a *Premio Ariel* (Mexico, 2003) in the category "best short documentary," a *Grand Coral First Prize* at the Havana Film Festival (Cuba, 2000), the second prize at the Festival Cinematografico Della Torino (Italy, 2004), and an honorable mention at the Festival "Voces Contra el Silencio" (Mexico, 2003); the latter three in the documentary category.

7. For a more detailed reading of the film's narrative strategies, see my article coauthored with Antonio Gómez, "Más allá del 'formato memoria'."

8. In Carri's words: *"El material se fue acumulando. . . . La madre de mi papá me entregó unas cuantas valijas que guardaban, intactos, desde los cuadernos escolares de su hijo hasta cada una de las burocráticas respuestas que obispos y funcionarios le enviaron cuando ella pedía por su vida. La tía de mi madre también me entregó cajas con documentos. . . . De la casa de cada persona que entrevisté, me retiraba con algún souvenir."* (Materials kept accumulating. . . . My dad's mother gave me many suitcases containing everything intact: from his son's school notebooks to every single bureaucratic reply sent by bishops and public officers

whenever she asked for his life. My mother's aunt also gave me boxes with documents. . . . I left each house from each person I interviewed with some sort of souvenir.) (*Los Rubios: cartografía* 9).

9. Gabriela Nouzeilles disagrees with Kohan's observation and claims that it is not authorship (or lack thereof) that matters in this scene but the fact that what is being read is a "specter of revolutionary thought" (271); the passage highlights the revolutionary potential of criminals. For Nouzeilles, Roberto Carri's book works in the film the same way as Iván Roqué's letter: as a political testament. What matters in *Los rubios* is that Albertina Carri invokes this testament to break away from her father's revolutionary project. While I find this argument sound and a thorough anticipation of what will happen in *Cuatreros*, I believe that Kohan and Nouzeilles's readings are not really at odds with each other. I think that the scene alludes at the same time to a distortion of referentiality and to a displacement of the authority of 1960s and '70s-era revolutionary thought, two dimensions that are deeply linked in post-2000 documentary.

10. There is also another possible interpretation: based on the mimetic theory of trauma, these remarks allude to healing. After having finished the documentary, Roqué has reached the conclusion that she does not want to expose herself to her traumatic past any longer. She is no longer willing to hypnotically reenact the traumatic experience. I owe this insight to Adolfo Bejar.

11. Although not contemplated in the readings, the two films could also be seen as examples of "family" or "quiet" trauma: "the impact of a major public event on relatives indirectly involved in terror" (Kaplan, Ann, 1).

12. Breaking with the idea that a monolithic perspective represented by the camera rules the field of vision, Hirsch makes a distinction between the "gaze," which "is external to human subjects situating them authoritatively in ideology, constituting them in their subjectivity" ("Surviving" 23) and the "look," which "is located at a specific point; it is local and contingent, mutual and reversible, traversed by desire and defined by lack" ("Surviving" 23; *Family* 11). Postmemorial viewers, she argues, use repetition, repositioning, and reintegration as aesthetic strategies that allow for a transformation of gaze into look; a transformation that enables mourning.

13. Though they do not quite fit within this chapter, there are at least three other contemporaneous films that display similar strategies, confirming the existence of a broader tendency in Argentine documentary and alluding to testimonial cinema's canonization. Vanessa Ragone's *Un tal Ragone* (2002) only very indirectly talks about the dictatorship yet also shows the filmmaker wandering through the streets and collecting fragmentary testimonies on his father, a journalist who died some years prior to the shooting. As it happened in the other films in this chapter, testimonies do not result in a coherent narrative, and mobility does not lead to new findings. In *El tiempo y la sangre* (2004), Alejandra Almirón mixes unidentified, disconnected footage to explore how the military repression devastated Morón, a neighborhood in west Buenos Aires. Although only the director's voice appears in the film, the documentary becomes a parody of testimonial conventions, as reflected in the mobile shots disrupting the documentary's talking heads. Lupe Pérez García's *Diario argentino* (2006) goes beyond the dictatorship to stage the political contradictions of recent history broadly understood. The documentary shows how Pérez García, born in Argentina in 1973 and exiled in Spain since the 2001 economic crisis, returns to her home country to examine the roots of her confusion between left and right—a metaphor for the ideological confusion

she encounters, even after studying (and showing) archival footage and listening to people's narratives. While not exactly postdictatorship second-generation performative films, these narratives share several patterns with those in this chapter—in particular, the use of documentary to repeat, expose, and parody the conventions driving the testimonial genre. As I mentioned in the book's introduction, however, representation patterns at a specific moment constitute less a homogeneous entity than a tendency. Benjamín Ávila's *Nietos. Identidad y Memoria* (2004) and Joaquín Daglio's *Padres de la Plaza* (2010), for instance, can be quoted as contemporaneous examples of testimonial documentaries built around a quite conventional, albeit residual, format.

14. For further details on the multiplicity of meanings entailed by *performance*, see Bial; Schechner; Taylor, *The Archive and the Repertoire*; *Disappearing Acts*; and *Performance*.

15. I here say *can result* because, even though most performance scholars agree that performance entails repetition (of a repertoire, of culturally coded and recognizable patterns, of earlier gestures and behaviors), there are different views on the effects of such repetition. For Hutcheon, for instance, repetition tends to produce an ironic effect (24). For Taylor, performance can normalize behavior, transmit a sense of identity, reenact memory, or shock and challenge (*Performance* 41; *Archive* xiii–xix). For Carlson, repetition is grounded in a consciousness of doubleness that places actions in mental comparison with a potential, ideal, or remembered original model (71). For Parker and Sedgwick's more deconstructive view, performance breaks the causal relationship with an original referent and even empties this referent out of meaning (168). I believe that this chapter shows that, except perhaps for some of the effects that Taylor mentions (normalize behavior, transmit identity, and reenact memory), most second-generation performative documentaries combine all the other possibilities.

16. Gustavo Noriega clarifies this point in his *Estudio crítico*. Although the INCAA had originally rejected funding for the project, *Los rubios* was selected for participation at BAFICI, which obliged the INCAA to provide the necessary funds to finish the film (31, 70). I believe, however, that this fact does not alter the performative nature of the discussion, as it could have been edited out of the film once funds became available.

17. Ever since he found out about his real biological identity, Cabandié has served as a public officer for *kirchnerismo*. He was legislator between 2007 and 2013, national deputy between 2013 and 2015, and vice president of the Comisión de Defensa al Consumidor since 2015. He is also one of the most active militants in La cámpora, a Peronist youth organization founded by Kirchner's son in 2003 that strongly supported the Kirchner administration.

18. Here, *iconic* is by no means related to van der Kolk's claim that traumatic memories are nonrepresentational, nonsymbolic, and thus iconic (521). As Leys carefully explains (250–254), van der Kolk not only has poor evidence to sustain this claim but also confuses Peircean terminology—and, I add, is unaware of the triadic relationship among the symbolic, iconic, and indexical dimensions.

19. See Guglielmucci for a thorough ethnography of the process of institutionalization of memory during *kirchnerismo*. See Delgado and Sosa for a detailed summary of filmic trends in this period.

20. There are two other television series that, even though they could not be defined as "testimonial" in the sense that I have been using the term in this book, resemble *Televisión x la identidad* and point to the link between fictionalization and hegemony that I have emphasized in this chapter: *Montecristo* (2006), a soap opera also directed by Colom that received record high ratings, was awarded a *Martín Fierro de Oro*—the Argentine version of an

Emmy—and was granted special distinction by the Argentine National Senate, and *Volver a nacer* (2012), a miniseries by Daniel De Felippo that aired on Argentine Public Television. In the two series, the hidden history of children born to disappeared parents drives the thriller-like and melodramatic narratives. Both tell the story of two opposing sets of characters: those who either took part in or were complicit with the abduction of children during the dictatorship and those who, in the 2000s, courageously solve the mystery and allow for their reunion with their biological families. Interesting is to note that both series rely on several characteristics also present in *Televisión x la identidad*: a solidification of naturalized emotions regarding the dictatorship, a privatization of state violence (here also most villains are civilians), and a romantic view of 1970s-era activism. The two series received government support, and *Montecristo*'s final episode broadcast at Luna Park, a huge theater in Buenos Aires, with Abuelas de Plaza de Mayo and several recovered grandchildren as special guests.

21. In this sense, my approach to second-generation production slightly differs from that of Ros and Blejmar. I think that Ros's concept of self-aware memory and Blejmar's notion of playful memory do not fully take into account the more iconic and hegemonic versions portrayed in fictions that are also part of the second generation, such as those analyzed in the next chapter.

4 Emotion and History in Post-2000 Second-Generation Iconic Fictions

After examining family photographs, wearing her father's clothes, and recreating multiple versions of his death, Carla Crespo—who is in her thirties—reaches a counterintuitive conclusion that is commonly heard in contemporary Argentina: she is now older than her father. This insight marks a turning point in Lola Arias's *Mi vida después* (2010), a play in which six men and women explore how 1970s-era collective history molded their own family narratives. Following Crespo's statement, the stage is all motion. The scenery changes quickly, the six stories interrupt one another, and the music becomes so loud that the audience is tempted to cover their ears. For Crespo, being older than her own father is more disturbing than the hole left by his absence or the impossibility of a shared future. It distresses her even more than the uncertainty of his death. Being older than her father seems to define the limit of what she can take. This scene of age recognition is not limited to Arias's play; Albertina Carri makes a similar statement in *Los rubios*, Martín Mórtola Oesterheld and Úrsula Méndez acknowledge the temporal convergence in Habegger's *(h)istorias cotidianas*, and María Inés Roqué opens *Papá Iván* with an analogous observation. In contemporary Argentina, the disquieting recognition of "out-aging" one's parents has become an identity marker and a collective sign of affiliation for members of the second generation.

Although members of the second generation are now older than their parents, they are exactly the same age as postdictatorship cinema. Postdictatorship films grew up as the second-generation members were growing up, evolved as they were evolving, and reached adulthood (perhaps even a saturation point) as they became adults. In fact, looking back at the history of the field, we notice that there has always been a strong correlation between the second generation's age and these films' formal choices—a correlation marked by the three consecutive stages in the postdictatorship period that I have been emphasizing in this book. As the second generation was growing up (the first stage), children and teenagers played a crucial role in narrative development. This protagonism is evident in three of the most canonical films of those years: María Luisa Bemberg's *Camila* (1984), Luis Puenzo's *La historia oficial*, and Héctor Olivera's *La noche de los lápices*. Here, as we saw in the first chapter, an unborn child, a young girl, and a group of high school–aged teenagers respectively encompassed the key features of the early democracy. It was because of these characters that the plots unfolded, that the films were able to undo the official version of history, and that an alternate version was asserted from the victim's perspective. More importantly, these figures enabled the creation of the childlike vision that marked the early years of the new democracy: the eagerness to know, the first attempts to tell, and even the innocence that was necessary in order to simplify. In this sense, Argentine films from the 1980s embodied typical modern discourse, which, as Karen Lury points out, has mapped out a narrative of progress whereby the child acts "as the personification of development itself" (25).

Both inheritor of the past and vehicle for the future, the modern figure of the child is, like the idea of the modern nation, a "mutually consolidating myth," especially in postwar periods (Lury 26). In the late 1990s, as second-generation members became young adults who were able to interrogate the past and give voice to their own stories, postdictatorship cinema began a new (second) stage and was henceforth dominated by a new genre: testimonial documentary. Attuned to the increasing visibility of organizations such as Abuelas de Plaza de Mayo and H.I.J.O.S., young adults born to disappeared parents were the leading narrators in stories about the regime, as in Blaustein's *Botín de guerra*. Given the close connections between the second generation and postdictatorship cinema, it is unsurprising that after 2000 (the third stage), several of the most prominent cultural representations of the military dictatorship have been performative documentaries created by second-generation filmmakers who reexamine the recent past from an adult's perspective. In these documentaries, as analyzed in the previous chapter, the second-generation members are not simply protagonists interviewed to narrate their own stories (like in the documentaries of the second stage) but also filmmakers who create them, direct them, and organize their narratives from an adult lens.

Yet, there is another post-2000 trend that seems to go against the history of the field: fiction films by second-generation filmmakers that return to a child's or a teenager's perspective and to an "archaic" 1980s format. Films in this line include Gastón Biraben's *Cautiva* (2005), Pablo Agüero's *Salamandra* (2008), Daniel Bustamante's *Andrés no quiere dormir la siesta* (2009), Paula Markovitch's *El premio* (2011), and Benjamín Ávila's *Infancia clandestina* (2012). In *Infancia clandestina*, Ávila reenacts his own experience as a child of radical Montoneros through a fictional character, twelve-year-old Juan. *El premio* narrates the story of a seven-year-old girl who, like director Markovitch herself, lives as an internal exile in a small coastal town and must keep an important secret to save her family—a plot that resembles *Salamandra*, a fictionalization of Agüero's childhood in Patagonia. In *Cautiva*, Biraben chooses an illegally adopted female protagonist as a synecdoche for all the members of his generation who have been deprived of their identity by the military. Biraben's strategy also drives *Andrés no quiere dormir la siesta*, where a fictional Andrés metonymically represents all children—including Bustamante, the director—who gradually register the horrific political environment surrounding them. These films are thus, to borrow Lury's term, "double-voiced": children and adolescents' views of the world are framed by the adult's retrospective understanding and projection (109). There is a form of ventriloquism in which the adult author speaks for the child that she or he remembers, a retroactive inner dialogue that yields an in-between temporality (Lury 111). As we will see later on, this double voice and its resulting temporality bear highly paradoxical ideological connotations in the Argentine case.[1]

Staging a child or adolescent's gaze is not, however, exclusive to post-2000 Argentina. As Vicky Lebeau has carefully examined, cinema has laid claim to this type of portrayal since its inception (20–55). Shaping notions of childhood and adolescence was inseparable from their visual representation, as evidenced by the volume of early films focusing on these figures, such as Louis Lumiére's *Repas de Bébé* (1895). In Latin America, Rocha and Seminet specify, children and teenagers have served as narrative focalizers since at least Luis Buñuel's *Los olvidados* (Mexico, 1950) and Leonardo Favio's *Crónica de un niño solo* (Argentina, 1965) (Rocha and Seminet 6–20). In the early 2000s, such films became one of the most popular genres, both in Latin America and around the world, as in *El espinazo del diablo* (Mexico-Spain 2001); *Kamchatka* (Argentina, 2002); *Valentín* (Argentina, 2002); *Machuca* (Chile, 2004); *Voces inocentes* (Mexico-El Salvador, 2005); *O ano em que meus pais saíram de férias* (Brazil, 2006); *Persepolis* (United States, 2007); *Paisito* (Uruguay, 2008); and *Boyhood* (United States, 2014), to name but a few.[2] Indeed, Sarah Thomas proposes that this recent proliferation has given rise to a well-defined subgenre, the "child-centered (post)-civil conflict film" (236)—a type of film featuring more affluent child protagonists whose lives have been affected by their nations' civil conflicts. In this sense, then, post-2000 second-generation Argentine films are not archaic but rather attuned to the latest developments in the transnational industry.

That being said, if we consider the particular history of postdictatorship cinema in Argentina, we see that these films go against the grain, as they return to a (much earlier) 1980s format. In other words, although the films belong to the third postdictatorship stage in terms of the historical moment of their production, aesthetically they return to the first stage, interrupting what seemed to be a diachronic tendency. This cultural exception raises a number of questions: Why do these second-generation filmmakers choose a format at odds with the one that apparently corresponds to their own generation? What are the aesthetic implications of moving backward in the history of the field? What are the ideological connotations of narrating the military dictatorship from a child or teenager's perspective after 2000, when the recent past lies at the center of public discourse and its crucial aspects are already known both nationally and internationally?

These questions have rarely been addressed by scholars working on Argentine cinema. Most of them have analyzed the films as if there were no significant differences between their own aesthetic configurations and those pursued by the other members of the second generation. David Blaustein, for example, considers *Cautiva* a good fictional representative of the "enhancement of criteria regarding memory" that is typical of contemporary documentaries (155). Rodolfo Hermida sees in its aesthetic makeup the traces of a whole generation influenced by professional film schools (15). These films have also been commonly interpreted as if there were no distinction between documentary and fiction. For instance, Susana Kaiser points out that since the end of the military dictatorship, the "cinematic camera [acts] as a historian" (101) in both genres. Moreover, the fictional works in this category have been examined as if there were no substantial differences between creating a narrative from a nonadult perspective after 2000 and using the same approach in the early democracy. In fact, it is common to compare the use of children or teenagers after 2000 with the representational strategies evident in *La historia oficial* (Blaustein 153; Dufays; Kaiser 106; Gorodischer; Scholz).

The current chapter proposes an alternative interpretation of this phenomenon. Instead of analyzing the above-mentioned films as additional examples of post-2000 second-generation narratives with no significant variations, I contend that their cultural exception has important ideological consequences. In these films, which I call "iconic fictions," the use of fiction allows for the cinematic images' iconic dimension to predominate over their indexical dimension. This predominance solidifies emotions, precludes examination, and to some extent conflicts with the commonplace belief that a child's or teenager's viewpoint is the basis for a successful historical representation. As an illustration, the first section of my chapter centers on *Cautiva*, a film that I find paradigmatic of this recent trend. I explain how this film's use of fiction results in an anachronism that both alludes to a stable consensus regarding the dictatorship and impedes further exploration—a result found, as I briefly analyze, in other representative films such as *Andrés no quiere dormir la siesta*, *El premio*, and *Salamandra*. In the second section, focusing on *Infancia clandestina*, I explore the fictional construction of 1970s-era activism as a highly iconic sign. This type of iconicity facilitates emotion yet prevents the configuration of new affects.

Before beginning my analysis, however, I find it necessary to clarify what I mean by a "child or teenager's point of view." As several scholars have carefully explained, childhood and adolescence are not biological categories so much as notions that have been socially constructed (Ariés; Calvert; Jenkins; Lury; Steedman). These notions, which first appeared in the Middle Ages, became especially relevant in the nineteenth century, alongside the emergence of modern disciplines such as psychoanalysis, history, pedagogy, and anthropology. Rather than referring to a clearly determined age population with fixed physical and psychological attributes, these categories helped conceptualize (and naturalize) ideas that were crucial to modern discourse: development, progress, evolution, and the self. As Henry Jenkins notes, the expansion of commercial capitalism and the rise of the middle classes were essential to the modern conception of the child as the future of market economy, as the vehicle for the bourgeois desire for social betterment, and as the core of the transfer of property (16)—a conception that, as Nick Lee and Patricia Holland rightly observe, is also open to constant historical transformation and has indeed changed in light of the social instability brought forth by the global economic crisis (Lee 15; Holland ix–xv). Moreover, as Jenkins claims, the myth, likewise questioned by globalization (Holland 12), that childhood innocence is eternal, natural, and universal, as well as the resulting idea that children are apolitical, have led adults to project their own anxieties, demands, and ideologies onto them (Jenkins 1–15). Such mythologies, Holland states, "allow abstract 'childhood' to become a depository for many precious qualities that 'adulthood' needs but which are incompatible with adult status. . . . Ultimately, childhood cannot be contained, the boundaries will not hold. The relationship between childhood and adulthood is not a dichotomy but a variety of fluctuating states, constantly under negotiation" (15–16).[3]

When I say, then, that post-2000 fiction films stage a child or teenager's point of view, I do not mean to imply that they reflect perspectives unanimously shared by a fixed set of natural human beings called children or adolescents. What I mean is that these films resort to socially constructed notions of the child and the adolescent in creating their narrative viewpoints. Further, this perspective can be formed in several ways. Anette Kuhn, for example, claims that any film, regardless of its content, is capable of replaying mental states typically experienced during childhood. Drawing from object-relations psychoanalysis, Kuhn argues that the filmic medium—through spatiality, liminality, and motion—is especially suitable for recreating preconscious experiences and thus echoes the way in which children negotiate the boundaries between inner and outer worlds (95–96). After surveying extensive scholarship on childhood and cinema, Carolina Rocha and Georgia Seminet have noted two fundamental possibilities for narrative construction: films are either produced *by* or *for* children and teenagers (as is the case with US teen-pic dramas appealing to young cinemagoers) or they involve children and teenagers as "narrative devices or focalizers in plots written by adults" (3). It is the latter possibility that, as I have explained in the previous paragraphs, best describes second-generation fiction films in Argentina. Unlike the performative documentaries that reexamine the past from an adult perspective, in these narratives the filmmakers return to a 1980s "archaic" format to recreate their own perspectives as children and teenagers growing up during the dictatorship.[4] The ideological effects of this archaic return are the main focus of this chapter. In sum, if the previous chapter analyzes how second-generation documentaries perform hegemony, this chapter elaborates on what I anticipated with *Televisión x la identidad*: second-generation iconic fictions enable hegemony, revealing ideological tensions that ultimately urge a reading of post-2000 second-generation cultural production as a site of political confrontation.

Anachronistic Resemblances: The Use of a Teenager's Perspective in *Cautiva*

Starting with its very first scenes, *Cautiva*—shot between 2001 and 2002, released at international film festivals in 2004 and in Argentina in October 2005— emphasizes the tension between documentary and fiction that insinuates the film's ideological implications. A caption highlighting the narrative's hybrid stance on reality ("This film is a fiction film based on real events")[5] precedes two opening sequences. Archival footage displaying Argentina's victory in the 1978 FIFA World Cup is followed by a sequence of fictional scenes in which Cristina (the protagonist) and her family celebrate the girl's birthday in 1994. This initial time loop aside, Gastón Biraben's debut feature has a clear-cut chronological plot. One day, fifteen-year-old Cristina is forced to leave during school hours to see a judge, who tells her that her parents are actually her adoptive parents and that her biological parents disappeared in 1978, during the military dictatorship. The rest of the film narrates how the teenager gradually learns both about her real parents and about recent Argentine history, finally coming to terms with her new identity.

Cautiva's connections with adolescence are not restricted to the choice of a young protagonist. The film also links the spectator to a teenage perspective through two interrelated strategies: the development of the narrative structure and the emphasis on psychological characteristics traditionally associated with teenage subjectivities. Biraben's film is organized as a coming-of-age story in which Cristina undergoes a series of identity crises and progressively detaches herself from her (adoptive) parents' values until she attains a new and more mature subjectivity. The filmic structure follows this development and enhances it through the choice of a particular genre: the political thriller. In *Cautiva*, age and genre are inextricable. As the girl matures, suspense intensifies; as she confronts her new identity, the film reaches its climax and history yields its final truth. Cristina's quest for her biological identity is told in the vein of a detective story in which the characters' lives always seem to be in danger; the critical clues to reconstructing the truth are whispered urgently in a dark basement, and the spectator ultimately realizes that the keys to solving the problem had been in plain sight from the very beginning—the baby was born during the final soccer game documented in the archival footage. As most of the film's reviews announce, *Cautiva* is a political thriller in every possible sense, one based on (indeed, dependent on) the psychological characteristics that have been historically linked to the concept of adolescence: identity crises, disengagement from the adult world, the influence of peer groups, periods of stress and storminess, and moments of self-consciousness.[6] These characteristics create an emotional atmosphere of doubt, increasing knowledge, and revelation. As the viewer accompanies Cristina in her subjective turmoil, she is also emotionally readied for the thriller's resolution and its political implications.

It is because of these very strategies that most readings (Blaustein 153; Kaiser 106; Gorodischer; Scholz) trace a parallel between *Cautiva* and the canonical *La historia oficial*. In both films, the private details associated with a child born to disappeared parents force the protagonists (and the spectator) to reexamine collective history, while the choice of an innocent character underscores the traumatic effects of the recent past, creating a narrative to denounce its atrocities. In the two fictions, then, the mystery surrounding a child impels a thriller, and the truth hidden in the thriller's plot ultimately unveils a political truth. In other words, according to these readings, both films employ a child's or adolescent's gaze as the basis for effective historical representation.[7]

Although the choice of age and genre certainly invite a parallel reading of *Cautiva* and *La historia oficial*, the two films are also marked by significant difference due to the specific historical moments of their release. *La historia oficial* confronts the spectator with unknown (or untold) aspects of the recent past. As with a detective, the audience joins the protagonists in deciphering clues that will simultaneously reveal Gaby's history and a new version of collective history that is missing in the early democracy. *Cautiva*, however, employs a teenage perspective to finally reveal what the spectator has known for at least thirty years—a strategy that, referring to the film, Inela Selimovic has called "mnemonic straightforwardness" for its uncomplicated thematic representation of memory (423). The closing captions make the difference quite visible: "Although the number of victims of Argentina's last military dictatorship is uncertain, they are supposed to be around 30,000. Those who are responsible, except for some cases of home arrest, are free, protected by laws that were created in their benefit by subsequent democratic governments. To date, 74 children of disappeared people have been identified. The fate of many more is still unknown. The search for them continues." If watching Puenzo's film introduces the audience to a new historical map, the viewer of *Cautiva* is eventually faced with recent Argentine history's best-known facts, both at home and abroad. The implied assumption, post-2000, that these facts have yet to be revealed, is as counterintuitive as Cristina's character; as late as 1994, she still knows nothing about the military dictatorship.[8] *Cautiva*, a post-2000 second-generation film released at a moment when the history of the military dictatorship lies at the center of public discourse, is told using a typical 1980s format.

The film's climax further attests to this temporal slippage. After furtively examining documents, asking questions that in 1994 are strangely perceived as dangerous, and secretly navigating the city, Cristina meets an old nurse who witnessed her birth and who is supposed to finally tell her the truth about her parents. This final revelation is accompanied by the only formal variation, except for the opening archival footage, that the film incorporates into its own texture: a sequence of scenes composing a flashback that was shot with a handheld camera and uses a different color scheme and filter. These temporal and formal changes underscore the spectator's impression of watching both Cristina's hidden history and the resolution of the political thriller. Yet, just like Cristina upon finishing the flashback—which confirms what she had known all along: that she was born to disappeared parents—the viewer's acquired knowledge of recent history equals her prior knowledge. Despite the film's detective-like atmosphere and constant allusions to undisclosed dimensions of the recent past, the spectator's only task is, as Kaiser suggests, "to verify if what is being represented matches the already-documented facts" (103). As opposed to post-2000 second-generation documentaries, Biraben's film requires that the viewer return to a perspective grounded in the early democracy, to the beginnings of postdictatorship cinema.

In her analysis of *Cautiva*, Selimovic suggests two possibilities for this return to an earlier viewpoint: the film could be staging a delayed process of grief, as it refers to losses that have been "both ongoing and entirely delayed for those directly stricken by such grief since 1985" (426), or it could be the result of Biraben's "delayed" perspective as an exile who has been living in Los Angeles for twenty years and might be unaware of subsequent developments in postdictatorship Argentine cinema (424). In either case, we could say that the in-between temporality stemming from the film's double voice (i.e., from Biraben's retrospective understanding of the past) results in an anachronism. Released in 2004 and 2005, *Cautiva*, a second-generation debut, is built like a 1980s film.

This being said, one need not address the history of postdictatorship cinema in order to perceive *Cautiva*'s anachronistic nature; the filmic texture itself reveals this temporal dissonance. A brief analysis of how the symbolic, indexical, and iconic dimensions merge in *Cautiva* reveals the connections between the film's formal exceptionality and its ideological implications. Released after 2000 and set in 1994, the first formal contradiction is, as I have already suggested, the anachronism of the film's symbolic dimension. The viewer notices this temporal disparity not only in its narrative format, but also in its language. The main characters, for example, speak as they would have spoken in the 1980s, in the first years of the new democracy—an anachronism that also attests to the indexical aspect of verbal language, which "depend[s] for full intelligibility on knowledge of the point in time at which a message was uttered" (Wollen 122).

Cristina's high school friends are probably the best example of this archaism, confirming the connections between a teenage perspective and the film's temporal dissonance. One of Cristina's friends is expelled because she aggressively complains to her teacher about the presidential decrees releasing members of the military—decrees that were in fact signed five years prior to the film's primary action. Another classmate claims that the former girl's parents were subversive communists who killed priests during the war against communism and that the disappeared are actually people who fled the country and are now happily living abroad. In both cases, the classmates' statements sound too old for 1994; indeed, Argentines would instantaneously associate them, as documented in *La historia oficial*, with the 1980s. In *Cautiva*, an adolescent perspective allows for a filmic language that is registered as an anachronistic discourse, a crystallized residue of the past manifesting itself in the present. A similar temporal gap emerges in some of the details that are meant to provide historical context: the crowded protests held by the Madres de Plaza de Mayo that Cristina involuntarily witnesses (too crowded for 1994, thus transporting the viewer back to the 1980s) and the newspapers that insist on denouncing US involvement in Argentine recent politics (an insistence also typical of the early democracy, when the first details regarding the dictatorship came to light).

While the symbolic dimension is archaic as compared to both the film's main temporal setting (1994) and the historical context in which it was produced (2001–2005), its indexical dimension alludes to a future time that further underscores the clash of temporalities. The indexicality of the cinematic image—the fact that the image is a trace of a real referent—forces the viewer to realize that what she is watching was shot after 1994. This realization is tied to some of the real objects that penetrate the film and denote a future time: an automatic machine from which Cristina retrieves her ticket when boarding a bus, a card she uses to call her adoptive parents from a pay phone, and, more evidently, the graffiti signed by H.I.J.O.S. across the city. Although these objects do not actually belong to a distant future—the organization H.I.J.O.S. was formed in 1995, the automatic ticket machine was inaugurated at the end of that same year, and it was possible to use a card at a Telefónica pay phone toward the end of the decade—the slight anachronism is emphasized by a sharp contrast with the antiquatedness of the symbolic dimension. In other words, these objects strike the viewer as almost futuristic when compared to the film's older format, plot, and language.

In "The Indexical and the Concept of Medium Specificity," Doane agrees with Peirce that cinema is "primarily indexical, subordinating the iconic dimension to secondary status" (134). Although cinematic and photographic images might look exactly like the object they represent, their resemblance is ultimately based on a physical correspondence to the represented object. The cinematic image's special credibility is more closely tied to physical correspondence—to the fact that the represented object testifies to the existence of a real object that was once before the camera—than to visual likeness. It is grounded more in referentiality than in resemblance. In this sense, iconicity is ultimately a "by-product of its indexicality" (134). While Doane's remarks are an accurate account of the tendency found in the cinematic field as a whole, we could say that in *Cautiva* the temporal clash inverts the equation. The "futuristic objects," though evidenced by indexicality, join an archaic format in reminding the spectator that what she is watching is less a product of referentiality than of resemblance—that the film is less an index (a document of a real referent) than an icon (a sign that visually duplicates a referent, regardless of its real connections to the latter). Simply put, *Cautiva*'s anachronism—the mixture of components specific to the post-2000 period, the 1980s, and 1994; a mixture enabled by a double-voiced teenage perspective—reminds the viewer that she is experiencing a fictional account of recent history. As with the home movie in the first episode of *Televisión x la identidad*, the images in *Cautiva* remind the viewer that the representation of historical facts *resembles* the postdictatorship period but by no means *documents* it. The film's temporal dissonance thus results in a loss of referentiality and in an intensification of iconicity.

In this sense, *Cautiva* is not an isolated example. As mentioned in the introduction, there are several second-generation fiction films, all contemporary with Biraben's, in which iconicity overtakes the other dimensions. Daniel Bustamante's *Andrés no quiere dormir la siesta*, for instance, follows a similar path. The film tells the story of an eight-year-old boy who is forced to move in with his grandmother after his mother's death. Set in 1978, the family drama intersects with Argentine history in a way that is reminiscent of *Cautiva* and *La historia oficial*. As in these films, melodrama and coming of age codify a political thriller. Individual suspense and private revelation run parallel to collective disclosure. As Andrés adjusts to his new life, he gradually discovers hidden aspects of the society around him. In the course of a transformational year, he learns about a clandestine detention center in the neighborhood, that people are being brought there by force, and that friends and relatives are aware of this facility but prefer not to interfere—and even work to hide all traces of it. Unlike Gaby's adoptive mother in 1985, Andrés ultimately conforms to his complicit surroundings. Toward the end, he betrays his mother's left-leaning boyfriend, identifying him to a military officer as the owner of "subversive flyers."

Although the film was released in 2009, the combination of symbolic, indexical, and iconic signs makes its narrative another anachronistic representation of dictatorial Argentina in the 2000s. The first indications of the temporal clash are, as with *Cautiva*, the outdated plot and genre. By means of a thriller-like coming-of-age narrative, Bustamante also takes us back to the allegorical melodramas and political thrillers of the early democracy. Even so, if we pay special attention to the dialogues, we will notice another conflicting temporality. On the one hand, adults speak as they would have spoken in 1978, using the typical vocabulary that films, documents, and scholarship have led us to immediately associate with the military years. One of the officers, for example, emerges from the clandestine center saying, *"Se me fue la mano con la máquina."* (I might have overused the device)—a familiar euphemism for having killed someone during a torture session. As neighbors and relatives peruse the dead mother's belongings and find left-leaning propaganda, they leave the house with the familiar phrase *"Yo no tengo nada que ver. Yo no ando metida en nada."* (I have nothing to do with this. I am not involved in anything.) Through such remarks, civil society signaled a lack of involvement in left-leaning politics. On the other hand, children use words that point to a future time, to the film's present of enunciation. *"Dale, no seas bolacero"* (Come on, don't tell a tall tale) serves as the most frequent example: a more recent colloquial expression accusing the addressee of exaggeration. In this way, symbolic signs indicate two conflicting temporalities: the early democracy and the 2000s. The interrelation of these two temporalities thus affects the representation of the military years. As contrasted with a historical moment yet to come, the military years seem antiquated. In other words, affected by the surprising irruption of the future, especially as materialized in the children's vocabulary, the representation of the dictatorship acquires archaic qualities.

This anachronistic effect is, as in *Cautiva*, emphasized by indexicality. Although all images in the film are indexical, one sign is even more prominently so: the grandmother. Norma Aleandro, one of Argentina's most famous actresses, plays this role, and her presence immediately highlights the images' indexical status. As an already-recognizable body, she instantly indicates the existence of an afilmic world—the same world in which Aleandro walks the streets, receives awards, is interviewed, and so forth. In other words, the shots of the grandmother interrupt the internal narrative to remind us both that an outside universe exists and that this universe is what constitutes cinematic images themselves. If indexicality is always linked to historicity by definition, then, the link is even more explicit in this case. Norma Aleandro became famous precisely because she is the actress who played Alicia, Gaby's adoptive mother, in *La historia oficial*. Aleandro is thus the most visible index of historicity in the film. Her older features and more mature gestures are a constant reminder that time has passed; although set in 1978, the film was clearly shot at least two decades later. *Andrés no quiere dormir la siesta* is not another allegorical melodrama of the early democracy; it is an outdated melodrama that was shot and released in the 2000s. An overtly indexical and historical sign, the grandmother produces an effect similar to that of the dialogues. The sudden irruption of the future—of the film's present of enunciation—destabilizes the temporal narrative, turning the military years into an archaic image.

Aleandro does not exemplify only the archaic qualities of such representations of the Argentine dictatorship, but also its iconic status: she establishes a connection with the dictatorship in which visual resemblance overcomes referentiality. Aleandro's body, her image, instantaneously evokes the military years, the past unveiled in *La historia oficial*. As with all icons, the link between sign and referent is a visual one. In short, we visually associate Norma Aleandro with the (steady, conventionalized) referent that we call "military dictatorship." In fact, the inclusion of this particular actress helps us perceive that iconicity itself is the dimension that dominates representation in this film. The dictatorship comprises a series of iconic signs: Norma Aleandro, a garage-style door leading to a detention camp, an enchained woman giving birth, a black hood in the middle of the night, and especially, the canonical green Ford Falcon, which appears in almost all of the suspenseful scenes.

The types of iconic representations at work in Biraben's and Bustamante's films have ideological consequences that must not go unnoticed. As Peirce claims, and as I have explained in the introduction to this book, iconicity emerges from a mixture of repetition and stability (Peirce 78). An icon is formed because a sign continually resembles a stable referent. To cite an everyday example: since a map consistently refers to a stable geographical area, people visually associate the map with the area in question. Iconic signs require both the repetition of a particular image (the map) and the stability of a steady referent (the area). Yet the process is even more complex. For Peirce, the referent (the immediate object) does not exist independently of the sign; it only exists within the semiosis. Because reality remains impervious to thought until we represent it, the referent is available only when linked to a particular sign. In other words, the geographical area is a geographical area only because we codify it as such. The symbolic thus plays a key role in the constitution of the referent; habit, convention, and law make the referent possible. Thus, iconic signs imply a close relationship among convention, image, and referent—among the symbolic, the iconic, and the immediate object. An icon results from a conventionalized association between an invariable sign and an invariable referent, an association that is repeated and sedimented over time.

Like the map and the area, then, the representation of recent Argentine history in these films is based on the repetition of iconic images that instantly recall familiar aspects of the past. The dark basement and the dangerous streets in *Cautiva* trigger conventional sensations. Norma Aleandro, the black hood, and the green Ford Falcon in *Andrés no quiere dormir la siesta* allow the viewer to identify and assimilate an existing piece of knowledge. In other words, these iconic representations evoke (and solidify) a given referent that is immediately recognized by the audience as the military dictatorship. Borrowing Laclau and Mouffe's language, we could say that these iconic signs have formed an empty signifier ("military dictatorship") that both articulates hegemony and points to a totalizing yet impossible referent. As I initially noted in chapter 2, because of the relational logic inherent to signification, the configuration of a hegemonic identity is always "catachrestical" (Laclau 72). Like the arm of a sofa, an empty signifier arises from the need to name an object that is necessary and unachievable, universal and contingent. The identity and unity of the referent result from this very process of naming—a process, however, that is possible only if naming is not subordinated either to description or to a preceding designation, but rather to repetition. Like the arm of a sofa, "military dictatorship" should thus be seen as a *point de capiton* (nodal point), a "word which, as a word, on the level of the signifier itself, unifies a given field, constitutes its identity" (Laclau 103).[9]

These iconic representations, first noticeable in *Cautiva*, became quite typical of a highly specific moment in Argentine history: *kirchnerismo*. Like other popular post-2003 films, such as the Academy Award–winning *El secreto de sus ojos*, these fictions join Kirchnerist discourse in making the dictatorship an empty signifier, a nodal point articulating hegemony.[10] This move has paradoxical implications. On the one hand, the very existence of an empty signifier that enabled a social consensus is what yielded actions as important as trials. As Laclau observes, an empty signifier emerges from an inseparable articulation between signifying and affective dimensions (111). Naming requires radical investment (i.e., recognizable emotion, codified feeling, qualified intensity). Simply put, because a sedimented convention existed against the atrocities of the regime, there was enough of a consensus to put ex-officers on trial. Given that, upon being confronted with certain iconic signs (a black hood, a green Ford Falcon), people evoked a shared, specific referent (an atrocious military dictatorship), there was enough support to take the perpetrators to court.

On the other hand, as mentioned earlier, empty signifiers rely on a given referent that prompts agreement while precluding further examination. Empty signifiers point to an impossible object that is both universal and contingent. A map instantly evokes a geographical area that is codified by the map itself and requires no additional consideration. During *kirchnerismo*—unlike what happened in the early democracy, when, as *La historia oficial* suggests, the dictatorship was a referent in progress—the military years became a sealed, totalizing, and already-given referent. The moment in which, in María Delgado and Cecilia Sosa's words, "grief was transformed into a state matter" (240) the dictatorship became a retro-style object, an archaic item that grew iconic—as *Cautiva* and *Andrés no quiere dormir la siesta* have helped us perceive. With respect to this shift, Janis Breckenridge remarks, referring to *Andrés no quiere dormir la siesta*, "The impact of now-iconic imagery. . . . remain[s] entirely lost on the naïve protagonist. Refusing to provide overt and didactic commentary within the narration, Bustamante instead relies on the viewer's knowledge of Argentina's recent history" (105). Iconic images reference a reality that is already familiar to the viewer and thus demands no further interpretation. In this way, the films become paradigmatic examples of what I call an "iconic fiction" (i.e., a fiction film in which iconicity takes precedence over indexicality). Iconic fictions evoke an already-given referent with universal (yet contingent) content that seems to lie outside of time, untouched by history or politics.

The inclusion of family photographs in *Cautiva* illustrates this predominance of iconicity and its implications. As in most postdictatorship narratives, photographs occupy a central space in *Cautiva*. The typical postdictatorship scenes in which the protagonists sort through family albums and revisit the first generation's past are recurrent in Biraben's film, constituting the coming-of-age rituals that, as Selimovic has carefully analyzed (425–429), gradually lead to the teenager's new subjectivity. Cristina's aunt and grandmother use photographs to recall details about her parents, Cristina's friend shares pictures of a detention center to explain their fate, and family portraits are all over her grandmother's place. Photographs accompany (and haunt) the girl in her coming-of-age story and in the quest for her new identity. In this sense, *Cautiva* seems to fit perfectly into second-generation culture as understood by Hirsch. The film's photos, however, are *fictional* photos—photos in which, as with the home movie in *Televisión x la identidad*, iconicity has priority over indexicality. In other words, the fact that these images resemble the recent past (that, for example, they portray people who look like disappeared people) is more important than the fact that there were once real objects in front of the camera (precisely because those real objects are known to be actors and actresses representing disappeared people). The inclusion of fictional photographs condenses the film's movement as a whole: the use of fiction, as opposed to documentary, emphasizes the iconic representation of Argentine history. The recent past is visually evoked, but its lack of referentiality means that it never becomes an object of interpretation.

Cristina's response to the fictional photographs further exemplifies this point. For her, photos aren't a resource for examining the past or for witnessing, by adoption, the first generation's memories; rather, photos are proof of her own identity (proof that she was born in 1978) and of the successful development of her teenage subjectivity. Something similar transpires with the flyers that are the medium of Andrés's betrayal in Bustamante's film. Although these flyers advance the plot and link the narrative elements together, we never see them in their entirety. Thus, the audience is never able to attribute a specific party affiliation to the mother's boyfriend, understand the characters' confrontation as part of a broader ideological struggle, or situate the drama within a concrete political moment. As is true of the other iconic signs in the film, the flyers evoke politics but prevent the audience from immersing themselves in those politics. They arouse a swift association with the dictatorship while precluding further interpretation.

I opened the chapter with an account of a recurrent scene in contemporary second-generation narratives: the moment of age recognition. After examining family photographs, manipulating their parents' objects, and even wearing their clothes (as Crespo does), members of the second generation are confronted with unsettling evidence that they are older than their parents. Indexicality plays a crucial role in these scenes of age recognition. Unlike the fictional photographs in *Cautiva* and the elusive flyers in *Andrés no quiere dormir la siesta*, the objects' indexical status forces intergenerational identification. Because these objects are traces of their parents' lives and thus hold referential value, second-generation viewers are able to identify with them. Unsurprisingly, too, since members of the second generation are now adults who are telling their stories from an adult perspective, the moments of age recognition in these narratives are concurrent with the moments of addressing first-generation political projects. With the disturbing realization that they are now older than their parents, the second generation is confronted with the question of political commitment—of their parents' political ideas and of how they in turn respond to those ideas.

The answers do not follow a homogeneous pattern. Carla Crespo proudly recalls her father's leadership and suggests (joining the other actors in the play) its continuity in the reemergence of political militancy during *kirchnerismo*. Albertina Carri distances herself from her parents' ideals and even alludes to this distance in the title of the documentary. María Inés Roqué's voiceover expresses her ambiguous feelings toward her father's radical activism. Úrsula Méndez states that, although she tries to situate her mother's choice within its historical context, she struggles to see her as a heroine. Martín Mórtola Oesterheld says that the radical rhetoric of the 1960s and '70s, such as in *La hora de los hornos*, sounds quite ridiculous to him. Nonetheless, as heterogeneous as these narratives may be, a striking coincidence connects them: in each and every one, an indexical sign (a photograph, a piece of authentic clothing, a real neighbor, a specific street, a handwritten letter, a former comrade) forces the members of the second generation to examine—and to take a position on—recent history, especially the first generation's political projects. In many cases, too, as in *Los rubios* and *Papá Iván*, it is the open redeployment of these objects' indexicality—such as the blurred photos in both documentaries—that hints at the adult filmmakers' stance on 1960s and '70s-era activism.

In fiction films by second-generation filmmakers, the movement is exactly the opposite. The use of fiction allows for a configuration of a child's or a teenager's perspective that, as illustrated by a close reading of *Cautiva* and *Andrés no quiere dormir la siesta*, both solidifies consensus and eludes the interpretation of controversial aspects of the recent past. As Marcela Jabbaz and Claudia Lozano suggest, people under thirty are typically perceived as oblivious to larger political or economic causes (102). Unlike an adult who is confronted with his or her own adulthood, children and teenagers are seen as people who do not usually question their own place in history, their own political agency, or their predecessors' ideological projects—which is probably why the only information we have about Cristina's disappeared parents is that they were architects. History acts as a given referent that accompanies (and influences) the search for their individual and social identities. Hence, the use of fiction (and of a child or teenager's perspective) enhances these films' iconic dimension and bridges the gap between sign and referent. As with all icons, the sign resembles a constant invariable referent, setting the question of referentiality aside. Unlike what happens in post-2000 second-generation documentaries, history in these iconic fictions (the 1970s as well as the postdictatorship period) is visually evoked and instantaneously remembered. Yet, as with the map and the area, the recent past (the 1970s as well as the postdictatorship period) is not an object for further analysis; it remains outside the task of interpretation.

Agüero's *Salamandra* and Markovitch's *El premio* are two other cases in point. In the former, Alba, a woman who has just been released from prison, takes Inti, the six-year-old son she barely knows, to El Bolsón, a small Patagonian town. Surrounded by all types of refugees and internal exiles, Inti gradually learns to navigate a mysterious environment and to understand his bitter, disturbed mother. In *El premio*, seven-year-old Cecilia follows her own mother to a precarious beach house to escape the military. Life in the coastal town is not easy; Cecilia must fake her identity to attend school and feign admiration for the army to participate in (and win) a contest. As in *Cautiva*, the use of a child's perspective is paramount to the films' 1980s-era format. The child's gaze creates a thriller-like suspense, as emphasized in *Salamandra*'s opening images—in which Inti mimics the waterboarding torture technique while taking a bath and then examines his dark house, carrying a toy gun—and in the windy and lonely sceneries that surround Cecilia in *El premio*. The infantile point of view allows for the circulation of a vague, ambiguous language that sets a general tone but requires no specific historical concerns. In Agüero's film, for instance, Alba whispers ambivalent phrases like "I was locked" or "I had a hard time during the military dictatorship," and her friend confesses that he "did a dark job during hard times." In Markovitch's film, Cecilia writes an obscure message about soldiers having killed her cousin and reads a telegram about her absent father that the audience never sees. In both films, as in *Cautiva*, the representation of history is constructed through the repetition of iconic images that resemble and instantaneously recall the recent past. These images prompt negative emotions against the dictatorship yet preclude the task of interpretation. Recent Argentine history becomes an invariable background that accompanies the main action. In turn, the recent past becomes a surrounding atmosphere, a familiar emotional environment—as the inclusion in *Salamandra* of María Elena Walsh's song "Canción de títeres," almost a repetition of the same element in *La historia oficial*, suggests.[11]

In a book primarily concerned with the process of intergenerational transmission of recent history, Sergio Guelerman asserts that, in order to avoid the risk of freezing the past and converting it into a mandate that is vertically controlled by the first generation, it is necessary to create a narrative in line with teenage and child subjectivities. A narrative based on the main psychological characteristics usually associated with an adolescent or a child—doubt, identity crisis, detachment from the adult worldview, curiosity—should allow for a discourse that serves as an analytical tool for exploration as opposed to a fixed order to be repeated (Guelerman 49–50). In other words, given that children and adolescents are commonly perceived as "human becomings" (Lee 7), they can destabilize those fixed conceptions that adults, as "human beings" (Ibid.), take for granted. In her study, Lury suggests that the dislocated temporality inherent to child and adolescent films—their double voice—offers opportunities for transgressing conventional modes of sexual, racial, and political identification (1–15). When talking about autofictions, Blejmar argues that the combination of adult and childlike voices results in a subversive polytemporality. Such temporality places special memory value on "anachronism," understood as the intrusion of a time into another time that invites us to read the past against the grain (25). Rocha and Seminet claim in their book that these narratives oblige adults to critique their own behavior and introduce topics of emerging social importance (16).In the same vein, Holland observes that "imagery may well aspire to an abstract universal concept of childhood, but it is inevitably placed within a specific historical moment, and itself contributes to political and social contestation" (18).

Iconic fictions, however, demand that we reevaluate these assertions. As I have showed in my analyses, children and teenager's perspectives are found at the core of filmic structures and emotional atmospheres that lead, in the 2000s, to political thrillers typical of the early democracy. These viewpoints enable anachronistic representations that result in an enhancement of iconicity. While iconicity strengthens social consensus, it also eludes consideration of larger political causes. In post-2000 iconic fictions, rather than constituting a successful means of historical exploration, the configuration of teenage and child subjectivities can serve as the exact opposite: the basis for converting the 1970s into a static referent that allows for consensus yet impedes further interpretation.

Private Activism: The Use of a Child's Perspective in *Infancia Clandestina*

Shot in 2011 and released in September 2012, Benjamín Ávila's *Infancia clandestina* has already been sold to over twenty countries, granted five prestigious international prizes and ten of the most important local prizes, nominated for at least twelve more, and selected to compete in the Best Foreign Language Film category at the 2013 Academy Awards. These achievements, though impressive, are far from surprising. An international coproduction featuring famous actors, the film condenses all the characteristics necessary to successfully attract a global audience: it is a moving story of the dictatorship narrated from a child's perspective and directed by the son of a disappeared activist. In fact, the film was conceived from the outset and marketed as a sequel to the Academy Award–winning *La historia oficial* and *El secreto de sus ojos,* two successful examples of how the so-called dirty war has become the country's most alluring trademark on the global stage.[12]

That said, even as many readings acknowledge these popular features, most highlight the film's originality. Although *Infancia clandestina* is a story about a highly recurrent topic—the dictatorship—such interpretations credit the film with a unique approach to this controversial era. As opposed to traditional cultural productions, which focus on the horrors of state violence, this movie openly addresses left-leaning violence as well. Breaking with the common representation of the disappeared as the passive victims of repression and torture, the film depicts them as active guerrilla fighters with guns, militant rituals, strong political affiliations, and a straightforward commitment to armed struggle. Appealing to a fictional framework, Ávila revisits a well-known historical period but provides an innovative angle: a highly politicized portrayal of revolutionaries, specifically radical Montoneros. Two interrelated cinematic strategies make this innovation possible: the use of a child's perspective and the inclusion of anime-style cartoons. The child's gaze allows for a firsthand account of activism. As the young protagonist witnesses his militant parents' daily life, he is able to provide an inside narration of the details characterizing their political organization. The cartoons help avoid the representation of state violence that dominates traditional cultural productions. Deaths, shootings, and kidnappings are obliquely exposed, mitigated by the animated techniques. In sum, most critics agree that these two strategies lie at the heart of the film's main achievements: eluding a naturalized view of the 1970s and offering an innovative structure based on an original representation of militancy (Aguilar, "Infancia"; Feinmann; Kairuz; Maguire; Pérez Zabala; Ranzani; Thomas).[13]

I argue, however, that what happens in the film—and what, in the end, makes it such a valuable cultural product—is in fact the opposite. Instead of providing a unique portrayal of the 1970s based on a novel exposition of left-leaning violence, this coming-of-age story fits within a version of militancy that has actually become quite common since the mid-1990s. Rather than presenting undisclosed aspects of the armed struggle, the film relies on a privatized and archaic image of the disappeared activist, which ultimately transforms 1970s militancy into an iconic sign. The prevailing interpretations, detailed above, are only accurate if, first, we consider that the figure of the disappeared as passive victim is the most common symbol (thus overlooking the representations of the disappeared as militants from the mid-'90s onward) and, second, if we disregard both Kirchnerist official discourse and second-generation fiction. Breaking with the leading interpretation that praises Ávila's film for its originality, then, I contend that its most interesting feature is, in fact, its commonality. *Infancia clandestina*'s repetitions help us perceive another pattern in the representation of activism that originates in the mid-1990s and solidifies after 2003 with the advent of the Kirchner administration. This pattern is found at the core of the contemporary iconization of 1970s militancy—an iconization that, as the film's international success implies, is also occurring at the global level. Hardly a brand-new creation, Ávila's film is a good example of how contemporary second-generation fiction both registers and participates in this iconizing process. Examining the use of a child's perspective and of anime-like cartoons illuminates this participation and elucidates the connections among such filmic strategies, the privatization of left-leaning violence, iconicity, and feeling.

At first glance, everything in *Infancia clandestina* is politically marked. Juan's childhood is entirely surrounded by revolutionary militancy. Challenging traditional concepts of childhood as "a time of innocence . . . and 'home' as a center of privacy, order, morality, and security" (Holland 57), Juan lives under the name Ernesto in a secret house. His parents and his uncle Beto belong to Montoneros and hold underground meetings with their fellow guerrillas right in front of him. He also has immediate access to firearms, bullets, hideaways, and dissident rituals. For Juan, political activism is not covert information that he needs to decipher; his mother allows him to witness everyday militancy and even uses Che Guevara's life as a model to explain how he should act. While Juan may still be considered a child, he is spared no violent details, no matter how painful. His father, for example, gives him an in-depth account of his uncle Beto's death, including how, upon being caught by a military officer, he decided to swallow a grenade, hug his captor, and put an end to both of their lives. It is this open account of left-leaning armed struggle, as I mentioned earlier, that led most critics to emphasize the film's originality. As opposed to the naturalized representation of the 1970s as a period dominated by state violence, Juan's coming-of-age story helps expose undisclosed aspects of this particular historical moment. In fact, according to Ávila, the search for an innovative angle is the film's starting point: *"Me parece que las historias que se habían contado en relación a la dictadura olvidaron dar cuenta de esos militantes que estaban dispuestos a dar sus vidas por sus ideales. . . . Yo asumí el desafío y el riesgo de contar la Historia desde ese costado."* (I think that previous stories on the dictatorship forgot to take into account the existence of militants willing to sacrifice their lives to achieve their ideals. . . . I accepted the challenge and told History from their perspectives) (Ávila n.p.). Breaking with traditional postdictatorship cultural productions, *Infancia clandestina* aims to denaturalize the most common constructions of the recent past, explore its hidden facets, and spotlight the forgotten image of disappeared activists.

Yet the widespread assertion of originality conflicts with the film's actual references to Argentine history, especially (and surprisingly) when alluding to the causes leading to the armed struggle and to the motivations for left-leaning violence. The generalizations voiced by the mother in explaining her organization's founding principles are a good example of this lack of innovation. According to her, Montoneros are waging revolution because they are hungry for justice and want to engage popular consciousness. Curiously enough, this is the only explanation for engaging in political activism that the film provides. A similar vagueness marks the closing captions: *"Dedicado a la memoria de mi madre, Sara E. Zermoglio, detenida-desaparecida el 13 de octubre de 1979. A mis hermanos, mi padre, mis hijos. Y a todos los Hijos, Nietos, Militantes y a todos aquellos que han conservado la fe."* (In memory of my mother, Sara E. Zermoglio, disappeared on October 13, 1979. To my siblings, my father, my children. And to all Children, Grandchildren, Militants, and Everyone who has kept their faith.) Throughout the film, as condensed in these final words, militancy is conceived as an everyday, domestic, and even family activity; as a personal virtue and abstract heroic faith; as a subjective and affective history. These features aren't only present in the closing dedication, a formula generally given to private emotions. The opening captions, designed to provide historical context and situate the narration within a particular period, are also based on a well-known simplification:

> *1975: tras la muerte del presidente Perón grupos parapoliciales comenzaron a perseguir y asesinar militantes sociales y revolucionarios. 1976: los militares tomaron el poder por la fuerza, se desencadenó la más violenta represión en la historia de la Argentina. 1979: desde su exilio en Cuba, los dirigentes de la organización revolucionaria montoneros lanzaron la Operación Contraofensiva. Algunos militantes regresaron a la Argentina con sus hijos.* (1975: after President Perón's death, paramilitary groups started to prosecute and kill social and revolutionary militants. 1976: military officers took power by force, the most violent repression in Argentine history began. 1979: from their exile in Cuba, the leaders of the revolutionary organization Montoneros launched a counteroffensive. Some militants returned to Argentina with their children.).[14]

Far from being an original account of activism, *Infancia clandestina* embodies the characteristics at the core of what Vezzetti calls the "subjective turn" in the representation of militancy (*Sobre la violencia* 110), a pattern that began in the mid-1990s and became dominant after 2003. According to Vezzetti, Argentine culture is marked by two common images of the disappeared: as victim of state violence and as militant. The former, which coincides with Crenzel's notion of the innocent victim, dominates 1980s cultural production (as seen in *Juan* and *La noche de los lápices*). Yet, in the mid-1990s, another pattern emerged: the disappeared as an activist often committed to armed struggle (as explored in chapter 2 with films like *Cazadores de utopías* and *Montoneros*). Vezzetti points to a series of motifs driving this second construction: abnegation, courage, heroism, sacrifice, and youth. Despite the public and collective claim on the notion of militancy, this second representation is based on private virtues, attesting to the above-mentioned subjective turn. Rather than constituting collective action, militancy is transformed into a private lifestyle, an everyday individual routine. This second representation thus erases the political dimension of activism, simultaneously privatizing and romanticizing revolutionary violence. Che Guevara's image becomes its most emblematic symbol: "*[Del] Che Guevara solo se toman las cualidades personales. . . . Es la leyenda del 'guerrillero esencial' en la que el ejemplo personal y la moral del sacrificio absoluto arrasan con la razón política.*" (Only Che Guevara's personal traits matter. . . . This is the myth of the "essential guerrilla," in which personal example and absolute sacrifice overtake political reason) (Vezzetti, *Sobre la violencia* 139).[15]

Although I agree with Vezzetti's periodization, I would argue that there are two opposing trends in the representations of the disappeared as militant from the mid-'90s onward. One, as exemplified by *Televisión x la identidad*, centers on subjective virtues. The other, as seen in *Montoneros, Papá Iván*, and *Los rubios*, shifts away from (and is even critical of) the subjective representation of activism. While the latter is closer to the documentary genre, the former often emerges in fiction, as is true for *Infancia clandestina*. Mediated by Juan's perspective, activism becomes an everyday routine, as normal and familiar as any household chore. Bullets and firearms, rather than being perceived as historical markers, are converted into picturesque domestic ornaments. Che Guevara, instead of serving as a political figure, embodies the fairytale features of a child's hero: he is an epic character who travels around the world and skillfully outwits his enemies by changing his clothes. The same romantic attributes are ascribed to all the militants Juan encounters. In his eyes, his parents, his uncle, and their friends are brave young soldiers, passionately fighting for their ideals. Every dialogue that he witnesses—especially when his father tells him about Beto's death and when his mother explains the values of fighting—unveils the private virtues mentioned by Vezzetti: abnegation, courage, heroism, sacrifice, and youth. Political militancy withdraws from collective action, becoming an individual trait. Ávila himself alludes to this subjective turn in an interview with Mariano Kairuz: "*Y yo quería justamente eso: dar una visión más humana de cómo fueron las cosas, como yo las recordaba, no esa construcción de mucho miedo, pánico y horror que se hizo luego. Hubo miedo y horror, por supuesto, pero también mucho humor, amor, risa, diversión; mucho cotidiano."* (And that's exactly what I wanted: to provide a more human view of how things really were, just like I recalled them. I did not want to offer a narrative filled with fear, panic, and horror. There were fear and horror, of course, but there were also lots of humor, love, laughter, fun; lots of every day [*sic*])) (Kairuz n.p.).

While the use of a child's perspective certainly challenges traditional notions of family, domesticity, and childhood, it is this very perspective, too, that enables a subjective, romanticized, and already-given representation of activism. But how exactly does the child's viewpoint play out in this film, and in what way does *Infancia clandestina* organize its strategies around this notion? At first, the answer seems obvious: the film's protagonist is a child, and the plot is based on his coming-of-age story. The audience accompanies him as he returns from exile, interacts with his parents, goes to school, falls in love, mourns his uncle's death, and celebrates a fake birthday. The answer grows less obvious, however, if we remember that the opening shot captures a sleeping Juan; that is, a child with no perspective. In fact, the first scene is related from the mother's viewpoint. The camera follows her gaze as she fixes it on her sleeping son, stares out at the raindrops on the car window, and looks onto the deserted streets. In spite of the child's presence in every scene and the careful way in which the cinematic sequences develop his story, some images (like the nap in the car in the opening shot) are neither based on his perspective nor use him as a focalizer. In *Infancia clandestina*, as Thomas has noticed, the child becomes a "partial focalizer" (236), because the film constantly shifts between internal and external points of view. Indeed, the film contains only two types of images that are strictly built around a child's perspective: a series of shots in which the camera mimics Juan's gaze and the anime-style cartoons. Although this distinction might seem like a technicality, it is of utmost importance in analyzing the film's ideological undertones—especially because these scenes are the ones that, instead of eluding a naturalized representation of the 1970s, transform them into an iconic sign.

As noted in the previous section, there is a close link between the use of fiction and the predominance of iconicity. Furthermore, scholars like Stephen Prince and Christian Metz argue that there is also a strong connection between iconicity and feeling. Since filmic images are visually isomorphic with real-world images, they are more eagerly apprehended than, for example, the written language that forms a novel:

> Via the technologies of motion picture recording, the camera is able to reproduce in clearly recognizable and even intensified form the familiar streams of facial and body motion cues. . . . These cues should be readily understood by cinema viewers, just as they are in real-world visual experience. If the distinctions between iconic and symbolic modes that we have been emphasizing are really relevant to differences between pictures and language, then one

would expect iconic modes to be processed more readily than symbolic ones. (Prince 114)

Because filmic images look like the real world, they resonate in a way that other types of images do not: they appeal to the viewer affectively. The mimetic qualities of visual resemblance connect to the viewer's subjectivity, eliciting a sentimental response. As Metz puts it, "Films give us the feeling that we are witnessing an almost real spectacle. . . . [They] release a mechanism of affective and perceptual *participation* in the spectator" (*Film* 4, emphasis in the original). Still, while the iconic status of all cinematic images makes them bearers of a sensorial component, some of them enhance it—especially close-ups, as Prince suggests, which "intensify and emphasize the most salient cues for the viewer's understanding in cognitive and affective terms" (113). Close-ups allow the viewer to delve into the screen, exploring in-depth objects that resemble those he or she finds in the real world. Close-ups also magnify the world in front of the camera, the world that the audience recognizes as their own. Simply put, the close-up enhances iconicity and intensifies feelings. Or, as Béla Balász, one of the first thinkers to theorize this representational technique, observes: "Good close-ups radiate a tender human attitude . . . a delicate solicitude, a gentle bending over the intimacies of life-in-the-miniature, a warm sensibility. Good close-ups are lyrical; it is the heart, not the eye, that has perceived them" (305).

If we analyze the scenes in *Infancia clandestina* that are strictly constructed through a child's perspective, we could say that this viewpoint enhances iconicity and intensifies feeling. This is especially evident when the camera mimics Juan's gaze. These images always follow the same sequence: first, a close-up of the child's face that draws the viewer to his eyes; next, a scene that seems to be perceived through these eyes; and, finally, a character who looks at Juan and whose external gaze (captured by a long shot) puts an end to the boy's own view. Here, the close-up is the predominant cinematic technique; it links the viewer's gaze to the child's and magnifies the objects he supposedly perceives. In line with what Lebeau has called the "subgenre of the child facial" (36)—the up-close representation of the child's gaze that has dominated child pictures from early cinema onward—the young gaze enlarges objects and people. As a result, the mimetic qualities of the filmic images are enhanced; sensorial responses are intensified. In other words, the child's gaze adds an additional layer of iconicity.

Interestingly, this sequence systematically occurs in two contexts: whenever Juan witnesses actions associated with militancy (a firearm exchange, an underground meeting, his mother singing a political anthem, an oneiric apparition of his dead uncle) and whenever he thinks about María, the girl he loves. In Ávila's film, militancy and feeling are inextricable: they are connected both formally (via the close-up) and thematically (via sentimental love). The recurrent parallel

Figure 4.1. Romantic close-up of Juan's mother in *Infancia clandestina*.

between Juan's mother (the main activist character) and María highlights this connection. Juan's daydreams about María immediately precede a bucolic picnic with his mother. At another point, his romantic contemplation of María's dance performance parallels the sentimental observation of his mother singing a political song. What's more, the two actresses look notoriously alike—and they also resemble Ávila's real mother, whose photograph appears in the final credits. If, as Metz argues, the close-up is always a synecdoche (*The Imaginary* 195) —a part of a whole—the close-up of the child's face is a synecdoche of sentimental militancy in *Infancia clandestina*.

Feeling and iconicity are further intensified in the staging of temporality. These sequences meticulously combine the close-up with slow-motion shots, creating the impression that the child's gaze interrupts the normal flow of things, removing people and objects from conventional time. Past, present, and future are indistinguishable and collapse into one. Causality is superseded by duration. Rather than offering an alternative temporality that productively disrupts adults' conventional understanding of history—as Lury suggests when analyzing the child's perspective in war films (105–144)—Juan's view seems to make things eternal, ahistorical, untouched by the passing of time.[16] Through his gaze, the movement-image gives way to the time-image: "the linkages of situation-action, action-reaction, and excitation-response" (Deleuze, *Cinema I* 211) give way to the privileging of "purely optical situations" over action (Deleuze, *Cinema II* 3). The logic of observation replaces the logic of cause and effect, of action and reaction, of progress. These slow-motion scenes do not advance the plot; in fact, they seem to interfere with its development. If, to borrow Metz's words, it is movement that prompts the spectator to perceive images as being present and thus produces a strong impression of reality (*Film* 7–8), slow motion submerges the audience into an unreal world where the conventional passing of time has been interrupted. In Walter Benjamin's terms, the child's gaze restores the aura to the scene: "its presence in time and space, its unique existence at the place where it happens to be" ("The Work" 733).

In Juan's eyes, militancy becomes auratic and is thus filled with cult value. Bullets and weapons are not just elements in the accompanying scenery; they occupy the entire frame, as if they were eternal works of art. The uncle and his fellow activists are more than additional characters; they conquer space and interrupt time, as if they were epic heroes. Juan's mother and girlfriend are much more than everyday people in the child's life; they are so close and move so slowly that, paradoxically, they become unreachable. Close-ups and slow motion transform them into two distant idols that Juan adores, evoking Benjamin's claim: "The definition of aura as a 'unique phenomenon of a distance however close it may be' represents nothing but the formulation of the cult value of the work of art in categories of space and time perception" ("The Work" 736). The firearm exchange, the underground meetings, and the political songs are not routine practices. They are auratic rituals, close yet unreachable, devoid of history, and embedded in cult value.

Feeling, according to Gonzalo Aguilar in his text "*Infancia Clandestina* or the Will of Faith," is also indivisibly linked to fiction. In Aguilar's view, Ávila's film shies away from conventional postdictatorship cinema to include a passionate representation of activism that breaks with the common notion of victimhood. Moreover, the film differs from second-generation cinema in that it chooses fiction as opposed to testimony. *Infancia clandestina*, Aguilar claims, "provides its story with the relative autonomy of fiction, shifting its discourse from the referential verification demanded by testimony and from the autobiographical experience of the first person, to one that condenses—with the immanent articulation of its own fictional narrative units—a tale of community identity over the historical past" (19). This choice allows for an emotional reconstruction of militancy whose strength subsumes the traumatic experience of the dictatorship. The film's unique representation of political passions (emotion, hope, heroism, will, and faith) is so powerful, the author asserts, that it recomposes the traumatic fragments of the past, providing closure and restoring community ties.

Although I agree that fiction allows for an emotional representation of activism, I do not believe that this representation engenders new feelings of collective militancy and posttrauma closure. Unlike what fictional testimony prompted in the early democracy, the fictional portrayal of militants in *Infancia clandestina* does not configure new sensibilities. The child's account of activism, far from creating a sense of urgency in interrogating the 1970s, repeats and solidifies an existing emotional discourse on left-leaning militancy. While the film shapes feelings, these feelings coincide with an already-given emotion toward radical militancy, precluding the emergence of a new type of sensation. In other words, had this particular representation materialized between the 1980s and the mid-1990s, when revolutionary violence was absent from public discourse, it might have facilitated an innovative interrogation of the recent past. But since the film was released in 2012, when the emotional appeal to militancy had already become hegemonic and now plays a central role in the prevalence of the subjective turn, this particular representation ultimately crystallizes the past, strengthens consensus, and prevents the audience from engaging with history.

Furthermore, the shaping of a new type of affect is precluded by the interlocking relationship between militancy and sentimental love. Romantic love (an already-given and socially-inscribed emotion) fuels the representation of activism, preventing new sensibilities from being formed. Instead of creating new kinds of affect or unsettling given emotions, the child's perspective mimics an existing feeling toward militancy and even enhances it via close-ups and slow motion. This gaze triggers well-known sensations, allows the viewer to identify and solidify an existing representation, and intensifies iconicity. Or, to put it in semiotic terms, the symbolic and the indexical dimensions contribute to the process of iconization, inhibiting new affective configurations. The repetition of historically marked social conventions (i.e., representations of militancy and sentimental love that are current in 2012) contributes to the sedimentation and enhancement of the 1970s as an iconic sign that is part of contemporary Argentina's "emotional hegemony" (Jaggar 60).[17]

The role of the indexical and symbolic dimensions in this iconization process becomes apparent, too, if we pay attention to *Infancia clandestina*'s photos and verbal language. Photographs of Ávila's childhood, especially of his missing mother, appear in the final credits, introducing, as Thomas puts it, "an additional temporal layer to the film's conclusion, as they signal to an extradiegetic past reality (the director's childhood) and introduce a trace of the present-ness into the film (as they are now objects of memory examined from a present vantage point)" (241). However, in this specific case—along the lines of what photos trigger in *Cautiva*—the indexical is somewhat erased. Although the pictures are not fictional, they are so small and distant that the actual images become indistinguishable. On several occasions, the audience wonders whether they are seeing the real mother's portrait or a photo of one of the two main actresses (a confusion that also stems from the resemblance among the three women). The photographs' referential value is undermined; contrary to what Thomas claims, it seems impossible to engage in postmemorial identification and restitch the generational fabric (242). Given the struggle to link sign and referent, pictures lose their indexical status; they become another iconic image of the 1970s.

Verbal language undergoes a similar shift. The film features dialogues between two different generations: militants and children. Although it seems initially that these dialogues forge an intergenerational connection, they actually create a dissonance—as in *Andrés no quiere dormir la siesta*—that separates them in time. While children use contemporary language (*"Te colgaste"*; *"Está para darle"* [You slept; She is so fuckable]), activists use typical 1970s-era vocabulary (*"Estaba podrida la cita"*; *"Beto cantó"* [The appointment was corrupted; Beto gave us away.]) Even though the children's language is actually the anachronistic one, pointing to a future time that does not coincide with the film's environment, it is the first generation's language, by contrast, that sounds archaic. Like the objects captured by Juan's gaze, the militants' vocabulary lies outside of time, untouched by history. Their words are an auratic residue of the past, a relic embedded in cult value. In *Infancia clandestina*, as Peirce suggests, the three semiotic dimensions overlap. Indexical and symbolic components join the child's gaze to intensify iconicity, transforming 1970s militancy into a highly iconic and emotional sign.

The inclusion of anime-style cartoons further heightens the iconizing process. These images appear whenever the film refers to militancy, thus paralleling the scenes in which the camera mimics the child's gaze. The anime-style cartoons portray shootings, deaths, and left-leaning violence. They depict the family's exile and summarize Che Guevara's epic journey. They serve, in short, as a graphic condensation of activism, a graphic summary of those images that had previously been presented, via close-ups and slow motion, through Juan's eyes. We could say, then, that the cartoons intensify the iconization of the already iconic. In adding a third layer of iconicity to 1970s-era activism, they further iconize a representation that was doubly iconic to begin with—both because of its filmic medium and because it had been emotionally enhanced through the child's lens. Or, as Argentine cultural critic Quintín observes, *"los fotogramas se convierten en cuadros de historieta y así quedan congelados como hechos de una historia que no se cuestiona."* (The drawings turn into cartoons and thus remain frozen, just like historical facts that are never called into question) (n.p.).

If we consider the relationship between repetition and stability that I have emphasized throughout the chapter, the ideological consequences yielded by the enhancement of iconicity become apparent. The iconic representation of activism in *Infancia clandestina* is based on a repetition that calls for an instantaneous response but prevents further analysis. The (triple) iconic representation repeats existing emotions and strengthens the archaic figure of a privatized, romanticized, and auratic militant. Cinematic images form an empty signifier that evokes a conventionalized, sedimented, and stable referent, one deeply familiar to the audience and which demands no further examination. Ávila himself inadvertently supports this interpretation when he says, in passing: *"Con* Infancia clandestina *espero varias cosas. . . . De mi generación, espero que se sienta identificada con la posibilidad de creer. Y en cuanto a la de mis hijos, espero que* Infancia clandestina *sea una película que les sirva para poder quitarle peso a la discusión política."* (With *Infancia clandestina* I expect many things. . . . With respect to my generation, I expect that they will identify with the possibility of believing. And regarding my children's generation, I hope that *Infancia clandestina* helps make political discussions lighter) (Ranzani n.p.).[18]

In *Latinamericanism after 9/11*, John Beverley suggests that a "paradigm of disillusion" (96) dominates the representation of armed struggle in contemporary Latin America:

> The armed struggle remains largely bracketed away from public memory in Latin America. . . . This is so partly because young people in Latin America today, unlike Sarlo's or my generation, have no direct biographical connection to the armed struggle. But that inevitable generation gap is aggravated in turn by the fact that the representation of the armed struggle they do have access to, like Castañeda's *Utopia Unarmed*, give on the whole a negative image of it. That image is in turn governed by what I am calling here the paradigm of disillusion [which] rests on a coming-of-age narrative. . . . Its underlying idea is something like the following: The illusion of the revolutionary transformation of society that was the inspiration of the armed struggle was a kind of romantic adolescence (99).

According to Beverley, this vision of armed struggle as an adolescent error is based both on the figure of the *"guerrillero arrepentido"* [the repentant guerrilla] (100) and on a teleological conception of history that sustains neoliberal hegemony. Since neoliberalism comes after the period of revolutionary upsurge, it appears as inevitable, a new historical stage that transcends the previous one. However, Beverley claims, new shifts in contemporary Latin American politics cannot be articulated without reassessing the heritage of the armed struggle and embracing a new historical paradigm: that of restoration. Following this paradigm, the 1960s and 1970s do not belong to an old and immature historical stage, but rather to a process that was repressed or deferred, the elements of which remain active and can reemerge and return to motion once again.

Beverley's claims are certainly thought-provoking; in particular, his idea that it is necessary to reassess the armed struggle's legacy in order to account for new shifts in Latin American politics. I believe, however, that his arguments do not entirely fit the reality of contemporary Argentina. As I have explained above, since the mid-1990s (and especially during the Kirchner administration), the representation of left-leaning violence has not been built on a paradigm of disillusion; rather, it has largely rested on a privatized and highly romanticized conception of activism. Its central figure, then, has been the everyday heroic militant, not the "guerrillero arrepentido." Various members of the second generation, chiefly those who share a biographical connection with the disappeared activists, are responsible for this centrality. In this sense, Ávila's film does not embody a marginal discourse but one that has become hegemonic, dominating national memory. The director himself enjoyed sponsorship by Argentine Public Television, recognized his sympathy for the Kirchner administration, and acknowledged his ties with H.I.J.O.S. (Ranzani). As Quintín notes, the film is a typical product of "cine kirchnerista" (Kirchnerist cinema) (n.p.). By contrast, far from being the dominant trend in the representation of armed struggle, the paradigm of disillusion is a view that, as *Infancia clandestina* suggests, has become peripheral in contemporary Argentina.[19]

Furthermore, Beverley's observations on the links between the representation of armed struggle and a teleological conception of history are also worth reexamining for the Argentine case. Although the repentant discourse underlying the paradigm of disillusion may be grounded in such a notion, the opposite representation (the most popular one in post-2000 Argentina) is grounded less in restoration than in archaization. Ávila's film is emblematic in this regard; in contemporary hegemonic discourse, militancy is perceived as an archaic and auratic practice, as a private virtue untouched by the passing of time, as an object for cult and contemplation, and as an iconic sign. Those elements that were repressed or deferred, and which could be set in motion once again, remain latent, far below the surface of public memory. The biographical connection with activism, instead of inviting a political reexamination, is the axis of the subjective turn that sees militancy as an everyday family routine. The child's perspective allows for a coming-of-age narrative that—rather than foregrounding the political dimension of left-leaning violence—privatizes, romanticizes, and converts revolutionary violence into an individual trait. In sum, the iconic representation of the armed struggle (and not the paradigm of disillusionment) allows for hegemony in contemporary Argentina.

Importantly, the particular representation evidenced in the films that this chapter has analyzed dominates not only contemporary Argentina but also the rest of the world. *Infancia clandestina*, *Cautiva*, *El premio*, *Salamandra*, and *Andrés no quiere dormir la siesta* successfully circulate in the sphere of global cinema. Through a child's or an adolescent's gaze, iconic fictions construct a version of recent Argentine history that has been internationally acclaimed. Rocha and Seminet offer a number of reasons for the global popularity of child and adolescent films: increased international concern for child safety, the emergence of a young generation of filmmakers eager to represent their own views of the past, the proliferation of women filmmakers who opt for alternative characters, the social and economic conditions of globalization that alter traditional forms of identity, the universal moral appeal of children, and the current interdisciplinary interest in the study of children and youth culture (12–15). Although there may be multiple causes for these films' success, I would like to argue that their popularity indicates a necessary link between iconicity and globalization. In the midst of late capitalism—in an age that, as Fredric Jameson famously stated, "has forgotten how to think historically" (*Postmodernism* ix)—the iconic sign best embodies global cultural logic. In the contemporary division of labor resulting from transnational business (with the transnational film industry being the paradigmatic example in the cultural field), Latin America's role seems relegated to providing iconic fictions that, like all icons, rely on instantaneous response and foster emotional consensus but preclude further examination.

Notes

1. In *Deleuze and World Cinemas*, David Martin-Jones calls this type of child figure, which appears in present-day films set during past historical conflicts, the "child-seer" (69). He compellingly proposes that this figure speaks more to the film's present of enunciation than to the past represented in the narrative.

2. See Holland 8–21; Lebeau, 20–55; Rocha and Seminet 6–20 for further details on the history of the child and adolescent genre in film and visual culture.

3. See Ariés; Calvert; Jenkins; Lee; Lury; Steedman for further details on the sociohistorical emergence of childhood, adolescence, and adulthood. See Jenkins 15–22 for a chronology of the notion of childhood prior to the nineteenth century. See Lee for a provocative study of how the notion of childhood has changed in recent decades in conjunction with the increasing instability of adulthood. See Qvortrup, Corsaro, and Honig, eds. for an introduction to key concepts in childhood studies and for a history of the field.

4. As Rocha and Seminet also explain, the first option (films produced by or for children and adolescents) is less typical in Latin America than in the United States, and it certainly does not apply to the adult-oriented and adult-created postdictatorship films I address in this chapter. Although I find Kuhn's observations quite interesting, I believe that they would lead my analysis far afield from a historical interpretation. Indeed, as I have already remarked with respect to trauma theory, the connotations of Kuhn's framework would not differentiate between specific historical moments in the postdictatorship period, as any film (regardless of historical context) could replay childlike mental states.

5. These captions and those that follow, unless otherwise stated, are quoted verbatim from the film's translated subtitles.

6. See Erikson; Hall; Harter; Lesko; Steinberg for further details on the qualities usually associated with the construction of teenage subjectivities.

7. See Dufays 131–154 for a more detailed analysis of the figure of the child in *La historia oficial*. Although she does not specifically compare the film with *Cautiva*, she argues that the filmic representation of the child between 1983 and 2008 should always be interpreted as an allegory of the nation—even if such allegory enables different psychological processes (mourning, melancholy, or nostalgia).

8. Marcela Jabbaz and Claudio Lozano (97–131) interviewed teenagers and young adults to assess their knowledge of recent Argentine history. Although they found certain disparities, especially regarding the causes of the military dictatorship, all of the interviewees were aware of the basic facts that *Cautiva* reveals: the dates, the number of disappeared people, and the quest for children born in captivity. We could thus say that *Cautiva*'s revelations are already shared by any possible public, be it an adult domestic audience, a young/teenage audience, or an international audience.

9. The impossibility of a fully universal referent indicates why the right-wing organization Argentinos x la Memoria Completa's demand for a complete memory—a memory that, unlike that of *kirchnerismo*, recalls everything that happened during the dictatorship—is both conceptually and practically unachievable. See the organization's website http://www.lahistoriaparalela.com.ar for further details. See Laclau, 116–117 for an in-depth analysis of the impossibility of universality.

10. See Tandeciarz for an analysis of how the military dictatorship is represented, conventionalized, and marketed in *El secreto de sus ojos*.

11. In *La historia oficial*, María Elena Walsh's song *"En el país de no me acuerdo"* appears throughout the film, allegorizing society's blindness during the military dictatorship and instilling a change in perspective for the new democracy. See Dufays 1–5, 131–150 for a more detailed analysis of the song's meaning in this film. In *Salamandra*, the soundtrack's primary song is *"Canción de títeres,"* another work by the same songwriter, who is usually considered an Argentine symbol of resistance against the military government. The use of this latter song thus creates an allegorical environment that transports the viewer back to the early democracy.

12. See Thomas (236–237) for a more detailed parallel between *Infancia clandestina* and *La historia oficial*.

13. Other readings do not focus on the representation of militancy, interpreting the film instead as another example of a postdictatorship narrative that comes to grips with a traumatic experience by engaging in memory work (Feierstein 124–144; Aon, 219–230; Young, Neil). I take these readings, once again, as a good example of how trauma theory yields a similar interpretation for every narrative, regardless of its specificity and production conditions.

14. As Vezzetti explains, the idea that left-leaning violence originated as a reaction against state violence has become a topic in postdictatorship Argentina. This topic, he argues, both precludes further historical examination and erases the ideology held by the armed activists themselves (*Sobre la violencia revolucionaria* 50).

15. The articles compiled by Crenzel in *Los desaparecidos en la Argentina* mostly coincide with Vezzetti's observations, both in chronological terms and with respect to the subjective and privatized elements of this second pattern. The texts also trace an itinerary that begins with the figure of the disappeared as an innocent victim in the early democracy and ends with the figure of the disappeared as "normalized militant" (102); this latter figure originates in the mid-1990s and solidifies after 2003.

16. In a chapter on child war films included in the above-mentioned book, Lury claims that these films productively pull the viewer in different directions. On the one hand, they seemingly simplify the narrative's historical context, inserting it within a fairytale temporal framework. On the other, this mythical temporal framework challenges the demand of chronological history-telling and thus offers possibilities for productive transgression (105–144).

17. Although carefully argued and thought-provoking, I deviate from Aguilar's interpretation on three important fronts. First, I find Aguilar's distinction between fiction and testimony to be misleading, as I further discussed in the first chapter. Second, as I have explained earlier in this chapter, I do not believe that this representation of activism is an original one; on the contrary, I find it a paradigmatic example of the subjective representation that has gained prominence since the 1990s. Finally, as I claimed in the third chapter, I find fiction films more popular (and more hegemonic) in second-generation cinema than the documentary genre.

18. For these reasons, I partially agree with Geoffrey Maguire's careful reading of *Infancia clandestina*. While I agree that the film challenges the idea of children lacking agency, and while I also believe that it offers a complex portrayal of the private consequences of political commitment, I do not think that it provides an innovative, politicized, or deeply historicized depiction of militancy.

19. Beverley himself indirectly suggests that this is the case when stating that "there is a relation between how one thinks about the armed struggle in Latin America and how one thinks about the nature and possibilities of the new governments of the *marea rosada*" (*Latinamericanism after 9/11* 95). Following his argument, if the paradigm of disillusion had dominated Argentina in the last decade, the Kirchner administration would not have had attained such strong support. Perhaps the problem with Beverley's assessment is that he has based his claims on Beatriz Sarlo, who was actually a marginal voice in this respect.

Afterword

From Counterhegemony to Hegemony

On August 10, 2016, Karla Zabludovsky, a journalist from BuzzFeed, interviewed Argentine president Mauricio Macri on his views of the country after almost a year of being in office. The interview, broadcast live on Facebook, received a fair amount of attention. The hottest, most criticized topic was Macri's opinion on how to deal with the aftermath of the dictatorship. In response to Zabludovsky's question of whether his administration was going to support the ongoing trials against those who committed crimes during the military regime, Macri said that he believed the judiciary power should continue the legal process without the executive power intervening. He then claimed that relatives of missing people deserved to know everything and that unveiling what happened during the horrible tragedy of the dirty war was a priority—even though his top priority, he further clarified, was to focus on the human rights of the twenty-first century. Finally, in an allusion to one of his public officers having previously stated that nine thousand—as opposed to thirty thousand—was a most accurate count for the number of people who had disappeared, Macri indicated that he had "no clue" about the numbers, as he considered them irrelevant. He then quickly added that the dictatorship had a huge importance already, regardless of the number of casualties; it was the worst thing that had ever happened in Argentine history.

There certainly are several issues worth criticizing in Macri's short answer. The assertion that the judiciary power should be independent from the executive power when dealing with state-sponsored violence not only eludes responsibility, but it also is oblivious to the role that the latter has played in this specific case. The executive power has historically been the one that has either enabled or inhibited the legal process, from Alfonsín's CONADEP and Menem's amnesties to Néstor Kirchner's repeal of the *leyes de punto final* and *obediencia debida*. Referring to the dictatorship as a "dirty war" is, as I explained in chapter 1, both conceptually and ideologically problematic. The notion that the human rights of the twenty-first century should take priority over those violated during the dictatorship fails to recognize how these seemingly past violations have spilled over into the present, as evident in the existence of around three hundred second-generation survivors who are still unaware of their real biological identity, to name but the most telling example. Finally, arguing that figures are irrelevant is, to say the least, clumsy. Though thirty thousand might not be an accurate count (see Vezzetti, *Pasado*), it has been deeply meaningful to those directly affected and a symbolic way of showing support for their cause.

What interests me most from this interview, however, is not Macri's already-criticized view but the fact that his words reveal the passage from counterhegemony to hegemony that I have emphasized throughout the book. His rhetoric ("horrible tragedy," "the worst thing that has ever happened") makes it clear that, in 2016, not even a right-wing administration can cast doubts on the catastrophic magnitude of the dictatorship without facing fierce opposition. Even in the midst of tensions, such as those existing between Macri and human rights organizations, it is impossible to call into question the legitimacy of the relatives of missing people without leading to social unrest.[1] After three decades of continuous antidictatorship discourse, even someone like Macri is forced to be (almost) politically correct when talking about the period. The president's vocabulary inadvertently proves that the narrative that once offered an alternative, subaltern version of history has become the dominant—even when not officially encouraged—view.

As my book has shown, testimonial films have both registered and contributed to this ideological trajectory. The transition from 1980s films such as *Juan* or *La noche de los lápices* and 1990s documentaries such as *Montoneros, Cazadores*, or *Botín de guerra* to post-2000 films such as *Los rubios, Papá Iván, Infancia clandestina*, or *Cautiva* has documented and enabled the transition of "military dictatorship" from what Laclau calls a "floating signifier" (131) to an empty signifier. In the first case, meaning is suspended and indeterminate between alternative equivalent frontiers. In the second, as explained in previous chapters, a particularity takes up universal signification and assumes the representation of a totality. In other words, in the first case, "military dictatorship" is open to contestation and articulation to different particular demands. The meaning of "military dictatorship" is still unstable, as an antagonistic frontier that could unify competing meanings into a stable system of signification has not yet formed. Notions like the innocent victim, the passionate activist, and the crime perpetrator and signs such as the green Ford Falcon bring about new feelings and offer alternative meanings. As the earlier films' staging of indexicality underscores, cinematic images are in the process of creating a new referent (a new immediate object) for "military dictatorship."

In the second case, the consolidation of antagonism has allowed previously heterogeneous meanings to unify into a stable system of signification. As is evident in post-2000 films, especially in fiction, images like the passionate activist, the innocent victim, the crime perpetrator, and the green Ford Falcon have been transformed into global iconic signs that further naturalize existing emotions.

Via a mixture of repetition and stability, these signs, along with others explored in previous chapters, have turned "military dictatorship" into an empty signifier (a *point de capiton*) that connects to a universal referent. This referent is, as exposed in second-generation performative documentaries, universal yet, at the same time, impossible and stable—even though stability is certainly contingent and open to transformation over time. Simply put, from 1983 to the present day, postdictatorship testimonial films have run the gamut from counterhegemony to hegemony.

This ideological trajectory resembles the one that goes from Eduardo Coutinho's *Cabra marcado para morrer* (1962–1984) to Cao Hamburger's *O ano em que meus pais saíram de férias* (2006) in Brazil, from Costa-Gavras's *Estado de sitio* (1972) to Ana Díez's *Paisito* (2008) in Uruguay, from Patricio Guzmán's *La batalla de Chile* (1975–1979) to his own *Nostalgia de la luz* (2010) in Chile, or from Víctor Erice's *El espíritu de la colmena* (1973) to Guillermo Del Toro's *El laberinto del fauno* (2006) in Spain. Beyond the Latin American or Spanish context, a parallel trajectory can be noted in films dealing with political conflicts that impacted the global imaginary over several decades. We can trace this type of shift, for instance, in the transition from Claude Lanzmann's *Shoah* (1985) to Roberto Benigni's *La vita è bella* (1998) in the case of the Holocaust or from Sharon Sopher's *Witness to Apartheid* (1986) to Clint Eastwood's *Invictus* (2009) in the case of apartheid South Africa. Such an ideological trajectory, on the one hand, ensures that not even a right-wing president can call these films' universal, stable referent into question without confronting fierce opposition, yet, on the other, it faces the numbing consequences of universalization and stability.

It is precisely this passage from counterhegemony to hegemony that explains the reticence against postdictatorship testimonial narratives that, as I observed in the book's introduction, came to light in the early 2000s and increased after 2003. This explains why the proliferation of unreliable testimonies in Gamerro's *El secreto y las voces*, the oxymoronic nature of Pauls's *Historia del llanto*, the irony in Pensotti's *Cuando vuelva a casa voy a ser otro*, and the critical views of scholars such as Sarlo, Vezzetti, Vallina, and Crenzel arose exactly as memory reached the center of public discourse. This transformation also explains why—as LaCapra, Tal, Nance, and Huyssen noticed—memory fatigue has set in. Yet, with these observations, I do not want to suggest that testimonial narratives are no longer relevant. Maintaining hegemony is of utmost importance in order to ensure continuity of trials, to help survivors reunite with their families and to make certain that atrocious events will not be repeated. In tracing this itinerary, rather than criticizing the testimonial genre, I have sought to advocate for a reading that places historicity at its core. This type of reading should be able to address the representation of history over time and to account for its different connotations since the 2000s, when the notion of working through the past has become a widespread moral imperative, when there already is a generalized consensus against dictatorships, when people already know the atrocities that happened in detention centers, and when the narratives that used to be the most subaltern version of history have shifted into the most hegemonic version.

Neither subaltern nor trauma theory are fully adequate in this respect. As I have analyzed throughout the book, several of their key concepts are oblivious to testimonial cinema's transformation. As a result, history remains a steady background, and the military dictatorship continues to be a stable and invariable referent—a founding trauma preserved by symptomatic, repetitive-compulsive readings. Contrary to their own stated purposes, these frameworks yield iconic interpretations that close the gap between sign and referent and preclude further examination. An approach grounded in a combination of semiotics and affect, on the contrary, provides the foundations to restore historicity. It helps elucidate how films materialize history and are inscribed in history. It contributes to an understanding of how films intersect with the present and are immersed in time. Arguably, this approach has other drawbacks. The burden on the reader is one of them. In order to read these films from this perspective, we need to delve into complex concepts such as icon, index, and affect, coming close to that hypertheoretical analysis that LaCapra rightly criticized. Furthermore, this approach requires that we be conversant with specific historical moments over time; that is, we would not be able to read these films' transformation without at least knowing something about Argentine postdictatorship culture and history. I believe, however, that reading the signs present in the cinematic field and their connection to history is no more complicated than appealing to intricate concepts such as postmemory, trauma, melancholy, and mourning. Moreover, if we consider the ideological implications of symptomatic, iconic interpretations, the adoption of an affective-semiotic approach becomes an ethical duty. Such an approach allows us, as I hope to have shown in this book, to overcome testimonial films' repetitive excess and to go beyond memory fatigue.

Note

1. Macri has indeed called into question the legitimacy of Hebe de Bonafini several times, even in that same interview. His accusations have, however, mostly been based on the legal case against Bonafini's embezzlement of federal funds and not on her rights as the mother of missing children. Indeed, a good example of how calling into question the legitimacy of relatives of missing people leads to social unrest is the government's decision, in March 2017, to put cement signs on top of the place where the Madres de Plaza de Mayo march every Thursday. This provocative gesture sparked a strong, generalized opposition materialized in rallies, newspaper articles, TV interviews, and so forth.

Works Cited

A los compañeros la libertad. Directed by Marcelo Céspedes and Carmen Guarini, Cine Ojo, 1987.
Abuelas de Plaza de Mayo. "Quiénes somos." n.p., Abuelas de Plaza de Mayo., https://www.abuelas.org.ar/abuelas/historia-9. Accessed Feb. 3, 2015.
Achugar, Hugo. "Leones, cazadores e historiadores." *Teorías sin disciplina (latinoamericanismo, poscolonialidad y globalización en debate)*, edited by Santiago Castro-Gómez and Eduardo Mendieta, Porrúa, 1998, pp. 207–218.
Achugar, Hugo and John Beverley, editors. *La voz del otro: testimonio, subalternidad y verdad narrativa*. Latinoamericana, 1992.
Acuña, Carlos, comp. *La nueva matriz política argentina*. Nueva Visión, 1995.
Agamben, Giorgio. *Homo Sacer: Sovereign Power and Bare Life*. Stanford: Stanford University Press, 1998.
———. *Lo que queda de Auschwitz: el archivo y el testigo*. Pretextos, 1999.
Aguilar, Gonzalo. "*Infancia Clandestina* or The Will of Faith." *Journal of Romance Studies*, vol. 13, no. 3, 2013, pp. 17–31.
———. "Maravillosa melancolía. A propósito de *Cazadores de utopías* de David Blaustein." *Cines al margen. Nuevos modos de representación en el cine argentino contemporáneo*, edited by María José Moore and Paula Wolkowicz. Libraria, 2007, pp. 17–32.
———. *Otros mundos. Un ensayo sobre el nuevo cine argentino*. Santiago Arcos, 2010.
Ahmed, Sara. *The Cultural Politics of Emotion*. Edinburgh University Press, 2004.
———. *The Promise of Happiness*. Duke University Press, 2010.
Alexander, Jeffrey. *Trauma. A Social Theory*. Polity Press, 2012.
Alexander, Jeffrey, Ron Eyerman, Bernard Giesen, Neil Smelser, and Piotr Sztompka. *Cultural Trauma and Collective Identity*. University of California Press, 2004.
Algarra, Giovanni and Andrea Noble. "'Transportamos sentimientos': Desafío para el estudio de las emociones en América Latina." *Pretérito indefinido. Afecto y emociones en las aproximaciones al pasado*, edited by Cecilia Macón and Mariela Solana. Título, 2015, pp. 43–65.
Altamirano, Carlos. "Montoneros." *Punto de vista*, no. 55, 1996, pp. 1–9.
Alvaray, Luisela. "Hybridity and Genre in Transnational Latin American Cinemas." *Transnational Cinemas*, vol. 4, no. 1, 2013, pp. 67–87.
Álvarez, Victoria. "'¿Habremos hecho bien?' Una aproximación a las zonas grises en *Montoneros: una historia*." n.p. *Revista Cine Documental*, no. 5, 2012, 9 Feb. 2015, www.revista.cinedocumental.com.ar/5/articulos_05.html. Accessed Feb. 9, 2015
Amado, Ana. *La imagen justa. Cine argentino y política (1980–2007)*. Colihue, 2009.
La amiga. Directed by Jeanine Meerapfel, Alma Films, 1988.
Andermann, Jens. "Expanded Fields: Postdictatorship and the Landscape." *Journal of Latin American Cultural Studies*, vol. 21, no. 2, 2012, pp. 165–187.
———. *Mapas de poder: una arqueología literaria del espacio argentino*. Beatriz Viterbo, 2000.

———. *New Argentine Cinema*. I. B. Tauris, 2012.
Andermann, Jens, Philip Derbyshire, and John Kraniauskas. "No Matarás ('Thou Shalt Not Kill'): An Introduction." *Journal of Latin American Cultural Studies*, vol. 16, no. 2 (2007, pp.111–113).
Andrés no quiere dormir la siesta. Directed by Daniel Bustamante. El Ansia Producciones, 2009.
Antze, Paul and Michael Lambek, editors. *Tense Past: Cultural Essays in Trauma and Memory*. Routledge, 1996.
Aon, Luciana. "Una cuestión de representación: las películas de los directores-hijos." *Estudios*, no. 25, 2011, pp. 219–230.
Appadurai, Arjun. *Fear of Small Numbers: An Essay on the Geography of Anger*. Duke University Press, 2006.
Aprea, Gustavo. *Cine y políticas en Argentina. Continuidades y discontinuidades en 25 años*. Universidad General Sarmiento, 2008.
Aprea, Gustavo, comp. *Filmar la memoria. Los documentales audiovisuales y la reconstrucción del pasado*. Universidad Nacional de General Sarmiento, 2012.
Arias, Arturo, editor. *The Rigoberta Menchú Controversy*. University of Minnesota Press, 2001.
Ariés, Philippe. *Centuries of Childhood. A Social History of Family Life*. Vintage Books, 1962.
Arfuch, Leonor. *Memoria y autobiografía. Exploraciones en los límites*. Fondo de Cultura Económica, 2013.
Assmann, Jan. *Cultural Memory and Early Civilization: Writing, Remembrance, and Political Imagination*. Cambridge University Press, 2011.
Avelar, Idelber. *The Untimely Present: Postdictatorial Latin American Fiction and the Task of Mourning*. Duke University Press, 1999.
Ávila, Benjamín. "Entrevista con Benjamín Ávila." n.p., *Revista Cabal*. 1 Oct 2012, www.revistacabal.coop/actualidad/entrevista-benjamin-avila-director-de-infancia-clandestina. Accessed March 23, 2013.
Balász, Béla. "The Close-Up." *Film Theory and Criticism: Introductory Readings*, edited by Leo Braudy and Michael Cohen, Oxford University Press, 1999, pp. 304–305.
Balderston, Daniel, comp. *Ficción y política: la narrativa argentina durante el proceso militar*. Alianza, 1987.
Balmaceda, Oscar and Antonio Fernández Llorente. *El caso Cabezas*. Planeta, 1997.
Basualdo, Eduardo. *Estudios de historia económica Argentina: desde mediados del siglo XX a la actualidad*. Siglo XXI, 2006.
La batalla de Chile. Directed by Patricio Guzmán, ICAIC, 1975–1979.
Bauman, Zygmunt. *Modernity and the Holocaust*. Cornell University Press, 1989.
Beasley-Murray, Jon. *Posthegemony: Political Theory and Latin America*. University of Minnesota Press, 2010.
Beceyro, Raúl. "Fantasmas del pasado." *Punto de vista*, no. 55, 1996, pp. 10–12.
Bekerman, Silvana. "Cultural Production: Contributions from Films to the Psychosocial Processing of Collective Trauma." *South Dictatorship and After. Psychosocial and Clinical Elaboration of Collective Traumas*, edited by Diana Kordon, EATIP, 2012, pp. 159–172.
Belzagui, Pablo, comp. *Sobre la responsabilidad. No matar*. Ediciones del Cíclope/La Intemperie, 2007.
Benjamin, Walter. *Illuminations*. Harcourt, Brace and World, 1968.

———. "Tesis de filosofía de la historia." *Discursos interrumpidos I*. Taurus, 1973.
———. "The Work of Art in the Age of Mechanical Reproduction." *Film Theory and Criticism: Introductory Readings*, edited by Leo Braudy and Michael Cohen, Oxford University Press, 1999, pp. 731–751.
Bennett, Jill. *Empathic Vision: Affect, Trauma, and Contemporary Art*. Stanford University Press, 2005.
Benveniste, Émile. *Problems in General Linguistics*. University of Miami Press, 1971.
Berlant, Lauren. *Cruel Optimism*. Duke University Press, 2011.
Bernardes, Horacio, Diego Lerer, and Sergio Wolf, editors. *Nuevo cine argentino: temas, autores y estilos de una renovación*. Fipresci, 2002.
Beverley, John. *Against Literature*. University of Minnesota Press, 1993.
———. *Latinamericanism after 9/11*. Duke University Press, 2011.
———. "The Neoconservative Turn in Latin American Literary and Cultural Criticism." *Journal of Latin American Cultural Studies*, vol. 17, no. 1, 2008, pp. 65–83.
———. *Subalternity and Representation*. Duke University Press, 1999.
———. *Testimonio: On the Politics of Truth*. University of Minnesota Press, 2004.
Bial, Henry, editor. *The Performance Studies Reader*. Routledge, 2004.
Bilyk, Pablo. "Memoria y subjetividad: Reflexiones desde el caso *Televisión por la identidad*." *Perspectivas de la comunicación*, vol. 6, no. 1, 2013, pp. 159–164.
Blaustein, David. "La mirada del cine: de la dictadura hasta hoy." *Psicoanálisis: identidad y transmisión*, compiled by Alicia Lo Giúdice. Abuelas de Plaza de Mayo, 2008, pp. 153–159.
Blejmar, Jordana. *Playful Memories: The Autofictional Turn in Post-Dictatorship Argentina*. Palgrave Macmillan, 2016.
Blejmar, Jordana and Natalia Fortuny. "Introduction." *Journal of Romance Studies*, vol. 13, no. 3, 2013, pp. 1–5.
Bonasso, Miguel. *La memoria en donde ardía*. Colihue, 1990.
Bordwell, David and Kristin Thompson. *Film Art: An Introduction*. McGraw-Hill, 1993.
Borón, Atilio, comp. *Peronismo y menemismo: avatares del populismo en la Argentina*. El Cielo por Asalto, 1995.
Bosteels, Bruno. *Marx and Freud in Latin America. Politics, Psychoanalysis, and Religion in Times of Terror*. Verso, 2012.
Botín de guerra. Directed by David Blaustein, Zafra, 1999.
Boyhood. Directed by Richard Linklater, IFC, 2014.
Breckenridge, Janis. "Enabling, Enacting, and Envisioning Societal Complicity. Daniel Bustamante's *Andrés no quiere dormir la siesta*." *Representing History, Class, and Gender in Spain and Latin America*, edited by Carolina Rocha and Georgia Seminet. Palgrave, 2012, pp. 101–114.
Brennan, Teresa. *The Transmission of Affect*. Cornell University Press, 2004.
Brunner, José Joaquín. *La cultura autoritaria en Chile*. Facultad Latinoamericana de Ciencias Sociales, 1981.
Bruzzi, Stella. *New Documentary: A Critical Introduction*. Routledge, 2006.
Bruzzone, Félix. *Los topos*. Mondadori, 2012.
Burke, Peter. *Eyewitnessing: The Uses of Images as Historical Evidence*. Reaktion, 2001.
Burton, Julianne, editor. *The Social Documentary in Latin America*. University of Pittsburgh Press, 1990.

Burucúa, Constanza. *Confronting the "Dirty War" in Argentine Cinema (1983–1993). Memory and Gender in Historical Representations*. Tamesis, 2009.
Butler, Judith. *Bodies that Matter: On the Discursive Limits of Sex*. Routledge, 1993.
Cabra marcado para morrer. Directed by Eduardo Coutinho, Gaumont, 1984.
Calveiro, Pilar. *Poder y desaparición. Los campos de concentración en Argentina*. Colihue, 1998.
Calvert, Karin. *Children in the House: The Material Culture of Early Childhood (1600–1900)*. Northeastern University Press, 1992.
Camila. Directed by María Luisa Bemberg, Gea, 1984.
Candau, Joël. *Antropología de la memoria*. Nueva visión, 2002.
Caparrós, Martín and Eduardo Anguita, comps. *La voluntad: una historia de la militancia revolucionaria en la Argentina*. Norma, 1997.
Carlson, Marvin. "What Is Performance?" *The Performance Studies Reader*, edited by Henry Bial, Routledge, 2004, pp. 68–73.
Carri, Albertina. *Los Rubios: cartografía de una película*. Ediciones Gráficas Especiales, 2007.
Carri, Roberto. *Isidro Velázquez. Formas prerrevolucionarias de la violencia*. Colihue, 2001.
Cartwright, Lisa. *Moral Spectatorship: Technologies of Voice and Affect in Postwar Representations of the Child*. Duke University Press, 2008.
Caruth, Cathy, editor. *Trauma: Explorations in Memory*. Johns Hopkins University Press, 1995.
Caruth, Cathy. *Unclaimed Experience: Trauma, Narrative, and History*. Johns Hopkins University Press, 1996.
Castro-Gómez, Santiago and Eduardo Mendieta, editors. *Teorías sin disciplina (latinoamericanismo, poscolonialidad y globalización en debate)*. Porrúa, 1998.
Casullo, Nicolás, editor. *Sobre Walter Benjamin: vanguardias, historia, estética y literatura: una visión latinoamericana*. Alianza, 1993.
Cautiva. Directed by Gastón Biraben, Cacerolazo Producciones, 2004.
Cazadores de utopías. Directed by David Blaustein, SBP, 1996.
Cenizas del paraíso. Directed by Marcelo Piñeyro, Patagonik, 1997.
Chanan, Michael, editor. *Twenty-Five Years of the New Latin American Cinema*. British Film Institute, 1993.
Chanan, Michael. *The Politics of Documentary*. British Film Institute, 2007.
Chapman, James. *Film and History*. Palgrave Macmillan, 2013.
Che vo cachai. Directed by Laura Bondarevsky, Hasta la victoria producciones, 2003.
Clarke, Simon, Paul Hoggett, and Simon Thompson, editors. *Emotion, Politics, and Society*. Palgrave Macmillan, 2006.
Cohan, Steven and Ina Rae Hark. *The Road Movie Book*. Routledge, 1997.
Colás, Santiago. *Postmodernity in Latin America: The Argentine Paradigm*. Duke University Press, 1994.
Comisión nacional sobre la desaparición de personas (CONADEP), comp. *Nunca Más: informe de la Comisión Nacional sobre la Desaparición de Personas*. Eudeba, 2003.
Connell, Raewyn W. *Masculinities*. Polity Press, 1995.
Connerton, Paul. *How Societies Remember*. Cambridge University Press, 1989.
Copjec, Joan. *Read My Desire: Lacan Against the Historicists*. MIT Press, 1994.
Crenzel, Emilio, comp. *Los desaparecidos en la Argentina. Memorias, representaciones e ideas (1983–2008)*. Biblos, 2010.

Crenzel, Emilio. *La historia política del* Nunca Más. *La memoria de las desapariciones en la Argentina*. Siglo XXI, 2008.
Crónica de un niño solo. Directed by Leonardo Favio, International Group, 1965.
Cuando vuelva a casa voy a ser otro. Directed by Mariano Pensotti, Teatro Centro Cultural San Martín, Argentina, 2016.
Cuarentena. Exilio y regreso. Directed by Carlos Echeverría, Clansud, 1983.
Cuatreros. Directed by Albertina Carri, Wankacine, 2016.
Da Silva Catela, Ludmila. "Lo invisible revelado. El uso de fotografías como (re) presentación de la desaparición de personas en la Argentina." *El pasado que miramos. Memoria e imagen ante la historia reciente*, compiled by Claudia Feld and Jessica Stites, Mor. Paidós, 2009, pp. 337–361.
———. "Prólogo". *La consagración de la memoria: Una etnografía acerca de la institucionalización del recuerdo sobre los crímenes del terrorismo de Estado en la Argentina*, edited by Ana Guglielmucci, Antropofagia, 2013, pp. 9–12.
Dalmaroni, Miguel. "La moral de la historia. Novelas argentinas sobre la dictadura (1995– 2002)." *Hispamérica*, no. 32, 2003, pp. 29–47.
Darse cuenta. Directed by Alejandro Doria, Rosafrey, 1984.
Davidson, Joyce, Liz Bondi, and Mick Smith, editors. *Emotional Geographies*. Ashgate, 2005.
Deleuze, Gilles and Félix Guattari. *Anti-Oedipus*. Continuum, 2004.
———. *Cinema I*. University of Minnesota Press, 1986.
———. *Cinema II*. University of Minnesota Press, 1989.
Delgado, María and Cecilia Sosa. "Politics, Memory and Fiction(s) in Contemporary Argentine Cinema: The Kirchnerist Years." *A Companion to Latin American Cinema*, edited by María Delgado, Stephen Hart, and Randal Johnson, Wiley-Blackwell, 2017, pp. 238–268.
Diana, Marta. *Mujeres guerrilleras*. Planeta, 1996.
Diario argentino. Directed by Lupe Pérez García, Ibermedia, 2006.
Doane, Mary Ann. *The Emergence of Cinematic Time: Modernity, Contingency, the Archive*. Harvard University Press, 2002.
———. "The Indexical and the Concept of Medium Specificity." *differences: a Journal of Feminist Cultural Studies*, vol. 18, no. 1, 2007, pp. 128–152.
Donatello, Luis Miguel. *Catolicismo y montoneros. Religión, política y desencanto*. Manantial, 2010.
Douglass, Ana and Thomas Vogel, editors. *Witness and Memory: The Discourse of Trauma*. Routledge, 2003.
Dove, Patrick. "Memory Between Politics and Ethics: Del Barco's Letter." *Journal of Latin American Cultural Studies*, vol. 17, no. 3, 2007, pp. 279–297.
Downing, John, editor. *Film and Politics in the Third World*. Automedia, 1986.
Dufays, Sophie. *El niño en el cine argentino de la posdictadura (1983–2008): alegoría y nostalgia*. Támesis, 2014.
Elsaesser, Thomas. "Postmodernism as Mourning Work." *Screen*, vol. 42, no. 2, 2001, pp. 193–201.
Encontrando a Víctor. Directed by Natalia Bruschtein, Centro de Capacitación Cinematográfica, 2005.
En memoria de los pájaros. Directed by Gabriela Golder, Vimeo, 2000.
Epstein, Edward and David Pion-Berlin, editors. *The Argentine Crisis and Argentine Democracy*. Lexington Books, 2006.

Erikson, Erik. *Identity, Youth, and Crisis*. Norton, 1968.
España, Claudio, comp. *Cine argentino en democracia (1983–1993)*. Fondo Nacional de las Artes, 1994.
El espinazo del diablo. Directed by Guillermo Del Toro, El Deseo Producciones, 2001.
El espíritu de la colmena. Directed by Víctor Erice, Elías Tejereta, 1973.
Estado de sitio. Directed by Costa-Gavras, Constantin Film, 1972.
Evita. Directed by Alan Parker, Patagonik, 1996.
Falicov, Tamara. *The Cinematic Tango: Contemporary Argentine Film*. Wallflower Press, 2007.
Feder, Elena. "In the Shadow of Race: Forging Images of Women in Bolivian Film and Video." *Frontiers: A Journal of Women Studies*, vol. 15, no. 1, 1994, pp. 123–140.
Feierstein, Liliana. "Por una e(sté)tica de la recepción. La escucha social frente a los hijos de detenidos-desaparecidos en Argentina." *Helix*, no. 5, 2012, pp. 124–144.
Feinmann, José Pablo. "El año que vivimos en peligro." *Página 12*, 16 Sept. 2012, www.pagina12.com.ar/diario/suplementos/radar/9-8231-2012-09-16.html. Accessed March 23, 2013.
Feld, Claudia. "'Aquellos ojos que contemplaron el límite': La puesta en escena televisiva de testimonios sobre la desaparición." *El pasado que miramos. Memoria e imagen ante la historia reciente*, compiled by Claudia Feld and Jessica Stites Mor. Paidós, 2009, pp. 77–109.
———. *Del estrado a la pantalla. Las imágenes del juicio a los ex comandantes en Argentina*. Siglo XXI, 2002.
Felman, Shoshana. *The Juridical Unconscious: Trials and Traumas in the Twentieth Century*. Harvard University Press, 2002.
Felman, Shoshana and Dori Laub. *Testimony: Crises of Witnessing in Literature, Psychoanalysis and History*. Routledge, 1992.
Ferro, Marc. *Cinema and History*. Wayne State University Press, 1988.
Fiorucci, Flavia and Marcus Klein, editors. *The Argentine Crisis at the Turn of the Millennium: Causes, Consequences and Explanations*. Cedla, 2004.
Firbas, Paul and Pedro Meira Monteiro. *Conversación en Princeton. Andrés Di Tella: cine documental y archivo personal*. Siglo XXI, 2006.
Forcinito, Ana. *Los umbrales del testimonio: Entre las narraciones de los sobrevivientes y las señas de la posdictadura*. Iberoamericana Vervuert, 2012.
Franco, Marina. *Un enemigo para la nación: orden interno, violencia y "subversión" (1973– 1976)*. Fondo de Cultura Económica, 2012.
Freud, Sigmund. *Beyond the Pleasure Principle*. Norton & Company, 1961.
Friedman, Régine Mihal. "Witnessing for the Witness: Choice and Destiny by Tsipi Reibenbach." *Shofar: An Interdisciplinary Journal of Jewish Studies*, vol. 24, no. 1, 2005, pp. 81–93.
Gabriel, Teshome. *Third Cinema in the Third World*. University of Michigan Research Press, 1982.
Gamerro, Carlos. *El secreto y las voces*. Norma, 2002.
———. *Un yuppie en la columna del Che Guevara*. Edhasa, 2011.
Garage Olimpo. Directed by Marco Bechis, Classic, 1999.
Garibotto, Verónica and Antonio Gómez. "Historical Stasis: Solanas and the Restoration of Political Film after the 2001 Argentine Crisis." *Studies in Hispanic Cinemas*, vol. 6, no. 2, 2010, pp. 125–138.

———. "Más allá del 'formato memoria': la repostulación del imaginario posdictatorial en *Los rubios* de Albertina Carri." *A contracorriente*, vol. 3, no. 2, 2006, pp. 107–126.

Garibotto, Verónica and Jorge Pérez, editors. *The Latin American Road Movie*. Palgrave Macmillan, 2016.

Garretón, Manuel, Saúl Sosnowski, and Bernardo Subercaseux, editors. *Cultura, autoritarismo y redemocratización en Chile*. Fondo de Cultura Económica, 1993.

Gellner, Ernest. *The Psychoanalytic Movement: The Cunning of Unreason*. Blackwell, 2003.

Gelman, Juan and Mara La Madrid, editors. *Ni el flaco perdón de dios. Hijos de desaparecidos*. Planeta, 1997.

Gillespie, Richard. *Los montoneros: soldados de Perón*. Grijalbo, 1998.

Gilman, Claudia. *Entre la pluma y el fusil: debates y dilemas del escritor revolucionario en América Latina*. Siglo XXI, 2003.

Goldberg, Amos and Haim Hazan, editors. *Marking Evil: Holocaust Memory in the Global Age*. Berghahn, 2015.

Gómez, Antonio. "Displacing the 'I': Uses of the First Person in Recent Argentine Biographical Documentaries." *Latin American Documentary Film in the New Millennium*, edited by María Guadalupe Arenillas and Michael Lazzara, Palgrave Macmillan, 2016.

———. "First-Person Documentary and the New Political Subject: Enunciation, Recent History, and the Present in New Argentine Cinema." *New Documentaries in Latin America*, edited by Vinicius Navarro and Juan Carlos Rodríguez, Palgrave Macmillan, 2014.

González Bombal, Inés. "Nunca más: el juicio más allá de los estrados." VVAA. *Juicios, castigos y memorias. Derechos humanos y justicia en la política argentina*, Nueva Visión, 1995, pp. 200–227.

González Canosa, Mora and Luciana Sotelo. "Futuros pasados, futuros perdidos. Reconfiguraciones de la memoria de los setenta en la Argentina de los noventa." *Nuevo Mundo. Mundos Nuevos*, 13 July 2011, https://nuevomundo.revues.org/61701. Accessed Feb. 9, 2015.

Gorodischer, Julián. "Hay toda una generación en juego." *Página/12*, 25 Oct. 2005. https://www.pagina12.com.ar/diario/suplementos/espectaculos/5-772-2005-10-20.html. Accessed 11 July 2015.

Gregg, Melissa and Gregory Seigworth, editors. *The Affect Theory Reader*. Duke University Press, 2010.

Grimson, Alejandro and Gabriel Kessler. *On Argentina and the Southern Cone. Neoliberalism and National Imaginations*. Routledge, 2005.

Grinberg-Plá, Valeria. "En defensa de la afectividad: cine, justicia y ciudadanía." *Revista de Historia*, no. 27, 2012, pp. 105–114.

Grossberg, Lawrence. *Bringing It All Back Home: Essays on Cultural Studies*. Duke University Press, 1997.

Grünbaum, Adolf. *The Foundations of Psychoanalysis: A Philosophical Critique*. University of California Press, 1984.

Grüner, Eduardo. "Open Letter to Jorge Jinkis and Juan Ritvo." *Journal of Latin American Cultural Studies*, vol. 16, no. 2, 2007, pp. 135–140.

Guarini, Carmen. "De lo real a la realidad. El documental de creación en América Latina." *Hacer cine. Producción audiovisual en América Latina*, compiled by Eduardo Russo, Paidós, 2008, pp. 347–362.

Guelerman, Sergio. "Escuela, juventud y genocidio: una interpelación posible." *Memorias en presente: identidad y transmisión en la Argentina posgenocidio*, compiled by Sergio Guelerman, Norma, 2001, pp. 37–65.

Gugelberger, Georg, editor. *The Real Thing: Testimonial Discourse in Latin America*. Duke University Press, 1996.

Guglielmucci, Ana. *La consagración de la memoria: Una etnografía acerca de la institucionalización del recuerdo sobre los crímenes del terrorismo de Estado en la Argentina*. Antropofagia, 2013.

Guha, Ranajit, editor. *A Subaltern Studies Reader (1986–1995)*. University of Minnesota Press, 1997.

Gundermann, Christian. *Actos melancólicos. Formas de resistencia en la posdictadura Argentina*. Beatriz Viterbo, 2007.

Guneratne, Anthony and Wimal Dissanayake, editors. *Rethinking Third Cinema*. Routledge, 2003.

Hacer patria. Directed by David Blaustein, Zafra, 2006.

Halbwachs, Maurice. *Los marcos sociales de la memoria*. Anthropos, 2004.

Hall, Granville Stanley. *Adolescence: Its Psychology and Its Relations to Physiology, Anthropology, Sociology, Sex, Crime, Religion and Education*. Appleton, 1904.

Harding, Jennifer and E. Deidre Pribram, editors. *Emotions: A Cultural Studies Reader*. Routledge, 2009.

Hardt, Michael. "Foreword: What Affects are Good For." *The Affective Turn: Theorizing the Social*, edited by Patricia Ticineto Clough and Jean Halley, Duke University Press, 2007, pp. ix–1.

Hardt, Michael and Antonio Negri. *Multitude: War and Democracy in the Age of Empire*. Hamish Hamilton, 2004.

Hart, Stephen. *Contemporary Latin American Cultural Studies*. Routledge, 2014.

Harter, Susan. *The Construction of the Self: A Developmental Perspective*. Guilford Press, 1999.

Herman, Judith. *Trauma and Recovery*. Basic Books, 1992.

Hermida, Rodolfo. "Cine nacional y diversidad cultural." *Diversidad cultural y políticas públicas*, edited by Carlos Moneta, Unesco, 2006, pp. 1–18.

H.I.J.O.S., el alma en dos. Directed by Carmen Guarini and Marcelo Céspedes, Cine Ojo, 2005.

H.I.J.O.S. "Quiénes somos." *HIJOS*, 1995, www.hijos-capital.org.ar/. Accessed Feb. 2015.

Hirsch, Marianne. *Family Frames: Photography, Narrative, and Postmemory*. Harvard University Press, 1997.

———. "Surviving Images: Holocaust Photographs and the Work of Postmemory." *The Yale Journal of Criticism*, vol. 14, no. 1, 2001, pp. 5–37.

La historia oficial. Directed by Luis Puenzo, Historias cinematográficas, 1985.

(h)istorias cotidianas. Directed by Andrés Habegger, Zafra, 2001.

Holland, Patricia. *Picturing Childhood: The Myth of the Child in Popular Imagery*. I. B. Tauris, 2004.

Hombre mirando al sudeste. Directed by Eliseo Subiela, Cinequanon, 1987.

La hora de los hornos. Directed by Fernando Solanas, Cinesur, 1968.

Hutcheon, Linda. *A Theory of Parody*. Methuen, 1985.

Huyssen, Andreas. *Present Pasts. Urban Palimpsests and the Politics of Memory*. Stanford University Press, 2003.

Infancia clandestina. Directed by Benjamín Ávila, Wandavisión, 2012.
Invictus. Directed by Clint Eastwood, Malpaso, 2009.
Irigaray, Luce. *Speculum of the Other Woman*. Cornell University Press, 1985.
Jabbaz, Marcela and Claudio Lozano. "Memorias de la dictadura y transmisión generacional: representaciones y controversias." *Memorias en presente: identidad y transmisión en la Argentina posgenocidio*, compiled by Sergio Guelerman, Norma, 2001, pp. 97–131.
Jaggar, Alison. "Love and Knowledge: Emotion in Feminist Epistemology." *Emotions: A Cultural Studies Reader*, edited by Jennifer Harding and E. Deidre Pribram, Routledge, 2009, pp. 50–68.
Jameson, Fredric. *The Geopolitical Aesthetic: Cinema and Space in the World-System*. Indiana University Press, 1992.
———. *The Political Unconscious: Narrative as a Socially-Symbolic Act*. Cornell University Press, 1981.
———. *Postmodernism, or the Cultural Logic of Late Capitalism*. Duke University Press, 1991.
Jara, René and Hernán Vidal, editors. *Testimonio y literatura*. Institute for the Study of Ideologies and Literatures, 1986.
Jauretche, Ernesto. *No dejés que te la cuenten. Violencia y política en los 70*. Colihue, 1997.
Jelin, Elizabeth. *Los trabajos de la memoria*. Siglo XXI, 2002.
———. "¿Víctimas, familiares, o ciudadanos/as? Las luchas por la legitimidad de la palabra." *Los desaparecidos en la Argentina. Memorias, representaciones e ideas (1983–2008)*, compiled by Emilio Crenzel, Biblos, 2010, pp. 227–239.
Jelin, Elizabeth and Ana Longoni, comps. *Escrituras, imágenes y escenarios ante la represión*. Siglo XXI, 2005.
Jelin, Elizabeth and Victoria Langland, editors. *Monumentos, memoriales y marcas territoriales*. Siglo XXI, 2003.
Jenkins, Henry, editor. *The Children's Culture Reader*. New York University Press, 1998.
Jinkis, Jorge. "A Reply to Oscar Del Barco." *Journal of Latin American Cultural Studies*, vol. 16, no. 2, 2007, pp. 119–125.
Juan, como si nada hubiera sucedido. Directed by Carlos Echeverría, HFF, 2005.
Kairuz, Mariano. "Esto es lo que creo." *Página 12*, 16 Sept. 2012, https://www.pagina12.com.ar/diario/suplementos/radar/subnotas/8231-1802-2012-09-16.html. Accessed March 23, 2013.
Kaiser, Susana. "Escribiendo memorias de la dictadura: las asignaturas pendientes del cine Argentino." *Revista Critica de Ciencias Sociais*, no. 88, 2010, pp.101–125.
Kamchatka. Directed by Marcelo Piñeyro, Patagonik, 2002.
Kaplan, Betina. "*Botín de guerra* by David Blaustein." *Chasqui*, vol. 31, no. 2, 2002, pp. 151–152.
Kaplan, E. Ann. *Trauma Culture: The Politics of Terror and Loss in Media and Literature*. Rutgers University Press, 2005.
Kaufman, Alejandro. "Aduanas de la memoria. A propósito de *Tiempo pasado* de Beatriz Sarlo." *Zigurat*, 6 Mar. 2008. http://rayandolosconfines.com/critica_kaufman.html. Accessed Apr. 30, 2008.
———. "The Paradoxical Legacy of a Lost Treasure." *Journal of Latin American Cultural Studies*, vol. 16, no. 2, 2007, pp. 145–153.
King, John. *Magical Reels: A History of Cinema in Latin America*. Verso, 2000.
Kirchner, Néstor. "Discurso por la creación del Museo de la Memoria." *Wikisource*, Mar. 24, 2004. https://es.wikisource.org/wiki/Discurso_de_N%C3%A9stor_Kirchner_por_la_creaci%C3%B3n_del_Museo_de_la_Memoria. Accessed Mar. 18, 2013.

Kohan, Martín. "La apariencia celebrada." *Punto de vista*, no. 78, 2004, pp. 24–30.
Kohen-Raz, Odeya. "Arnon Goldfinger's *The Flat* (2011): Ethics and Aesthetics in Third Generation Holocaust Cinema." *Studies in Documentary Film*, vol. 6, no. 3, 2012, pp. 323–338.
Koselleck, Reinhardt. *Futuro pasado*. Paidós, 1993.
Kuhn, Annette. "Cinematic Experience, Film Space and the Child's World." *Canadian Journal of Film Studies*, vol. 19, no. 2, 2010, pp. 82–98.
El laberinto del fauno. Directed by Guillermo Del Toro, Estudios Picasso, 2006.
LaCapra, Dominick. *History in Transit: Experience, Identity, Critical Theory*. Cornell University Press, 2004.
———. *Writing History, Writing Trauma*. Johns Hopkins University Press, 2001.
Laclau, Ernesto. *On Populist Reason*. Verso, 2005.
Laclau, Ernesto and Chantal Mouffe. *Hegemony and Socialist Strategy: Towards a Radical Democratic Politics*. Verso, 2001.
Laderman, David. *Driving Visions: Exploring the Road Movie*. University of Texas Press, 2003.
Latin American Subaltern Studies Group. "Founding Statement." *boundary 2*, vol. 20, no. 3, 1993, pp. 110–121.
Lazzara, Michael. "Kidnapped Memories: Argentina's Stolen Children Tell Their Stories." *Journal of Human Rights*, no. 12, 2013, pp. 319–332.
Lazzarato, Maurizio. "Immaterial Labor." *Radical Thought in Italy: A Potential Politics*, edited by Paolo Virno and Michael Hardt, University of Minnesota Press, 1996, pp.133–148.
Lebeau, Vicky. *Childhood and Cinema*. Reaktion Books, 2008.
Lee, Nick. *Childhood and Society: Growing Up in an Age of Uncertainty*. Open University, 2001.
Lefebvre, Martin. *Landscape and Film*. Routledge, 2006.
Lesko, Nancy. *Act Your Age! A Cultural Construction of Adolescence*. Routledge, 2001.
Levi, Primo. *Trilogía de Auschwitz*. El Aleph, 2005.
Levitsky, Steven and Leandro Wolfson. *La transformación del justicialismo: Del partido sindical al partido clientelista, 1983–1999*. Siglo XXI, 2005.
Leys, Ruth. *Trauma: A Genealogy*. Chicago University Press, 2000.
Longoni, Ana. *Traiciones: la figura del traidor en los relatos acerca de los sobrevivientes de la represión*. Norma, 2007.
Lorenz, Federico. *Combates por la memoria: huellas de la dictadura en la historia*. Capital Intelectual, 2007.
Lukács, György. *History and Class Consciousness: Studies in Marxist Dialectics*. MIT Press, 1971.
Lury, Karen. *The Child in Film: Tears, Fears, and Fairy Tales*. I. B. Tauris, 2010.
Lupton, Deborah. *The Emotional Self: A Sociocultural Exploration*. Sage, 1998.
Lusnich, Ana Laura and Pablo Piedras, editors. *Una historia del cine político y social en Argentina (1896–1969)*. Nueva Librería, 2009.
Lutz, Catherine. *Unnatural Emotions: Everyday Sentiments on a Micronesian Atoll and Their Challenge to Western Theory*. University of Chicago Press, 1988.
Lvovich, Daniel and Jacquelina Bisquert. *La cambiante memoria de la dictadura: discursos públicos, movimientos sociales y legitimidad democrática*. Univ. Nac. de General Sarmiento, 2008.

M. Directed by Nicolás Prividera, Trivial, 2007.
MacCabe, Colin, editor. *The Talking Cure: Essays in Psychoanalysis and Language.* St. Martin's, 1981.
Machuca. Directed by Andrés Wood, Tornasol, 2004.
Macón, Cecilia. "*Los rubios* o del trauma como presencia." *Punto de vista*, no. 80, 2004, pp. 44–47.
Macón, Cecilia and Mariela Solana, editors. *Pretérito indefinido. Afecto y emociones en las aproximaciones al pasado.* Título, 2015.
Las Madres: The Mothers of Plaza de Mayo. Directed by Susana Blaustein Muñoz and Lourdes Portillo, Women Make Movies, 1985.
Maguire, Geoffrey. "Entre la memoria y la imaginación: la politización de la niñez y la conciencia cinematográfica en *Infancia clandestina* (2012) de Benjamín Ávila. *El pasado inasequible. Desaparecidos, hijos y combatientes en el arte y literatura del nuevo milenio*, edited by Jordana Blejmar, Mariana Eva Perez, and Silvana Mandolessi, Eudeba, 2017, pp. 249–276.
Malvinas: historia de traiciones. Directed by Jorge Denti, Zafra, 1983.
Manetti, Ricardo. "Cine testimonial." *Cine argentino en democracia (1983–1993)*, compiled by Claudio España, Fondo Nacional de las Artes, 1994, pp. 257–271.
Margulis, Paola. *De la formación a la institución. El documental audiovisual argentino en la transición democrática (1982–1990).* Imago Mundi, 2014.
———. "Documentaries and Politics in Postdictatorship Argentina: *Cuarentena: Exilio y regreso* and *Juan, como si nada hubiera sucedido* by Carlos Echeverría." *Social Identities: Journal for the Study of Race, Nation and Culture*, vol. 19, no. 3, 2013, pp. 324–339.
———. "Imágenes de la violencia. Un acercamiento a algunas imágenes recurrentes en el cine documental posdictadura." *Oficios Terrestres* vol. 16, no. 25, 2010, pp. 117–128.
———. "A Professional Without Borders: The Case of the Documentary Film-Maker Carlos Echeverría in Germany and Argentina." *Studies in Documentary Film*, vol. 5, no. 1, 2001, pp. 3–15.
Martín Barbero, Jesús. "Nuevas visibilidades políticas de la ciudad y visualidades narrativas de la violencia." *Revista de Crítica Cultural*, no. 33, 2006, pp. 6–11.
Martin-Jones, David. *Deleuze and World Cinemas.* Continuum, 2001.
Martuccelli, Danilo and Maristella Svampa. *La plaza vacía: Las transformaciones del peronismo.* Editorial Losada, 1997.
Masiello, Francine. *The Art of Transition: Latin American Culture and Neoliberal Crisis.* Duke University Press, 2001.
Massumi, Brian. *Parables for the Virtual: Movement, Affect, Sensation.* Duke University Press, 2002.
Memoria del saqueo. Directed by Fernando Solanas, Cinesur, 2004.
Mestman, Mariano. "Postales del cine militante argentino en el mundo." *Kilómetro 111. Ensayos sobre cine*, no. 2, 2001, pp. 7–32.
Mestman, Mariano, comp. *Las rupturas del 68 en el cine de América Latina.* Akal, 2016.
Metz, Christian. *Film Language. A Semiotics of the Cinema.* Oxford University Press, 1974.
———. *The Imaginary Signifier. Psychoanalysis and the Cinema.* Indiana University Press, 1995.
———. *Impersonal Enunciation, or the Place of Film.* Columbia University Press, 2016.
Mi vida después. Directed by Lola Arias, Teatro La Carpintería, 2010.

Miss Mary. Directed by María Luisa Bemberg, Gea/New World, 1986.
Montaldo, Graciela. *De pronto, el campo: literatura argentina y tradición rural*. Beatriz Viterbo, 1993.
Montecristo. Directed by Miguel Colom, Telefé, 2006.
Montoneros, una historia. Directed by Andrés Di Tella, SBP, 1994.
Moraña, Mabel and Ignacio M. Sánchez Prado, editors. *El lenguaje de las emociones: Afecto y cultura en América Latina*. Iberoamericana/Vervuert, 2012.
Moreiras, Alberto. *The Exhaustion of Difference: The Politics of Latin American Cultural Studies*. Duke University Press, 2001.
Moreno, María. "Esa rubia debilidad." *Página/12*, 19 Oct. 2003, https://www.pagina12.com.ar/diario/suplementos/radar/9-1001-2003-10-22.html. Accessed June 21, 2006.
Mulvey, Laura. *Visual and Other Pleasures (Language, Discourse, Society)*. Palgrave Macmillan, 1989.
Nance, Kimberly. *Can Literature Promote Justice? Trauma Narrative and Social Action in Latin American Testimonio*. Vanderbilt University Press, 2006.
Negri, Antonio. "Value and Affect." *boundary 2*, vol. 26, no. 2, 1999, pp. 77–87.
Newman, Kathleen. "Notes on Transnational Film Theory: Decentered Subjectivity, Decentered Capitalism." *World Cinemas, Transnational Perspectives*, edited by Nataša Ďurovičová and Kathleen Newman, Routledge, 2010, pp. 3–11.
Nichols, Bill. *La representación de la realidad*. Paidós, 1997.
———. *Introduction to Documentary*. Indiana University Press, 2001.
Nietos. Identidad y memoria. Directed by Benjamín Ávila, Primer Primer Plano, 2004.
Nino, Carlos. *Juicio al mal absoluto*. Emecé, 2006.
Nisenson, Pablo. "Acerca de *Vidas Privadas*." *Página/12*, 8 Mar. 2014, https://www.pagina12.com.ar/diario/espectaculos/subnotas/4713-2372-2002-05-04.html. Accessed May 8, 2015.
No al punto final. Directed by Jorge Denti, Zafra, 1986.
La noche de los lápices. Directed by Héctor Olivera, Aries, 1986.
Nora, Pierre. *Les Lieux de Mémoire*. Gallimard, 1997.
Noriega, Gustavo. *Estudio crítico sobre "Los rubios."* Picnic, 2009.
Nostalgia de la luz. Directed by Patricio Guzmán, Atacama, 2010.
Nouzeilles, Gabriela. "Postmemory Cinema and the Future of the Past in Albertina Carri's *Los Rubios*." *Journal of Latin American Cultural Studies*, vol. 14, no. 3, 2005, pp. 263–278.
Nueve reinas. Directed by Fabián Bielinksy, Patagonik, 2000.
O ano em que meus pais saíram de férias. Directed by Cao Hamburger, Miravista, 2006.
Oberti, Alejandra and Roberto Pittaluga. *Memorias en montaje. Escrituras de la militancia y pensamientos sobre la historia*. El cielo por asalto, 2006.
Odin, Roger. "Dokumentarischer Film—dokumentarisierende Lektüre." *Bilder des Wirklichen. Texte zur Theorie des Dokumentarfilms*, edited by Eva Hohenberg, Vorwerk, 1998, pp. 286–303.
O'Donnell, Guillermo. *Modernization and Bureaucratic-Authoritarianism: Studies in South American Politics*. Institute of International Studies, University of California Press, 1973.
O'Donnell, Guillermo, Philippe Schmitter, and Laurence Whitehead. *Transitions from Authoritarian Rule. Latin America*. Johns Hopkins University Press, 1986.

O'Keeffe, Moira. "Evidence and Absence: Documenting the *Desaparecidos* of Argentina." *Communication, Culture & Critique*, no. 2, 2009, pp. 520–537.
Los olvidados. Directed by Luis Buñuel, Versatil, 1950.
Orgeron, Devin. *Road Movies: From Muybridge and Méliès to Lynch and Kiarostami*. Palgrave Macmillan, 2008.
Padres de la Plaza. Directed by Joaquín Daglio, Oruga Cine, 2010.
Page, Joanna. *Crisis and Capitalism in Contemporary Argentine Cinema*. Duke University Press, 2009.
Paisito. Directed by Ana Díez, Tornasol, 2008.
Palermo, Vicente and Marcos Novaro. *Historia reciente: Argentina en democracia*. Edhasa, 2004.
Papá Iván. Directed by María Inés Roqué, Zafra, 2004.
Parker, Andrew and Eve Kosofsky Sedgwick. "Introduction to *Performativity and Performance*." *The Performance Studies Reader*, edited by Henry Bial, Routledge, 2004, pp. 167–174.
Partnoy, Alicia. "*Cuando vienen matando*: On Prepositional Shifts and the Struggle of Testimonial Subjects for Agency." *PMLA*, vol. 121, no. 5, October 2006, pp. 1665–1669.
———. *The Little School: Tales of Disappearance and Survival*. Cleis Press, 1986.
Paulinelli, María, editor. *Cine y dictadura*. Córdoba: Comunicarte, 2006.
Pauls, Alan. *Historia del llanto: un testimonio*. Anagrama, 2007.
Peirce, Charles. *Writings of Charles Peirce: A Chronological Edition*, edited by Max Fisch. Indiana University Press, 1982.
Perdía, Roberto. *La otra historia. Testimonio de un jefe montonero*. Ágora, 1997.
Perez, Mariana Eva. *Diario de una princesa montonera*. Capital Intelectual, 2012.
———. "Their Lives After: Theatre as Testimony and the So-Called 'Second Generation' in Post-Dictatorship Argentina." *Journal of Romance Studies*, vol. 13., no. 3, 2013, pp. 6–16.
Pérez Zabala, Victoria. "La doble vida de Juan." *La nación*, 15 Sept. 2012. www.lanacion.com .ar/1508554-la-doble-vida-de-juan. Accessed Jan. 21. 2013.
Persepolis. Directed by Marjane Satrapi, Diaphana, 2007.
Pfeiffer, Erna, editor. *Alicia Kozameh: Ética, estética y las acrobacias de la palabra escrita*. Instituto Internacional de Literatura Iberoamericana, 2013.
Pick, Zuzana, editor. *Latin American Film Makers and the Third Cinema*. Carleton University Press, 1978.
Piedras, Pablo. *El cine documental en primera persona*. Paidós, 2014.
———. "The Contemporary Documentary Road Movie in Latin America: Issues on Mobility, Displacement, and Autobiography." *The Latin American Road Movie*, edited by Verónica Garibotto and Jorge Pérez, Palgrave Macmillan, 2016, pp. 217–235.
———. "La regla y la excepción: figuraciones de la subjetividad autoral en documentales argentinos de los ochenta y noventa." *Toma Uno*, no. 1, 2012, pp. 37–53.
Pines, Jim and Paul Willemen, editors. *Questions of Third Cinema*. British Film Institute, 1989.
Plantinga, Carl. *Rhetoric and Representation in Non-fiction Film*. Cambridge University Press, 1997.
Plotkin, Mariano Ben. *Freud en las pampas: orígenes y desarrollo de una cultura psicoanalítica en la Argentina (1910–1983)*. Sudamericana, 2003.

Podalsky, Laura. *The Politics of Affect and Emotion in Contemporary Latin American Cinema: Argentina, Brazil, Cuba, and Mexico.* Palgrave Macmillan, 2011.
Popper, Karl. *Conjectures and Refutations.* Routledge, 1963.
Portela, Edurne. *Displaced Memories: The Poetics of Trauma in Argentine Women's Writing.* Bucknell University Press, 2009.
El premio. Directed by Paula Markovitch, IZ Films, 2011.
Prince, Stephen. "The Discourse of Pictures: Iconicity and Film Studies." *Film Theory and Criticism: Introductory Readings*, edited by Leo Braudy and Michael Cohen, Oxford University Press, 1999, pp. 99–117.
Prohibido. Directed by Andrés Di Tella, Latin American Video Archives, 1997.
Quintín. "Llega el cine kirchnerista." *La lectora provisoria*, 30 Sept. 2012, www.lectoraprovisoria.wordpress.com/2012/09/30/llega-el-cine-kirchnerista/. Accessed Jan. 21, 2013.
Qvortrup, Jens, William Corsaro, and Michael-Sebastian Honig, editors. *The Palgrave Handbook of Childhood Studies.* Palgrave Macmillan, 2009.
Rabasa, José. "On Documentary and Testimony: The Revisionists' History, the Politics of Truth, and the Remembrance of the Massacre at Acteal, Chiapas." *Documentary Testimonies: Global Archives of Suffering*, edited by Bhaskar Sarkar and Janet Walker, Routledge, 2010, pp. 173–195.
Radstone, Susannah. "Trauma and Screen Studies: Opening the Debate." *Screen*, vol. 42, no. 2, 2001, pp. 188–193.
———. "Trauma Theory: Contexts, Politics, Ethics." *Paragraph*, vol. 30, no. 1, 2007, pp. 9–29.
Raggio, Sandra. "Narrar el terrorismo de Estado: de los hechos a la denuncia pública. El caso de 'La noche de los lápices.'" *Revista socio-histórica*, vol. 19, no. 20, 2007, pp. 99–125.
———. "La noche de los lápices: del testimonio judicial al relato cinematográfico." *El pasado que miramos. Memoria e imagen ante la historia reciente*, compiled by Claudia Feld and Jessica Stites Mor, Paidós, 2009, pp. 45–74.
Ranalletti, Mario. "El cine frente a la memoria de los contemporáneos. Historia y memoria en la Argentina sobre el terrorismo de Estado a partir de dos películas de Andrés di Tella." *Historia contemporánea*, no. 22, 2001, pp. 81–95.
Ranzani, Oscar. "Militancia no es sinónimo de muerte, sino de crecer." *Página 12*, 20 May 2012. www.pagina12.com.ar/diario/suplementos/espectaculos/2-25270-2012-05-20.html. Accessed Jan. 21. 2013.
Ray, Sangeeta. *Gayatri Chakravorty Spivak: In Other Words.* Blackwell, 2009.
Reati, Fernando. "El Ford Falcon: un icono del terror en el imaginario argentino de la posdictadura." *Revista de Estudios Hispánicos*, no. 43, 2009, pp. 385–407.
Renov, Michael. *The Subject of Documentary.* University of Minnesota Press, 2004.
Repas de Bébé. Directed by Louis Lumiére, YouTube, 1895.
La República perdida I. Directed by Miguel Pérez, Noran, 1983.
La República perdida II. Directed by Miguel Pérez, Noran, 1986.
Richard, Nelly, editor. *Cultural Residues: Chile in Transition.* University of Minnesota Press, 2004.
Richard, Nelly and Alberto Moreiras, editors. *Pensar en/la postdictadura.* Editorial Cuarto Propio, 2001.
Ricoeur, Paul. *La memoria, la historia, el olvido.* Trotta, 2003.

Ritvo, Juan Bautista. "Cruelty Is the Real Exposure (Intemperie)." *Journal of Latin American Cultural Studies*, vol. 16, no. 2, 2007, pp. 127–133.
Rocha, Carolina and Georgia Seminet, editors. *Representing History, Class, and Gender in Spain and Latin America: Children and Adolescents in Film*. Palgrave Macmillan, 2012.
Rodowick, David. *The Difficulty of Difference: Psychoanalysis, Sexual Difference, and Film Theory*. Routledge, 1991.
Rodríguez, Ileana, editor. *The Latin American Subaltern Studies Reader*. Duke University Press, 2001.
Romero, Luis Alberto. *Breve historia contemporánea de la Argentina (1916–2010)*. Fondo de Cultura Económica, 2012.
———. *La crisis argentina: Una mirada al siglo XX*. Siglo XXI, 2003.
Ros, Ana. *The Post-Dictatorship Generation in Argentina, Chile, and Uruguay. Collective Memory and Cultural Production*. Palgrave Macmillan, 2012.
Rosaldo, Michelle. "Toward an Anthropology of Self and Feeling." *Emotions: A Cultural Studies Reader*, edited by Jennifer Harding and E. Deidre Pribram, Routledge, 2009, pp. 84–99.
Rosen, Philip. *Change Mummified: Cinema, Historicity, Theory*. University of Minnesota Press, 2001.
Rosenstone, Robert. *Visions of the Past: The Challenge of Film to Our Idea of History*. Harvard University Press, 1995.
Los rubios. Directed by Albertina Carri, Primer Plano Films-Women Make Movies, 2003.
Salamandra: niños de la Patagonia. Directed by Pablo Agüero, Rohfilm, 2008.
Santner, Eric. *Stranded Objects. Mourning, Memory, and Film in Postwar Germany*. Cornell University Press, 1990.
Sarkar, Bhaskar and Janet Walker, editors. *Documentary Testimonies: Global Archives of Suffering*. Routledge, 2010.
Sarlo, Beatriz. *Tiempo pasado. Cultura de la memoria y giro subjetivo, una discusión*. Siglo XXI, 2005.
Scarry, Elaine. *The Body in Pain. The Making and Unmaking of the World*. Oxford University Press, 1985.
Schama, Simon. *Landscape and Memory*. Harper Collins, 1995.
Schechner, Richard. *Between Theater and Anthropology*. University of Pennsylvania Press, 1985.
Scholz, Pablo. "Saber, sentir y después decidir." *Clarín*, 25 Oct. 2005, www.ojala.do/pel%C3%ADculas-videos-teatro/contenido/saber-sentir-y-despu%C3%A9s-decidir. Accessed June 23, 2011.
El secreto de sus ojos. Directed by Juan José Campanella, Tornasol, 2009.
Sedgwick, Eve Kosofsky. *Touching Feeling: Affect, Pedagogy, Performativity*. Duke University Press, 2003.
Selimovic, Inela. "Gastón Biraben's *Cautiva* (2005): An Instance of Enduring Grief." *Bulletin of Hispanic Studies*, vol. 93, no. 4, 2016, pp. 421–438.
Semán, Ernesto. *Soy un bravo piloto de la nueva China*. Mondadori, 2011.
Seoane, María and Héctor Ruiz Nuñez. *La noche de los lápices*. Sudamericana, 1986.
Shoah. Directed by Claude Lanzmann, New Yorker Films, 1985.
Shumway, Nicholas. *The Invention of Argentina*. University of California Press, 1991.

Signer, Michael Alan. *Humanity at the Limit: The Impact of the Holocaust Experience on Jews and Christians*. Indiana University Press, 2000.

Silverman, Kaja. *The Subject of Semiotics*. Oxford University Press, 1983.

Solanas, Fernando and Octavio Getino. *Cine: cultura y descolonización*. Siglo XXI, 1973.

Sonderéguer, María. "Los relatos sobre el pasado reciente en Argentina: una política de la memoria." *Iberoamericana*, no. 1, 2001, pp. 1–18.

Sommer, Doris. *Proceed with Caution When Engaged by Minority Writing in the Americas*. Harvard University Press, 1999.

Sosa, Cecilia. "Humour and the Descendants of the Disappeared: Countersigning Bloodline Affiliations in Post-dictatorial Argentina." *Journal of Romance Studies*, vol. 13, no. 3, 2013, pp. 75–87.

———. *Queering Acts of Mourning in the Aftermath of Argentina's Dictatorship: The Performances of Blood*. Boydell, 2014.

Sosnowski, Saúl. comp. *Represión y reconstrucción de una cultura: el caso argentino*. Eudeba, 1988.

Stam, Robert. "*The Hour of the Furnaces* and the Two Avant-Gardes." *The Social Documentary in Latin America*, edited by Jullianne Burton, University of Pittsburgh Press, 1990, pp. 251–266.

Stearns, Carol. "'Lord Help Me Walk Humbly:' Anger and Sadness in England and America (1570–1750)." *Emotions: A Cultural Studies Reader*, edited by Jennifer Harding and E. Deidre Pribram, Routledge, 2009, pp. 170–190.

Steedman, Carolyn. *Strange Dislocations: Childhood and the Idea of Human Interiority (1780– 1930)*. Virago, 1995.

Steinberg, Laurence. *Adolescence*. McGraw-Hill, 1996.

Stewart, Kathleen. *Ordinary Affects*. Duke University Press, 2007.

Stiglitz, Joseph. *Globalization and Its Discontents*. Norton, 2002.

Strejilevich, Nora. *El arte de no olvidar. Literatura testimonial en Chile, Argentina y Uruguay entre los 80 y los 90*. Catálogos, 2006.

Sur. Directed by Fernando Solanas, Cinesur, 1988.

Svampa, Maristella. *La sociedad excluyente: la Argentina bajo el signo del neoliberalismo*. Taurus, 2005.

Tal, Kali. *Worlds of Hurt. Reading the Literature of Trauma*. Cambridge University Press, 1996.

Tandeciarz, Silvia. "Secrets, Trauma, and the Memory Market (or the Return of the Repressed in Recent Argentine Post-Dictatorship Cultural Production.)" *Cinej Cinema Journal*, vol. 1, no. 2, 2012, pp. 63–71.

Tangos: el exilio de Gardel. Directed by Fernando Solanas, Cinesur, 1986.

Tatián, Diego. "Lo impropio." *Crítica del testimonio. Ensayos sobre las relaciones entre memoria y relato*, edited by Cecilia Vallina, Beatriz Viterbo, 2009, pp. 49–65.

Taylor, Diana. *The Archive and the Repertoire: Performing Cultural Memory in the Americas*. Duke University Press, 2003.

———. *Disappearing Acts: Spectacles of Gender and Nationalism in Argentina's "Dirty War."* Duke University Press, 1997.

———. *Performance*. Duke University Press, 2016.

Teatro x la identidad. *Teatro x la identidad: obras de teatro del ciclo 2001*. Eudeba, 2001.

Televisión x la identidad. Directed by Miguel Colom, Telefé, 2007.

Thomas, Sarah. "Rupture and Reparation: Postmemory, the Child Seer and Graphic Violence in *Infancia clandestina* (Benjamín Ávila, 2012)." *Studies in Spanish and Latin American Cinemas*, vol. 12, no. 3, pp. 235–254.
Thrift, Nigel. *Non-Representational Theory: Space, Politics, Affect*. Routledge, 2008.
Ticineto Clough, Patricia. "Introduction." *The Affective Turn: Theorizing the Social*, edited by Patricia Ticineto Clough and Jean Halley, Duke University Press, 2007, pp. 1–33.
Tiempo suspendido. Directed by Natalia Bruschtein, Centro de Capacitación Cinematográfica, 2016.
El tiempo y la sangre. Directed by Alejandra Almirón, Cine Ojo, 2004.
Todo es ausencia. Directed by Rodolfo Kuhn, TVE, 1984.
Todorov, Tzvetan. *Los abusos de la memoria*. Paidós, 2000.
Tomkins, Silvan. *Affect Imagery Consciousness*. Springer, 1991.
Torchin, Leshu. *Creating the Witness. Documenting Genocide on Film, Video, and the Internet*. University of Minnesota Press, 2012.
Traverso, Antonio and Mick Broderick. "Interrogating Trauma: Towards a Critical Trauma Studies." *Continuum: Journal of Media and Cultural Studies*, vol. 24, no. 1, 2010, pp. 3–15.
Trímboli, Javier, editor. *La izquierda en la Argentina: conversaciones*. Manantial, 1998.
Triquell, Ximena. "Proyectar la historia. Testimonio, denuncia y memoria en el cine argentino postdictadura." *DeSignis. Revista de la Federación Latinoamericana de Semiótica*, no. 10, 2006, pp. 167–178.
Turim, Maureen. *Flashbacks in Film: Memory and History*. Routledge, 1989.
Un tal Ragone (deconstruyendo a pa). Directed by Vanessa Ragone, Cruz del sur, 2002.
Vaisman, Noa. "Posmemoria y memoria desaparecida en dos obras de la posdictadura argentina." *El pasado inasequible. Desaparecidos, hijos y combatientes en el arte y la literatura del nuevo milenio*, edited by Jordana Blejmar, Silvana Mandolessi, and Mariana Eva Perez, Eudeba, 2017, pp. 185–203.
Valentín. Directed by Alejandro Agresti, Patagonik, 2002.
Vallina, Cecilia, editor. *Crítica del testimonio. Ensayos sobre las relaciones entre memoria y relato*. Beatriz Viterbo, 2009.
van der Kolk, Bessel, Alexander McFarlane, and Lars Weisaeth, editors. *Traumatic Stress: The Effects of Overwhelming Experience on Mind, Body, and Society*. Guilford, 2007.
Verdesio, Gustavo, editor. "Latin American Subaltern Studies Revisited." *Dispositio/n. American Journal of Cultural Histories and Theories*, vol. 25, no. 52, 2005, pp. 5–373.
Vezzetti, Hugo. *Aventuras de Freud en el país de los argentinos: de José Ingenieros a Enrique Pichon-Rivière*. Paidós, 1996.
———. *Pasado y presente. Guerra, dictadura y sociedad en la Argentina*. Siglo XXI, 2002.
———. *Sobre la violencia revolucionaria: memorias y olvidos*. Siglo XXI, 2009.
———. "El testimonio en la formación de la memoria social." *Crítica del testimonio. Ensayos sobre las relaciones entre memoria y relato*, edited by Cecilia Vallina, Beatriz Viterbo, 2009, pp. 23–34.
Viñas, David. *Indios, ejército y frontera*. Siglo XXI, 1982.
———. *Menemato y otros suburbios*. Adriana Hidalgo, 2000.
La vita è bella. Directed by Roberto Benigni, Miramax, 1998.
Voces inocentes. Directed by Luis Mandoki, Altavista, 2005.
Volver a nacer. Directed by Daniel De Felippo, Televisión Pública Argentina, 2012.

Williams, Gareth. *The Other Side of the Popular: Neoliberalism and Subalternity in Latin America.* Duke University Press, 2002.
Williams, Raymond. *Marxism and Literature.* Oxford University Press, 1977.
Williams, Simon. *Emotion and Social Theory.* Sage, 2001.
Witness to Apartheid. Directed by Sharon Sopher, Lifting the Veil, 1986.
Wollen, Peter. *Sign and Meaning in the Cinema.* Indiana University Press, 1972.
Young, James. *The Texture of Memory. Holocaust Memorials and Meaning.* Yale University Press, 1993.
Young, Neil. "Clandestine Childhood: Cannes Review." *The Hollywood Reporter,* 21 May 2012, www.hollywoodreporter.com/review/clandestine-childhood-cannes-review-327182. Accessed May 19, 2013.
Zajko, Vanda and Miriam Leonard, editors. *Laughing with Medusa: Classical Myth and Feminist Thought.* Oxford University Press, 2006.
Žižek, Slavoj. *The Art of the Ridiculous Sublime: On David Lynch's "Lost Highway."* University of Washington Press, 2000.
Zuker, Cristina. *El tren de la victoria.* Sudamericana, 2003.

Index

Abuelas de Plaza de Mayo, 3, 21, 78, 93–94, 103n16, 129–30, 139n20, 141. *See also* H.I.J.O.S.; Madres de Plaza de Mayo
adolescence, 25, 142–43, 145–46, 167, 169n3. *See also* teenagers
affect, 19–24, 27, 36–37n33–34, 37n35, 61–62, 65–67, 76, 99, 165, 175; aliens, 88, 97, 99; reason and, 41, 60; theories of, 36n32, 37n35, 40, 61–62. *See also* emotion
affective labor, 92–93
affective turn, 19, 36n33
Agüero, Pablo, 25, 141, 155; *Salamandra: niños de la Patagonia*, 25, 141, 143, 155, 168, 170n11
Aguilar, Gonzalo, 23, 35n27, 36n30, 79, 81, 87, 89, 164, 171n17
Ahmed, Sara, 20, 67, 88
Aleandro, Norma, 150–51
Alfonsín, Raúl, 2, 38–39, 41, 45–47, 49, 51, 57, 68nn1–2, 70n14, 73, 77, 172. *See also* CONADEP
A los compañeros la libertad (Céspedes and Guarini), 24, 55
Amado, Ana, 27, 42, 75, 100–101, 117–18, 126
amnesia, 123; Menemist, 4; official, 3, 74, 100
Andermann, Jens, 27, 42, 70n13, 74–75, 79, 81, 89, 99–101, 103n21, 108, 113, 115–17, 120, 134
Andrés no quiere dormir la siesta (Bustamante), 19, 25, 141, 143, 149–54, 166, 168
Anguita, Eduardo, 3, 102n6
Aprea, Gustavo, 26–27, 42, 58, 75, 90
archival footage, 23–24, 47, 49, 77, 84, 86, 89–90, 92–93, 97–98, 124, 138n13, 145, 147
Arfuch, Leonor, 12, 25–27, 36n34
Arias, Lola, 3, 102n6, 140
armed struggle, 12, 39, 80–81, 105, 157–60, 167–68, 171n19
Astiz, Alfredo, 47, 100, 104n22
Avelar, Idelber, 7, 30n2

Ávila, Benjamín, 141, 157–58, 160, 163, 165, 167; *Infancia clandestina*, 19, 22, 25, 141, 143, 156–68, 170n12, 171n18, 173; *Nietos. Identidad y memoria*, 138n13

Basterra, Víctor, 62, 72n24
Bayer, Osvaldo, 41, 46, 96
Benjamin, Walter, 7–8, 31n9, 91, 164
Bennett, Jill, 21, 34n23, 37n35, 63
Benveniste, Émile, 27–28
Bettini, Marta Francesa de, 46, 52, 58
Beverley, John, 5–6, 8, 10, 32n12, 134, 167–68, 171n19
Bilyk, Pablo, 131–32
Biraben, Gastón, 31n6, 141, 147; *Cautiva*, 23, 25, 141, 143, 145–55, 165, 168, 169–70nn7–8, 173
Blaustein, David, 29, 78–79, 82, 94, 98, 143; *Botín de guerra*, 24, 29, 75–76, 78, 94–98, 100–101, 105–106, 111, 126, 128–31, 134, 141, 173; *Cazadores de utopías*, 24, 75, 77–83, 89–94, 98, 101, 103nn9–10, 106, 112, 116, 128, 131, 134, 160, 173
Blaustein, Susana, 2, 46. *See also Las Madres: The Mothers of Plaza de Mayo*
Blecho, Francisco, 81, 89, 92
Blejmar, Jordana, 25–27, 31n6, 72n31, 116, 121, 139n21, 156
Bonafini, Hebe de, 46, 175n1
Bonasso, Miguel, 78, 102n6, 108
Bondarevsky, Laura, 123–24; *Che vo cachai*, 25, 107, 123–24, 136n5
Botín de guerra (Blaustein), 24, 29, 75–76, 78, 94–98, 100–101, 105–106, 111, 126, 128–31, 134, 141, 173
Bruzzi, Stella, 106, 136n4
Buch, Esteban, 17–18, 41–43, 47–49, 53–54, 59, 58–60, 86
Buenos Aires Independent Film Festival (BAFICI), 78, 138n16

195

Bustamante, Daniel, 31n6, 142, 149, 151–52;
    Andrés no quiere dormir la siesta, 19, 25,
    141, 143, 149–54, 166, 168
Bruschtein, Natalia, 3, 25, 107, 122–23;
    Encontrando a Víctor, 3, 25, 100, 107,
    122–23, 136n5

Cabandié, Juan, 129, 133, 138n17
Cabezas, José Luis, 89, 94, 103n14
Caparrós, Martín, 3, 81, 102n6
capitalism, 25, 87, 93, 97, 144, 169
Carlson, Marvin, 125, 138n15
Carri, Albertina, 1–4, 14, 23, 25, 105, 107,
    111–28, 136n4, 136–37nn8–9, 140, 154;
    Cuatreros, 25, 107, 123–24, 136nn4–5, 137n9;
    Los rubios, 1–2, 14, 21, 23–26, 42, 75, 100,
    105–107, 111–28, 134, 136n5, 137n9, 138n16,
    140, 154, 160, 173
Carri, Roberto, 105, 113–15, 124–25, 127, 137n9.
    See also Caruso, Ana María
Cartwright, Lisa, 37n35, 56
Caruso, Ana María, 105, 113–14, 125, 127
Caruth, Cathy, 7, 31n8, 31–32nn10–11, 33n18,
    34n25, 118–19
Cautiva (Biraben), 23, 25, 141, 143, 145–55,
    165, 168, 169–70nn7–8, 173
Cazadores de utopías (Blaustein), 24, 75,
    77–83, 89–94, 98, 101, 103nn9–10, 106, 112,
    116, 128, 131, 134, 160, 173
censorship, 13, 38–39, 68, 100
Céspedes, Marcelo, 24, 37n37, 98–99
Chanan, Michael, 23, 37n36, 43–44, 68,
    70nn10–11, 75, 83, 127
Che vo cachai (Bondarevsky), 25, 107,
    123–24, 136n5
child, the, 141–44, 155–56, 169n1; filmic
    representation of, 169n7
childhood, 25, 123, 142–44, 156, 161, 169n3;
    objects of, 116. See also adolescence
children, 2, 59, 65–67, 112, 140, 144, 155–56,
    159, 166; abducted, 31n6, 94, 96–97;
    agency of, 171n18; of disappeared/missing
    persons, 3, 16, 93, 98, 101, 102n5, 103n16,
    121, 126, 129–30, 139n20, 141, 146–47, 170n8,
    175n1; moral appeal of, 169; perspective of,
    19, 132, 135, 141–43, 154–55, 157–58, 161–63,
    165, 168; trauma and, 11

cinema, 11, 17, 21, 25–26, 28, 56, 66, 88, 128,
    142; 1960s, 90; 1980s, 40–42, 50, 60, 62,
    67, 69n5, 80–81, 101; apparatus of, 42,
    52, 124–25; Argentine, 16, 23, 27, 35n27,
    45, 74–75, 143, 147; childhood and, 144;
    didactic, 75; early, 162; European, 106;
    fictional, 39; global, 168; indexicality of,
    148; Kirchnerist, 168; Latin American,
    36n32; militant, 90–91; new Argentine, 45,
    70n13, 74; performative, 24; post-1990s,
    42, 45; postdictatorship, 8, 21–22, 27,
    29–30, 37n37, 41, 47, 75, 124, 140–42, 147,
    155, 164, 169n4, 174; as record of the past,
    35n28; second-generation, 135, 164, 171n17
    (*see also* second-generation filmmakers);
    semiotic and, 35n29; testimonial (*see*
    testimonial cinema); viewers, 161; world,
    30. *See also* documentaries; *kirchnerismo*:
    cinema and; postdictatorship: cinema;
    road movies; semiotics: cinema and
cinematic images, 37n36, 43, 46, 52, 64,
    127, 150; as empty signifiers, 167; iconic
    dimension/status of, 25, 143, 162;
    indexicality of, 35n29, 50, 70n11, 148, 173
close-up shots, 22, 35n29, 47, 49, 66, 90, 92,
    108–109, 113, 162–66
collectivity, 56, 81–82, 98; damaged, 106
Colom, Miguel, 128–29, 138n20
CONADEP (National Commission on the
    Disappearance of Persons), 38, 49, 57, 65,
    172
Copjec, Joan, 34n26. *See also* historicism
counterhegemony, 24–25, 29, 32n14, 75–77,
    80, 93, 98, 104n19, 107, 130, 134, 173–74. *See
    also* hegemony
Crenzel, Emilio, 2, 56–57, 160, 170n15, 174. *See
    also* victims: innocent
Cuando vuelva a casa voy a ser otro
    (Pensotti), 2, 174
Cuatreros (Carri), 25, 107, 123–24, 136nn4–5,
    137n9

De la Rúa, Fernando, 73, 99
Del Barco, Oscar, 12, 33n20
Delgado, María, 138n19, 152
democratic participation, 41, 53
democratization, 35n27, 40, 45, 58, 60, 67, 73

Denti, Jorge, 24, 46, 49
detention centers, 2, 38, 40, 55, 62, 66, 72n24, 72n26, 75, 115, 149, 153, 175. *See also* disappeared; military dictatorship; torture
Diario del juicio, 50, 64, 71n16. *See also juicio a las juntas* (trial of the juntas)
Diario de una princesa montonera (Perez), 26, 102n6
Díaz, Pablo, 40, 62–65, 72n27
disappeared, 59; activists, 112, 157–59, 168; bodies of the, 101; children of the, 3, 16, 93, 102n5, 103n16, 121, 126, 139n20, 141, 146–47; films about, 128; images of, 159–60; as innocent victims, 170n15; parents, 2, 39, 93, 100, 112, 114, 121, 123, 145–47, 155; as passive victims, 157–58; persons, 3, 9, 16, 29, 40, 56, 71nn20–21, 74, 78, 97–98, 114, 148, 153, 170n8, 172; photographs/portraits of the, 57–58, 120; relatives of the, 117, 131; students, 62. *See also* detention centers; military dictatorship; torture
distortion, 113, 115–16, 123, 137n9; generic, 24; parodic, 18
Di Tella, Andrés, 78–79, 82; *Montoneros: una historia*, 24, 71n20, 75, 77–91, 98–99, 101, 103n10, 106, 111–12, 128, 131, 160, 173; *Prohibido*, 24, 88–89
Doane, Mary Ann, 18, 23, 44, 52, 127, 148–49
documentaries, 11, 23–24, 64, 69n4, 76, 78, 82, 98–101, 106, 123–24; 1990s, 130, 173; Di Tella's, 89; first-person, 136n4; inconclusive, 118–19; performative, 18, 49, 106–107, 109, 125, 127–28, 134–35, 138n15, 141, 144, 174 (*see also* cinema: performative); post-1990s, 42; post-2000, 127; reflective, 40; second-generation, 3, 23, 106, 119–22, 125, 144–45, 147, 155, 174; social, 90; testimonial, 24–25, 27, 37n37, 45, 70n14, 77, 100–101, 108, 125, 128, 138n13; by women filmmakers, 37n34, 136n5, 168
domesticity, 13, 16, 25, 57, 161

Easter uprising, 45, 71n16
Echeverría, Carlos, 41, 50; *Juan, como si nada hubiera sucedido*, 17, 23, 40–42, 44, 47, 49–50, 52, 54, 57–61, 67, 101

economic crisis of 2001, 47, 73, 135n1, 137n13
emotion, 20–21, 36n33, 40, 60, 62–63, 67, 143, 152, 164–65. *See also* affect; feeling
Encontrando a Víctor (Bruschtein), 3, 25, 100, 107, 122–23, 136n5
empty signifier, 134–35, 151–52; cinematic images as, 166; military dictatorship as, 76, 128, 151–52, 173–74. *See also* Laclau, Ernesto
En memoria de los pájaros (Golder), 25, 107, 123–24
enunciation, 28–29, 37n37, 105, 41, 118; aporia of, 117; level of, 28, 40, 113; present of, 15–18, 35n28, 40, 44–45, 75, 79, 88, 92, 95, 98, 101, 121–22, 132, 135, 150, 169n1
ESMA (Escuela Superior de Mecánica de la Armada), 62, 72n24, 84, 108, 129–30, 133
exile, 13, 38, 41, 68, 78, 84, 88, 90, 123, 137n13, 141, 147, 155, 159, 161, 166
Ezeiza massacre, 84, 90

Falcone, Claudia, 62, 67, 72n30
feeling, 19–20, 23–25, 27, 40, 51, 60–62, 67, 158, 161–65; codified, 152; queer archives of, 21–22. *See also* affect; emotion
Felman, Shoshana, 7–8, 13, 31n8, 32n11, 33n18, 34n25, 55, 118
fiction, 22–29, 37nn36–37, 39–40, 43, 62, 64–65, 67–68, 69n4, 70n10, 72n28, 72n31, 113, 128–35, 141, 143–45, 154–55, 160–61, 164, 171n17, 173; classical, 44; films, 17, 19, 22, 69n6, 77, 83; generic, 24, 39–40, 42, 45, 60; iconic, 25, 143, 145, 153, 155–56, 168–69; hegemony and, 135; melodramatic, 23–24; second-generation, 19, 23, 144–49, 154, 158
fictionalization, 25–26, 107, 123, 128, 132, 138n20, 141
film: history and, 17, 35n28, 36n30; industry, 35n28, 39, 74, 102n3, 169; nontestimonial, 25. *See also* cinema; documentaries; road movies
filmic images, 35n29, 36n32, 43, 106, 161–62; history and, 17, 19; as indexical traces, 18, 70n11
Firmenich, Mario, 79–80, 82, 85
Forcinito, Ana, 25, 35n27, 36n34

198 | Index

Freud, Sigmund, 7, 33n18, 100, 118. *See also* melancholy; mourning; psychoanalysis
Fuerzas Armadas Revolucionarias (FAR), 105, 108

Galimberti, Rodolfo, 79–80, 82, 85
Gamerro, Carlos, 1–2, 4, 102n6, 174
Gelman, Juan, 3, 102n6
genre, 22, 27, 35n29, 39, 53, 59–60, 62, 70n10. *See also* fiction: generic
Getino, Octavio, 37n37, 90
Golder, Gabriela, 31n6, 123–24; *En memoria de los pájaros*, 25, 107, 123–24
Gómez, Antonio, 27, 106, 113, 117–18
grief, 21, 99, 147, 152. *See also* melancholy; mourning
Grupo Cine Testimonio, 37n37, 69n9
Guarini, Carmen, 24, 42, 75, 98–99
guerrillas, 12, 57, 67, 71n19, 73, 78–79, 86, 157–58, 160; repentant, 167; urban, 72n30 (*see also* Montoneros)
Guevara, Ernesto "Che," 90, 158, 160, 166; image of, 67, 160

Habegger, Andrés, 136n2; *(h)istorias cotidianas*, 24, 98–100, 104n21, 111, 136n2, 140
hegemony, 24–25, 29, 76–77, 102n7, 132, 134–35, 151–52, 168, 173–74; emotional, 22–23, 82, 165; fictionalization and, 138n20; neoliberal, 167; performing, 145; of popular-subaltern texts, 11; of state historiography, 5; of testimonial films, 107, 128. *See also* counterhegemony; posthegemony
H.I.J.O.S. (Hijos por la Identidad y la Justicia contra el Olvido y el Silencio), 3, 9–10, 75, 89, 98, 100, 102n5, 116, 121–22, 126, 135, 141, 148, 168. *See also* Abuelas de Plaza de Mayo; disappeared; *H.I.J.O.S., el alma en dos* (Guarini and Céspedes); Madres de Plaza de Mayo
H.I.J.O.S., el alma en dos (Guarini and Céspedes), 24, 98, 100, 104n19, 111
Hirsch, Marianne, 30–31n6, 47, 111, 117, 119–21, 137n12, 153

Historia del llanto: un testimonio (Pauls), 2, 174
La historia oficial (Puenzo), 14, 16–17, 27, 35n29, 39, 60, 69n6, 140, 143, 146, 148–52, 156–57, 169n7, 170nn11–12
(h)istorias cotidianas (Habegger), 24, 98–100, 104n21, 111, 136n2, 140
historicism, 21, 34n26
historicity, 15–19, 21, 23, 26, 34nn22–23, 34n26, 37n35, 63, 89, 101, 122, 150, 174; of feelings, 62; of testimonial films, 37n37
Holland, Patricia, 144, 156
Holocaust, the: films about, 37n37, 174; images of, 119; survivors of, 121
La hora de los hornos (Solanas), 90–91, 103n15
human rights, 172; discourse, 21, 117; organizations, 3, 21, 38, 46, 71n16, 98, 102n4, 103n16, 116, 135, 173 (*see also* Abuelas de Plaza de Mayo; H.I.J.O.S.; Madres de Plaza de Mayo); violations, 2, 38, 57, 68n2; violence, 36n34
Huyssen, Andreas, 4, 14, 29, 174

iconicity, 19, 23, 37n36, 133, 135, 149, 151, 153, 156, 165–66; feeling and, 25, 143, 158, 161–63; globalization and, 16, 106, 154. *See also* cinematic images: iconic dimension/status of
iconic representation, 133, 135, 151–53, 166, 168
identity politics, 8, 15, 32n12, 49, 106
indexicality, 17–18, 23, 36n30, 37n36, 44–45, 50, 64, 70n13, 85–86, 110, 127, 133, 150, 153–54, 173; manipulation of, 52, 59, 101, 123, 128, 135; photography and, 120; referential quality of, 131. *See also* cinematic images: indexicality of
indigenous populations, 10, 37n37, 95–97, 130
Infancia clandestina (Ávila), 19, 22, 25, 141, 143, 156–68, 170n12, 171n18, 173
Instituto Nacional de Cinematografía (INC/INCAA), 39, 74, 126–27, 134, 138n16
intellectual ethics, 8, 11
intellectuals, 2–6, 9–10, 12–13, 82, 88–89, 127; Latin American, 30n5, 32n12; left-leaning, 2, 4, 12, 97; revolutionary, 30n5

Jabbaz, Marcela, 154, 170n8
Jaggar, Alison, 20, 22, 61, 82
Jameson, Fredric, 32–33n17, 58–59, 169
Jauretche, Ernesto, 78, 102n6
Jouvé, Héctor, 12, 33n20
Juan, como si nada hubiera sucedido (Echeverría), 17, 23, 40–42, 44, 47, 49–50, 52, 54, 57–61, 67, 101
juicio a las juntas (trial of the juntas), 38, 40, 46, 50–51, 62, 68n2

Kaiser, Susana, 143, 147
Kaufman, Alejandro, 6–7, 12
Kirchner, Néstor, 133, 172; administration of, 3, 9–10, 69n8, 73, 101, 102n5, 104n22, 129, 131, 138n17, 158, 167–68, 171n19
kirchnerismo, 16, 32n14, 74, 129, 131, 138n17, 138n19, 152, 154; cinema and, 22, 25, 75, 77, 128, 168; cultural production of, 105; discourse of, 132–33, 152, 158; memory and, 138n19, 170n9; testimonial genre and, 107
Kohan, Martín, 113, 115, 137n9
Kuhn, Annette, 144, 169n4
Kuhn, Rodolfo, 24, 46

LaCapra, Dominick, 4, 12, 15, 56, 174–75
Laclau, Ernesto, 76, 134, 151–52, 173. *See also* hegemony; populism
La Madrid, Mara, 3, 102n6
Las Madres: The Mothers of Plaza de Mayo (Portillo and Blaustein), 2, 24, 46–47, 49–50, 56
Laub, Dori, 7–8, 13, 31n8, 32n11, 33n18, 34n25, 118. *See also* testimony
Lauretta, Miguel, 108–109, 112
Lebeau, Vicky, 142, 162
Lee, Nick, 144, 169n3
ley de obediencia debida (Law of Due Obedience), 41, 45, 47, 49, 52, 69n8, 73, 172
ley de punto final (Full Stop Law), 41, 45, 47, 49, 52, 69n8, 73, 172
The Little School (Partnoy), 2, 9, 55–56
Longoni, Ana, 71n20, 103n11
love, 161; sentimental, 162, 165
Lozano, Claudia, 154, 170n8
Lury, Karen, 141–42, 156, 163, 170n16

M (Prividera), 2, 21, 25, 42, 107, 117, 122–23
Macón, Cecilia, 116–17
Macri, Mauricio, 32n14, 172–73, 175n1
macrismo, 32n14, 77
Madres de Plaza de Mayo (Mothers of Plaza de Mayo), 3, 21, 36n34, 46, 89, 123, 126, 148, 175n1
Malvinas: historia de traiciones (Denti), 24, 46
Margulis, Paola, 41–42, 45, 50, 53–54, 69n4, 77
Markovitch, Paula, 141; *El premio*, 25, 141, 143, 155, 168
Marxism, 11, 32n16; post–, 31n7
Massumi, Brian, 20–21, 37n35, 63
melancholy, 79, 99–100, 117, 119–20, 126, 169n7, 175. *See also* grief; mourning
melodrama, 39, 42, 60, 63, 66, 69n6, 139n20, 149–50; testimonial, 27
memory, 7–8, 11, 13, 25–26, 31n6, 33n18, 33–34n22, 37n34, 116–17, 120–21, 143, 174; acts of, 99, 104n21, 116; communal, 55; complete, 170n9; controlled, 10; discourse, 5, 14, 38; eclipse, 74; fatigue, 4, 9, 29, 174–75; fragmentary, 116; historicity of, 15; institutionalization of, 138n19; landscape and, 104n20; missing persons and, 58; narratives, 29; objects of, 165; public, 167–68; recovery of, 78; reenactment of, 138n15; representation of, 146; self-aware, 26, 116, 139n21; sense, 37n35; sites of, 34n22, 86, 99–100; social, 101; studies, 31n8, 32n11, 33n22; texts, 3–5, 9–10; trauma and, 4, 14; traumatic, 118–19, 126; value, 156; work, 170n13. *See also* amnesia; postmemory
Méndez, Úrsula, 100, 140, 154
Menem, Carlos, 3, 45, 73–74, 79, 82, 85, 87, 92, 94, 102n1, 103n12, 103n14; amnesties of, 73, 79, 82, 94, 130, 172. *See also* neoliberalism
menemismo, 3–4, 16, 74, 79, 82, 85, 87, 93, 95, 97, 99, 101–102nn1–3, 101n5, 131. *See also* neoliberalism
Metz, Christian, 14, 21, 28–29, 35–36nn29–30, 36n32, 105, 113, 124, 161–64

militancy, 22, 56, 67, 79, 82–84, 86, 98, 103n9, 110–11, 116, 159–60, 162, 164–66, 168; 1970s, 78, 92–93, 157–58, 166; erasure of, 57; left-leaning, 22, 77, 90, 94, 165; political, 154, 160; representation of, 159, 165, 170n13, 171n18; sentimental, 163. *See also* political commitment

military dictatorship, 19, 22, 30n2, 35n28, 68, 97, 102n1, 103n16, 104n22, 132, 142–43, 145–46, 155, 170n11, 175; causes of, 170n8; cultural representations of, 141, 170n10; as "dirty war," 30n2, 71n19, 157, 172; as empty signifier, 76, 128, 151–52, 173–74; testimonial films about, 74. *See also* detention centers; disappeared; torture

military junta, 3, 16, 71n19. *See also juicio a las juntas* (trial of the juntas)

Mi vida después (Arias), 3, 102n6, 140

Montaldo, María Luisa, 81, 92

Montoneros (Movimiento Peronista Montoneros),

Montoneros: una historia (Di Tella), 24, 71n20, 75, 77–91, 98–99, 101, 103n10, 106, 111–12, 128, 131, 160, 173. *See also* Testa, Ana

Moreiras, Alberto, 7, 77

Moreno, María, 114–15, 122

Mórtola Oesterheld, Martín, 100, 140, 154

Mouffe, Chantal, 76, 134, 151. *See also* hegemony

mourning, 4, 6, 8, 13–15, 21, 25–26, 58, 99–100, 116–20, 137n12, 169n7, 175; work of, 99, 104n21, 118. *See also* grief; melancholy

neoliberalism, 8, 24, 35n27, 62, 73–74, 82, 87–88, 91–93, 97–98, 102n1, 128, 130–31, 167. *See also* Menem, Carlos; *menemismo*

Nichols, Bill, 69n10, 106, 136n4

Ni el flaco perdón del dios (Gelman and La Madrid), 3, 102n6

No al punto final (Denti), 24, 49

La noche de los lápices (Olivera), 23, 40–41, 62–63, 140

Noriega, Gustavo, 115, 138n16

Nouzeilles, Gabriela, 114–17, 120, 137n9

Oberti, Alejandra, 82, 103n9, 109, 116

O'Keeffe, Moira, 95, 101

Olivera, Héctor, 40, 62, 67; *La noche de los lápices*, 23, 40–41, 62–63, 140

Onganía, Juan Carlos, 84, 90, 109

Page, Joanna, 35n27, 69n5, 117–18, 126

Papá Iván (Roqué), 18, 23–25, 29, 75, 78, 100, 104n21, 105–11, 113, 116–23, 134, 136n6, 140, 154, 160, 173

Parker, Andrew, 126, 138n15

parody, 1, 18, 24, 28, 31n6, 35n28, 111–12, 122, 124–25, 127–28, 134, 136n4, 137–38n13. *See also* distortion: parodic

Partnoy, Alicia, 2, 5–6, 9–11, 55–56

Pauls, Alan, 2, 174

Peirce, Charles S., 19, 35n29, 36n31, 148, 151, 166. *See also* semiotics

Pensotti, Mariano, 2, 174

Perdía, Roberto, 80–81, 102n6

Perez, Mariana Eva, 102n6, 121

performativity, 126–27

peronismo (Peronism), 74, 84–85, 94, 102n2

photography, 25, 41, 72n22

Piedras, Pablo, 27, 37n34, 42, 86, 99–100, 106, 109–10, 136n4

Pittaluga, Roberto, 82, 103n9, 109, 116

Podalsky, Laura, 61–62

political commitment, 39, 56, 58, 67, 126, 154, 171n18. *See also* militancy

populism, 74, 76

Portela, Edurne, 8, 31n10

Portillo, Lourdes, 2, 45. *See also Las Madres: The Mothers of Plaza de Mayo*

postdemocratization, 73–74, 80, 105. *See also* democratization

postdictatorship, 13, 30n2, 34n23; abduction of children during, 103n16; Argentina, 9, 25, 31n6, 35n27, 36n34, 53, 71n21, 72n24, 73, 82, 99, 149, 170n14, 175; cinema, 8, 21–22, 27, 29–30, 37n37, 41, 47, 75, 124, 140–42, 147, 155, 164, 169n4, 174; corpus, 37n34; cultural productions, 159; history, 2, 129; narratives, 1–2, 10–11, 32n12, 34n25, 100, 153, 170n13, 174; novelty and, 70n15; photography and, 72n22; scholarship, 26,

32n11; studies, 7–8, 31n9; trauma studies and, 34n22; women's testimonies and, 36n34
posthegemony, 32n14, 76–77, 102n8
postmemory, 25, 116–22, 134, 175
poststructuralism, 17, 31n8
present in progress, 44, 47, 86
Prince, Stephen, 161–62
privatization, 13, 55, 73–74, 87; of left-leaning violence, 157–58, 160, 166–68; of state violence, 139n20
Prividera, Nicolás, 2–3, 25, 107, 117, 123
Prohibido (Di Tella), 24, 88–89
psychoanalysis, 7–8, 11, 13–14, 31nn8–9, 32–33nn17–18, 34n24, 36n33, 143–44; Lacanian, 32n16, 35n29
Puenzo, Luis, 14, 16, 39, 140, 146. See also *La historia oficial*

queer theory, 21, 36n34
Quintín, 166, 168

Rabasa, José, 5–6, 108
Radstone, Susannah, 31n8, 33n18
Raggio, Sandra, 62–65, 67
reconstruction, 26, 59, 75, 78, 93, 114, 129; emotional, 112, 164; historical, 86, 112, 116, 123; of the past, 105; political, 112; social, 99
referentiality, 17, 113, 119, 127, 137n9, 149, 151, 155; of documentary, 43; lack of, 153; recovered, 13. See also iconicity; indexicality
reflexivity, 23, 42–43, 45, 60, 62
restoration, 44, 167–68
reticence, 2–5, 8, 11, 132, 174
Richard, Nelly, 7–8, 61, 70n15
road movies, 37n34, 88–89, 99, 125; documentary, 86
Rocha, Carolina, 142, 144, 156, 168, 169n2, 169n4
Roqué, Juan Julio "Iván," 105, 108, 116
Roqué, María Inés, 23, 29, 105, 107–10, 112, 119, 121–23, 134, 137n10, 154; *Papá Iván*,
Ros, Ana, 25–26, 116, 139n21
Rosaldo, Michelle, 19–20, 61

Rosen, Philip, 17, 70n11, 83
Los rubios (Carri), 1–2, 14, 21, 23–26, 42, 75, 100, 105–107, 111–28, 134, 136n5, 137n9, 138n16, 140, 154, 160, 173

Salamandra: niños de la Patagonia (Agüero), 25, 141, 143, 155, 168, 170n11
Sarlo, Beatriz, 2, 4–10, 13, 32n12, 61, 121, 167, 171n19, 174
second-generation filmmakers, 25, 141–42, 154. See also cinema: second-generation
second-generation survivors, 3–4, 11, 29, 30n6, 75, 100, 116, 123, 126, 131
El secreto de sus ojos (Campanella), 152, 157, 170n10
Sedgwick, Eve Kosofsky, 126, 138n15
Selimovic, Inela, 146–47, 153
Seminet, Georgia, 142, 144, 156, 168, 169n2, 169n4
semiotics, 11, 17–19, 22–23, 32n16, 175; cinema and, 35n29, 36n30, 36n32, 43, 165–66; Peircean, 17, 36n31, 138n18. See also affect; iconicity; indexicality; Peirce, Charles S.; psychoanalysis
Silverman, Kaja, 27, 35n29
Solanas, Fernando, 37n37, 69n6, 90, 106
Sosa, Cecilia, 21–22, 31n6, 36n34, 116–17, 138n19, 152
speaking subject, 6, 27–29, 40, 62, 89, 98, 101, 105, 108–10, 112, 121, 136n2
spoken subject, 28–29
Stearns, Carol, 19–20
subaltern theory, 6, 8–11, 24, 32n12, 32n15, 175
subjectivity, 9, 17, 26, 35n29, 118, 137n12; Albertina Carri's, 112–13; deprivation of, 54; polyphonic, 56; private, 59; teenage, 153; of the viewer, 162. See also speaking subject; spoken subject; subject of speech
subject of speech, 28–29, 40, 58, 62, 105, 121, 136n2

Tal, Kali, 4, 29, 174
Taylor, Diana, 36n34, 125–26, 138n15
teenagers, 25, 65–66, 140–46, 148–49, 153–56, 169n9, 170n8. See also adolescence; children

television, 83; images, 18, 47, 49, 71n16; primetime, 101, 129; public, 45, 74; strategies, 23, 50–52

Televisión x la identidad (Colom), 3, 25, 101, 107, 128–35, 138–39n20, 145, 149, 153, 160

Testa, Ana, 79–81, 83–88, 103n11

testimonial cinema, 1, 22–24, 26–27, 29, 34n22, 34n26, 67–68, 80, 107, 134, 175; Argentine film industry and, 74–75, 102n8, 122, 124, 134; canonization of, 137n13; counterhegemonic role of, 76; deixis and, 116; democracy in Argentina and, 40–41, 50, 135; documentary and, 27; historicity of, 17; *kirchnerismo* and, 25; postdictatorship, 30; referential nature of, 106; semiotics and, 19; Third Cinema and, 37n37

testimonial discourse, 10–11, 13, 123, 128

testimonial genre/*testimonio*, 3–6, 9–10, 14, 17–18, 27, 31n7, 125, 174; development of, 122; fictionalization of, 25; hegemony of, 107, 128; homogenization of, 11; parodies of, 35n28, 138n13. *See also* testimony

testimonial narratives, 2–3, 5–11, 13–17, 30n2, 30n4, 32n14, 35n27, 77; Argentine postdictatorship, 1–2, 100, 174; in *Botín de guerra*, 95; in *Cazadores* (Blaustein), 90; fiction and, 135; hegemony of, 134; Latin American, 4, 6, 31n7; in *Tiempo suspendido* (Bruschtein), 123

testimonial subjects, 9–12, 24. 55–56, 79–81, 99–101

testimony, 7, 13, 16, 26–27, 53–56, 164; authentic, 64; authority of, 111–12; fictional, 35n28, 41, 62–63, 67, 164, 171n17; personal, 108; politics of, 34n23

Third Cinema, 37n37, 39, 69n3, 90–91, 103n15, 106

Thomas, Sarah, 142, 161, 165

thriller (genre), 13, 39, 42, 60, 69n6, 139n20, 155; melodramatic, 62; political, 145–47, 149, 156

Ticineto Clough, Patricia, 19–20

Todo es ausencia (Kuhn), 24, 46–47, 50, 52, 56

Todorov, Tzvetan, 4, 29

torture, 12, 38, 47, 54–55, 59, 65, 67–68, 78, 102n4, 150, 155, 157

trauma, 4, 7, 11–15, 21, 25–26, 31n8, 32nn10–11, 33n18; cultural, 30n6, 34nn22–23, 34n25, 100–101, 110, 116–21, 175; founding, 15, 175; literatures of, 4; mimetic theory of, 137n10 (*see also* trauma theory); quiet, 137n11

trauma studies, 8, 31n8, 32n11, 33n22

trauma theory, 6–8, 11–14, 24, 31n8, 34nn22–23, 42, 107, 118–19, 122, 169n4, 170n13, 175

utopia, 67, 79, 92, 132–33

Vallina, Cecilia, 2, 174

Van der Kolk, Bessel, 7, 138n18

Vélez, Ignacio, 80–81

Vezzetti, Hugo, 2, 4, 15, 38, 54–55, 71n19, 159–60, 170nn14–15, 174

victimhood, 32n13, 57, 67, 164

victims, 11, 33n18, 52, 58; of Argentine military dictatorship, 3, 53–56, 98, 146, 159–60; child, 121; first-generation, 30n6; innocent, 56–58, 60, 63, 68, 80–82, 117, 131, 160, 170n15, 173 (*see also* Crenzel, Emilio; disappeared persons); middle-class, 32n13; passive, 157–58; perspective of, 141; relatives of, 51; in testimonies, 2; underrepresented, 10

Videla, Jorge Rafael, 73, 110

violence, 12, 54, 59, 84, 89, 132; gender, 36n34; left-leaning, 157–59, 166–68, 170n14; military, 3, 52; political, 57; revolutionary, 12, 35n27, 71n21, 80, 123, 160, 165, 168; state, 53, 55, 71n19, 93, 139n20, 157–58, 160, 170n14, 171

La voluntad (Céspedes and Anguita), 3, 9–10, 102n6

Walger, Silvina, 80–81

Walsh, María Elena, 155, 170n11

witnessing, 26, 108, 121; retrospective, 30n6, 120, 153; secondary, 134

VERÓNICA GARIBOTTO is associate professor of Latin American literary and cultural studies at the University of Kansas. She is the author of *Crisis y reemergencia: el siglo XIX en la ficción contemporánea de Argentina, Chile y Uruguay* and editor (with Jorge Pérez) of *The Latin American Road Movie*.

www.ingramcontent.com/pod-product-compliance
Lightning Source LLC
Chambersburg PA
CBHW061939220426
43662CB00012B/1967